STUDIES
IN
REVELATION

Books by M. R. De Haan

Adventures in Faith
Bread for Each Day
Broken Things
The Chemistry of the Blood
Daniel the Prophet
The Days of Noah
Dear Doctor: I Have a Problem
508 Answers to Bible Questions
Genesis and Evolution
Studies in Hebrews
The Jew and Palestine in Prophecy
Studies in Jonah
Law or Grace
Our Daily Bread
Pentecost and After
Portraits of Christ in Genesis
Studies in Revelation
The Romance of Redemption
The Second Coming of Jesus
Signs of the Times
Simon Peter
Studies in First Corinthians
Studies in Galatians
The Tabernacle

M. R. De Haan Classic Library

STUDIES IN REVELATION

M. R. De Haan

kregel
PUBLICATIONS

Grand Rapids, MI 49501

For more information about Kregel Publications, visit our
web site at http://www.kregel.com.

Cover photo: Copyright © 1998 Kregel, Inc.
Cover design: Art Jacobs

Library of Congress Cataloging-in-Publication Data
De Haan, M. R. (Martin Ralph), 1891–1965.
[Revelation]
   Revelation / by M. R. De Haan.
      p.   cm.
   Originally published: Revelation: Grand Rapids, Mich.:
Zondervan, 1946.
    1. Bible. N.T. Revelation—Sermons. I. Title.
BS2825.4.D44   1998   228'.06—dc21   98-26807
                                                       CIP

ISBN 0-8254-2485-2

4 5 6 7 8 / 07 06 05 04 03

Printed in the United States of America

Contents

6   *Contents*

Introduction

Blessed is he that readeth, and they that hear the words
of this prophecy, and keep those things which are written
therein: for the time is at hand. (Rev. 1:3).
Behold, I come quickly: blessed is he that keepeth the
sayings of the prophecy of this book. (Rev. 22:7).

The author of the book of the revelation is Jesus
Christ (Rev. 22:16). The Lord intended that this book
should be read and studied especially by His people
(Rev. 1:3). It is not a sealed book, as many suppose, but
one which is open and easy to understand (Rev. 22:10).
Bearing these facts in mind, we find the study of Revelation to be fascinating, illuminating and deeply profitable, instead of difficult and confusing. The messages
in this volume constitute thirty-five radio sermons
which were preached first over the Mutual Network and
by foreign and short-wave stations around the world,
from August, 1945, to April, 1946. The response to
these radio messages was so enthusiastic and the evident desire for light on the book of the Revelation so
general that we soon decided to print these studies on
one volume. Hence this book.

No attempt has been made to present an exhaustive
verse-by-verse exposition of the book, but, rather, we
have tried to present the general outline, the basic
structure and the framework. We have dwelt at length
on certain passages because they constitute the pillars
of the book. Our purpose is to present clearly the
general outline and structure, and then the details
will fall naturally into their proper places.

If certain simple rules are followed in reading and
studying it, the book of the Revelation becomes clear,
logical and easily understood. We present here a few

rules which should be observed before studying the book:

1. Revelation is *not* a dark book. It is a *revelation*.
2. It is not necessary for one to understand all the symbols and details if he is to gain a deeper knowledge of the book as a whole. One need not be able to identify every tree in the forest to appreciate the beauty of the forest as a whole.
3. Observe the rule of literal interpretation. The greatest curse of the Christian Church is the evil of spiritualizing the Bible. Although there are many symbols and signs in the book, as in every other book and in our daily conversation, the context indicates whether a passage is to be interpreted literally or symbolically. Interpret literally, except where the context or grammatical structure clearly indicates that the reference is a symbol or a sign.
4. Approach the Book with a "fresh" mind. Try to forget the views you have held concerning the Book because others have declared it to be mysterious and beyond our understanding. Thousands of believers never read Revelation, but carefully avoid it simply because someone told them it is a dark book and impossible to understand. *Study the book for yourself.*
5. Read the book prayerfully, realizing that the Holy Spirit who infallibly inspired the book is also the person Who must illuminate the book. Never read a portion of scripture without first asking Him for light and guidance.

We submit for your help the following simple outline of Revelation. Remember these five rules as you study it. If you will memorize the outline thoroughly, and keep it clearly before your mind, you will have no trouble filling in the details.

Grand Rapids, Michigan   *M. R. De Haan*

Outline of Revelation

I. *Introduction:* Revelation 1
An introduction to the author and object of the book, Jesus Christ Himself.

II. *The History of the Professing Church:* Revelation 2–3
The seven churches, representing the course of Christendom's history from Pentecost to the Rapture.

III. *The Translation of the Body of Christ:* Revelation 4:1–3
The true Church within the professing Church.

IV. *The Church in Heaven:* Revelation 4:3–11

V. *The Seven-Sealed Book:* Revelation 5
The key to Revelation.

VI. *The First Half of the Tribulation Period:* Revelation 6–10
Corresponds to the first half of Daniel's Seventieth Week.

VII. *Parenthetical Portion:* Revelation 11–13
An introduction to the chief participants in the last half of the Tribulation period.

VIII. *The Great Tribulation:* Revelation 14–19:11
The last half of Daniel's Seventieth Week.

IX. *The Second Coming of Christ:* Revelation 19:11–21

X. *The Millenium:* Revelation 20
The binding of Satan and the first resurrection.

XI. *The Final Judgment:* Revelation 20:11–15

XII. *Eternity:* Revelation 21–22

God's Prophetic Program for This Age

Blessed is he that readeth, and they that hear the words of this prophecy, and keep those things which are written therein: for the time is at hand (Rev. 1:3).

There is probably not a book in the entire Bible which is less read and understood than the book of the Revelation. To the average person the last book of the Bible is a deep mystery, consisting of strange fantastic predictions which cannot be understood, and as a result the average Bible-reader knows little or nothing about either its contents or its meaning. No greater delusion, however, could occur than to call the book of the Revelation a dark book and one difficult to understand. In these messages we shall try to prove that if we are willing to believe the book and read it with an unprejudiced mind, it is not only one of the most instructive and important books, but also one of the easiest to understand. The very title of the book gives the lie to the statement that Revelation is a dark book and impossible of understanding. The name is "revelation," the translation of the Greek word apocalypsis, meaning "unveiling." If, then, the book is a dark book, then the author, the Holy Spirit, made a grave mistake in calling it "Revelation." Start, therefore, with this thought: the book is an unveiling, a revelation. Many people, preachers, teachers and others have complained that the

11

book is hard to understand; consequently the average person has believed this misinformation and carefully avoids this most important book for these last days.

A SPECIAL BLESSING

Not only is the book called "Revelation" to encourage us to read it, but it is the only book in the Bible in which God promises a special blessing to those who will read and study it. No wonder, then, that the devil has tried to delude men and women with the lie that the average person cannot understand this last book of the Scriptures, and therefore had better leave it alone. Satan would like to rob you of the special blessing God has promised to those who will read it. Listen to the promise again:

> Blessed is he that readeth, and they that hear the words of this prophecy, and keep those things which are written therein: for the time is at hand (Rev. 1:3).

A PROPHETIC BOOK

The book is not only a source of blessing to all who study it, and a revelation, but it is a prophecy of things to come. How all of us would like to look into the future! How man longs to know what lies ahead! He has turned to inane and insane delusions and magicians, soothsayers, charlatans, crystal-gazers, fortune-tellers and ouija boards in his endeavor to know the future. He has neglected the one and the only book the Bible which does tell the future without fail.

Thousands of prophecies were fulfilled in the past, and not one failed. There are hundreds of prophecies concerning the first coming of Christ, all of which were fulfilled when He came the first time. Hundreds of years before Jesus was born it was foretold where He would be born, of what tribe, in what province and in what city. His birth, His life, His miracles, His betrayal,

His crucifixion, His death, His resurrection after three days and His ascension into heaven were all foretold. The coming of the Holy Spirit and God's program for the Church were all foretold and fulfilled in minutest detail. These same prophets, writing at the same time and under the inspiration of the same infallible Spirit, also foretold the course of this age and the coming again of the Lord Jesus Christ. Yet many accept the prophecies of His first coming as being literal because they are literally fulfilled, whereas they spirtualize the unfulfilled prophecies of His second coming, and argue them away. How inconsistent! The prophecies of His First and Second advents were written at the same time by the same men, indicted by the same Holy Spirit, and if those which have already come to pass were literally fulfilled, then simple logic must cause us to expect the same literal fulfillment of those which are yet to be fulfilled.

THE BOOK OF REVELATION

While prophecies of the future are found throughout all the Scriptures, both in the Old and the New Testaments, there is one book in particular which is called prophetic. That book is the one we shall study, the Book of Revelation. It is called a prophecy in verse 3. That is what God called it, and we shall see that it deals with the events in God's program beginning with the time when John wrote it some nineteen hundred years ago on the Isle of Patmos.

THE PERSON OF THE BOOK

The name of this last book is "The Revelation of Jesus Christ." In your Bibles you have the caption "The Revelation of St. John the Divine," but that is quite incorrect. That is the name mere men who translated the book gave to it: the book is not the revelation of John,

but the revelation of Jesus Christ. Remember this simple
rule, and it will simplify many otherwise difficult passages. Christ is the subject of the book, the center and
the consummation. Throughout the book He is pre-
eminent, as we shall see, and it ends with the final revelation of Jesus Christ at the end of the Tribulation period
and the setting up of the Kingdom of Jesus Christ. Remember that it is the revelation of Jesus Christ, and it
was given to John to be passed on to us, that we might
study it and particularly in these last days might know
what the appalling events in the world today mean in the
light of the Scriptures. Remember these rules as you
study the book:

1. Revelation is *not* a dark book.
2. A special blessing is promised to those who study
   it.
3. It is a prophetic book, telling of the future.
4. It deals with the final coming of Christ.

THREE DIVISIONS OF THE BOOK

The book of the Revelation of Jesus Christ is divided
into three well-defined parts given by the Holy Spirit in
chapter 1:19:

Write the things which thou hast seen, and the things
which are, and the things which shall be hereafter.

You will notice the three divisions here: past, present
and future. "The things which thou hast seen," are
chapter 1, the vision of the glorious Christ. "The things
which are," cover the present age, the age of the Church.
John lived during its early days, and we are living at the
close of the same age, called here "the things that are."
This division ends with chapter three with the Laodicean
Church, and in chapter 4:1 the third division begins with
the Rapture of the Church at the end of this present age,
to be followed by the description of the Tribulation in

chapters 6-19, and closing with the personal glorious appearing of the Lord Jesus Christ spoken of in Revelation 19 and the setting up of His millennial kingdom described in chapters 20 and 21. The entire first chapter deals with the glory of Christ in His coming again and are thus the things which John had seen in the vision and are called "the things which thou hast seen." Chapters 2 and 3 are "the things which are," the present Church Age, ending in apostasy, war and destruction and the coming of Christ for His Church in the Rapture. The third part, "the things which shall be hereafter," that is, after this present age, covers the remainder of the book.

THE OUTLINE OF THE BOOK

In the chapters to follow we shall study the details of the book, but before we do, we want you to have a general idea of the main outline of the book. Chapter 1, as we pointed out, is the picture of the Person of Christ, the center of the book. Chapters 2 and 3 give us the history of the Church pre-written from Pentecost to the Rapture of the Church. This history is in seven periods, represented by the seven churches of chapters 2 and 3: Ephesus, Smyrna, Pergamos, Thyatira, Sardis, Philadelphia and Laodicea. These seven churches represent the successive chronological history of professing Christendom. It is a history of declension, apostasy and progressive decline. The history of the professing Church closes with chapter 3 where Jesus is pushed outside the door. In the first period of history under the figure of the Church of Ephesus we see the Lord in the Church walking in the midst of the seven golden candlesticks, which are the seven churches. In the last days of the Church we see Him pushed outside professing Christendom, typified by the Church of Laodicea, knocking at the door from the outside. He is now outside, having been turned

out by the mass of professing Christendom. The door
is shut to Him, and the place He should occupy has been
taken by social service, the social gospel, banqueting
and feasting, bloodless preaching and denial of His
deity, atonement, resurrection and coming again. When
Christendom shuts the door on earth to Him, something
happens in heaven.

ANOTHER DOOR

Chapter 4 begins by telling of another door in heaven.
Revelation 4:1 reads as follows:

> After this (that is, after the Church has turned the
> Saviour outside the door) I looked, and, behold, a door was
> opened in heaven: and the first voice which I heard was as
> it were of a trumpet talking with me; which said, Come up
> hither, and I will shew thee things which must be hereafter.

This verse speaks of the Rapture of the Church. When
all appears to be lost in Laodicea, and it seems that the
Gospel will perish from the earth and the preaching of
the Gospel is so hindered that it seems hopeless, the
door in heaven will open and the Lord will ''descend
from heaven with a shout, with the voice of the archangel,
and with the trump of God: and the dead in Christ
shall rise first: then we which are alive and remain
shall be caught up together with them in the clouds, to
meet the Lord in the air.'' The Church will be taken out
to be with her Lord.

THE SCENE IN HEAVEN

In the remainder of Chapter 4 and all of 5 we have
a record of what the Church will see when it gets to
heaven at the Rapture. Beginning with Chapter 6 we
have a description of the period of time between the
Rapture and the second coming of Christ spoken of in
Revelation 19:11. Almost fourteen chapters are devoted to this brief period of the world's greatest trib-

ulation, of war and death and destruction greater than any in all history, when the demons from the pit shall be loosed upon the earth, hailstones weighing a hundred pounds shall fall from the sky, when the man of sin, the world-dictator and the Satanic superman, will unite the world in a great political federation, kill all the believers and set up his devilish kingdom on the earth. He will marshall the kingdoms of the world in the greatest battle of all history just north of Palestine in the battle of Armageddon, and were it not for the intervention of the Lord no flesh should be saved. Man would be annihilated and perish. When that seems about to happen, the Lord will come, as we read in Revelation 19:11:

> And I saw heaven opened, and behold a white horse; and he that sat upon him was called Faithful and True, and in righteousness he doth judge and make war.

This is the coming of Christ after the Tribulation to put an end to the battle of Armageddon and the reign of man. Before the Tribulation He came *for* His Church to take them *out;* now He comes *after* the Tribulation *with* His Church to reign.

THE DEVIL BOUND

Revelation 20 speaks of the devil bound, the millennial kingdom established, the creation restored and blessed, wars come to an end, peace over all the earth, even the vegetable and animal creation at rest and peace one with the other. For one thousand blessed years Jesus will reign according to the promises of His Word. At the end of the thousand years Satan will be loosed for a moment only to be cast into the lake of fire with all his followers. Then will follow the judgement of the Great White Throne where all wicked will be judged and cast into the lake of fire and brim-

stone, and in chapter 22 we have a picture of the eternal
state and rest.

This, in brief, is the outline of the clearest book in
the Bible and the easiest to understand, the most illuminating and instructive in these dark days. In the following messages we shall fill in the details. In this chapter
we have merely tried to give you an introductory outline so that you may be able to insert the details where
they belong. In our next message we shall consider the
history of the Church as given in Revelation 2 and 3.

Behold, I come quickly.

CHAPTER TWO

The History of the Church

The surest thing in the world is neither death nor taxes. The surest thing is the Coming again of the Lord Jesus Christ to reign and rule over the earth and to vindicate and explain His First Coming, when He was rejected and slain. In our preceding chapter we began a study of the last book of the Bible, the Book of the Revelation of Jesus Christ. We pointed out that its central theme is the Coming of Christ and the central Person is Christ. The Book begins with a vision which John the Seer saw on the Isle of Patmos where he had been banished because of his witnessing for Christ. We took special note of Revelation 1:3 where God promises a peculiar blessing to all who will read this book, hear its message and follow its teaching. Then we gave the broad outline of the book as follows:

Chapter 1: The Person of the Book.
Chapters 2 and 3: The History of the Church.
Chapters 4:1 to 4: The Rapture of the Church.
Chapters 4 and 5: The Church in Heaven.
Chapters 6 to 19:11: The Tribulation.
Chapters 19:11 to 21: The Second Coming of Christ.
Chapters 20 and 21: The Millennium.
Chapter 22: The Eternal State.

In this message we consider the seven churches spoken of in Revelation 2 and 3. It would be well to mem-

orize them in their order, for in them we have the
Revelation of Jesus Christ to us concerning the program of this present Church Age, and what we may
expect during the years between our Lord's ascension
and His return according to His promise. Here are the
seven churches in correct order:

1. Ephesus.
2. Smyrna.
3. Pergamos.
4. Thyatira.
5. Sardis.
6. Philadelphia.
7. Laodicea.

These seven churches are called "candlesticks" in
Chapter 1 and Jesus Christ is seen at the beginning
walking among them. Chapter 1 gives us the most complete picture of Christ in the glory of His Coming again
to be found anywhere in the Scriptures. Read it carefully and behold the Holy Spirit's own portrait of the
Coming Glorious King. After this vision of the Head
of the true Church and the King of the world, we are
given a prophetic picture of what will become of
Christendom during the absence of this Lord and Saviour Jesus Christ.

Various Interpretations

Various views have been held by Bible students regarding the meaning of these seven churches in Revelation. First of all, we believe that they represent seven
literal assemblies of churches which were in existence at
the time of John and that the description is that of these
historic assemblies. Secondly, these seven churches also
present a picture of seven different kinds of assemblies
in the world during this entire Church Age. There are
churches today which are warm and on fire like the

Church of Ephesus, and there are others which are cold and dead like Laodicea. We know of churches which like Thyatira are full of ritualism and ceremonialism and differ little from paganism, while others like Sardis are mere dead formalism.

All these applications can be made to these seven churches, but we are reminded in chapter 1 that Revelation is a prophetic book, and so we look for a prophetic meaning in the description of these seven assemblies in Asia. Now that the present age is almost run out we can look back and see that these seven churches are a progressive picture of the history of the professing Church from the First Coming of Christ to His Second Coming. Each of them describes in unmistakable detail and clearness a certain period of Church history. Even the names are prophetic and revelatory. Remember, therefore, the following order and then see how the names fit in:

Ephesus was the Church of the first century.

Smyrna was the persecuted Church of the second and third centuries.

Pergamos was the church from about 312 A. D. to 500 A. D.

Thyatira represents the Church of the Dark Ages, to the sixteenth century.

Sardis is the Church of the Renaissance and the Reformation.

Philadelphia is the Church of the Revival of the nineteenth century.

Laodicea is the end-time Church of apostasy.

The Names

Bearing this fact in mind, consider the churches. Ephesus is the first named and represents the Church of the first century. It includes the Church in the book of Acts and is often referred to as the "Apostolic Church."

The name "Ephesus" means the "desirable one." It
was the Early Church with all the zeal of its first love
burning for Christ. It was during this age that Paul
made his missionary journeys and the apostles went
everywhere preaching the Gospel. Read Revelation
2:1-3:

> Unto the angel of the church of Ephesus write; These
> things saith he that holdeth the seven stars in his right hand,
> who walketh in the midst of the seven golden candlesticks;
> I know thy works, and thy labour, and thy patience, and
> how thou canst not bear them which are evil: and thou
> hast tried them which say they are apostles, and are not,
> and hast found them liars: And hast borne, and hast patience,
> and for my name's sake hast laboured, and hast not failed.

Here we have a description of the early Apostolic
Church, the "desirable one." But toward the end of the
first century and toward the close of the period represented by Ephesus, the leaven of evil was already at work
and the Church began to cool off and become indifferent,
and so the Holy Spirit, through John, continues in verse
4:

> Nevertheless I have somewhat against thee, because thou
> has left thy first love.

According to the Bible this present Church Age will
not end in a great revival of religion, in which the masses
will accept Christ and the world will be converted. That
is man's dream and Satan's delusion. Instead of this,
the entire body of Scripture teaches unmistakably that
this age will become worse and worse and worse until the
Coming again of Christ. Internationally it will become
worse and worse, with wars and destruction increasing,
and while men talk of peace there will be more wars and
destruction. Religiously it will become worse and worse,
until the Church of Ephesus with its zeal and love and
devotion and service has degenerated into the Church of
Laodicea with its lukewarmness and apostasy, until God

Himself says that He will spew her out of His mouth. There will be no wholesale world-conversion through the channels of preaching and religion and education, but on the contrary, conditions will be worse and worse until Christ comes. We read that the Church of Ephesus left her first love, and there follows a warning in verse 5:

> Remember therefore from whence thou art fallen, and repent, and do the first works; or else I will come unto thee quickly, and will remove thy candlestick out of his place, except thou repent.

Ephesus is no more; its candlestick has been removed, and the mass of those who professed have gone. But the faithful ones were given the promise that while the mass of professing Christendom even in Ephesus never repented, God still saves and rewards the individual believer in every age. The record of Ephesus, therefore, ends with a gracious promise:

> He that hath an ear, let him hear what the Spirit saith unto the churches; To him that overcometh will I give to eat of the tree of life, which is in the midst of the paradise of God.

THE SECOND PERIOD

Let us consider now the second period of the history of the professing Church as prophesied in Revelation. This period is given under the figure of the Church of Smyrna. Again we remind you that there was an actual Church in Smyrna, which answered to the description given here, but which at the same time was prophetic of the second period of Church history. This covers the second and third centuries of persecution of the Church by the pagan Roman emperors. Here is the brief record:

> And unto the angel of the church in Smyrna write; These things saith the first and the last, which was dead, and is alive; I know thy works, and tribulation, and poverty, (but thou art rich) . . . Fear none of those things which thou

shalt suffer: behold, the devil shall cast some of you into
prison, that ye may be tried; and ye shall have tribulation
ten days: Be thou faithful unto death, and I will give thee
a crown of life (Revelation 2:8-10).

This is the persecuted Church. The words that are
prominent in this passage are "tribulation," "poverty,"
"suffer," "prison," and, again, "tribulation." The last
term perfectly describes the Church of the second and
third centuries, when the ancient Roman Empire sought
to eradicate the faith of Jesus from the earth. The
Christians were burned and beaten, hanged and crucified,
cast to the lions and tortured to death. It seemed that
Christianity must cease to be. Under ten tyrants from
Nero to Constantine the Great the Church was persecuted unto the death. The history of those two hundred
years is the blackest in the history of the Church. Smyrna
was chosen the symbol, therefore, of this Church period.
The word "Smyrna" comes from the word "myrrh,"
one of the spices used in the ritual of Israel. It was a
fragrant spice but had to be crushed and beaten small
in order to give forth its full fragrance and perfume.
What a perfect figure for the Church of the persecution
of those days! The Christians, too, were crushed and
persecuted, but the more they suffered, the more fragrant
was their testimony. This period of Church history has
produced the most amazing records of fortitude and
faith on the part of the martyrs of Smyrna who stood
upon the fagot piles praising God and met the lions
quoting Scripture and singing psalms. In them we see
the truth of the age-old statement "The blood of the
martyrs is the seed of the Church."

CONSTANTINE THE GREAT

The second age of Church history, represented by
Smyrna, lasted for some two hundred years during
which time tens of thousands of Christians were put to

death for their faith and sealed their testimony with their blood. In 312 A. D. Constantine the Great, the emperor of Rome, was carrying on his conquests of the world. He was suffering serious reverses, and then one day he announced that he had seen in the sky a giant cross, and over it were these words: "In this sign thou shalt conquer." The pagan king took this to mean that if he would embrace the Cross he would be victorious, and so in what probably was an act of desperation he professed to become a Christian and decreed that the religion of the Roman Empire must henceforth be Christianity. After his victory he made the religion of Christianity the state religion, compelled all his armies to be baptized, and began that era of Church history which by many historians is hailed as a great blessing, but which in reality became a curse.

The Church became the ward of the state, and the Roman Empire began to paternalize and subsidize the Church. Church and state became one. The Church was supported by the state and the wealth of the empire was placed at the disposal of the Church officials. Soon the emperor also became the head of the Church and so the union of Church and state was complete. The Church married to the state soon began to dictate not only the powers of religion but also the powers of government. Everyone accepted Christianity. How many embraced Christ we do not know, probably very, very few, for from this day we can date the decline of the spiritual power of the Church. With all this wealth at her disposal and with the state to subsidize and protect her the Church soon became cold, worldly, indifferent, proud and powerless. Many *professed* Christianity because it was popular, but few *possessed* Christ.

PERGAMOS

Let us consider now the Church of Pergamos, that period beginning with the supposed conversion of Constantine and lasting until approximately 500 A. D. when the Thyatira age began. "Pergamos" means "married," and the name of this Church tells its character. It was the Church which was married to the world, and the next two hundred years were years of revelry, the rise of the hierarchy of the clergy and the dominion of a special class of so-called clergy over the laity. Hence the history of this period is a gloomy one spiritually and is described in Revelation 2:12-16:

> And to the angel of the church in Pergamos write; These things saith he which hath the sharp sword with two edges; I know thy works, and where thou dwellest, even where Satan's seat is: and thou holdest fast my name, and hast not denied my faith, even in those days wherein Antipas was my faithful martyr, who was slain among you, where Satan dwelleth. But I have a few things against thee, because thou hast there them that hold the doctrine of Balaam . . . So, hast thou also them that hold the doctrine of the Nicolaitanes, which thing I hate. Repent; or else I will come unto thee quickly, and will fight against them with the sword of my mouth.

Two outstanding doctrines are mentioned here: the doctrine of Balaam and the doctrine of the Nicolaitanes. The doctrine of Balaam was the doctrine of tolerance. Balaam, even in the time of Israel's early history, encouraged Israel to mingle with the Gentile nations about them thereby losing their separated position. During the Pergamos Age when the Church became rich and independent, worldly practices and alliances crept in and corrupted the Church. The *way* of Balaam refers to preaching and prophesying for money and gain, making a "racket" of the Gospel. This, too, crept in about this time, but the *doctrine* of Balaam refers to a laxness and losing our separated position.

In our next message we shall consider briefly the doctrine of the Nicolaitanes, the setting up of a distinct class of men called clergymen and the denial of the common priesthood of all believers.

I am sure you can see that in these seven churches we have a prewritten prophecy of the course of the professing Church. In the remaining four churches the picture becomes still clearer. We believe that the clock of this age will soon strike the hour of the coming of the Lord. Laodicea is upon us and the coming of the Lord draweth nigh. May the Lord help us to be ready and to search His own blueprint, the Scriptures, that we may not be ashamed at His appearing.

CHAPTER THREE

The Failure of Reformation

> This know also, that in the last days perilous times shall
> come. For men shall be lovers of their own selves, covetous,
> boasters, proud, blasphemers, disobedient to parents, un-
> thankful, unholy, without natural affection, trucebreakers,
> false accusers, incontinent, fierce, despisers of those that
> are good, traitors, heady, highminded, lovers of pleasures
> more than lovers of God; having a form of godliness, but
> denying the power thereof (II Tim. 3:1-5).

This passage might well be taken from a modern
newspaper, but it is from the Word of God. Written
almost two thousand years ago by Paul, these words
describe the very days in which we are living. The
greatest delusion which Satan has ever foisted upon
religious Christendom is the unscriptural theory that
as the age progresses conditions will become better and
better, more and more people will become Christians
and finally, through the efforts of men in education,
religion, morality, invention and reformation, the world
will culminate in a millenium, when everybody will love
everybody, the world will be converted, and the golden
age of which man has dreamed will be ushered in. There
is not a shred of evidence in the Bible to support this
false Utopian theory. Instead, the Bible teaches that as
the age progresses, conditions will become worse and
worse, and then the Lord will come and judge the nations, punish the wicked, catch away His Church, the true

body of Christ, and by His personal presence establish
that wonderful age of peace and righteousness. In spite
of the clearness of Scripture in regard to the course of
this age, which will decay morally, politically and religiously, millions of people believe this bad dream of a
human man-made golden age of peace and these deluded
folk do not search the Scriptures to see if these things be
true.

The Evidence of History

Even aside from the clear teaching of the Word of
God, history itself contradicts this vain theory. Each
age has been worse than the one preceding. True, we
have inventions and discoveries in science, medicine,
art, music and education, but all of them, instead of
making men better, are used only to express the corruption of the human heart. The new inventions and discoveries, instead of being used for the good of men,
increase destruction, suffering and sorrow. They are
the instruments which make possible the recent brutal
conflict with its global implications. Never has there
been more crime, divorce, drunkenness, immorality,
atheism, unbelief and violence than in this so-called
"enlightened" age. After six thousand years of human
history the world is scourged by hatred and brutality
such as it has never seen.

The Record of Revelation

In our previous messages we pointed out that this is
precisely what the Bible predicted. In the second and
third chapters of the book of the Revelation of Jesus
Christ we have a prophecy of this present age of Christendom under the teaching of the seven churches mentioned in these two chapters. From the almost ideal
Church of Ephesus, the Apostolic Church, we trace a
gradual decline till it culminates in Laodicea, of which

God says that He will spew her out of His mouth. We
studied briefly the first three of these churches, Ephesus,
Smyrna and Pergamos. Ephesus typifies the state of
Christendom in the first century. Smyrna is the persecuted Church of the second and third centuries. Pergamos is a picture of the Church joined in an unholy
union with the world. After Constantine the Great, the
emperor of Rome, nominally accepted Christianity, the
Church became wealthy and worldly. Two evils crept
in, according to Revelation 2: Balaamism and Nicolaitanism. Balaamism is the doctrine of worldly compromise.
Nicolaitanism is the rise of hierarchal clergy. Certain
men lusting for religious power declared themselves
above the rest of the people, upon whom they laid bur-
dens, and virtually made them slaves of this self-ap-
pointed group of religious dictators. This was followed
as a matter of course by the next period of Church history represented by the fourth church mentioned in Revelation 2:18-29. Here is the description of the Church of
Thyatira, and you will see, if you are familiar with medi-
eval history, how well it describes those centuries known
to historians as the "Dark Ages," when the Word of God
became corrupted and the Church turned from the teaching of pure grace to a religion of works and religion, ceremonies and sacrifices. Here is the record:

> And unto the angel of the church in Thyatira write; These
> things saith the Son of God, who hath his eyes like unto a
> flame of fire, and his feet are like fine brass; I know thy
> works, and charity, and service, and faith, and thy patience,
> and thy works; and the last to be more than the first.

The word "Thyatira" means literally "a continual
sacrifice." It was during the centuries typified by the
Church of Thyatira, called the Dark Ages, that the completeness of the finished work of Christ was denied, and
to it were added works, ceremonies, ritual and sacrifices.
That is why works are mentioned twice in the passage

describing this church, which had a religion of works and not of grace. Then the Holy Spirit accuses this church in Revelation 2:20 of suffering the woman Jezebel to seduce the Church. Jezebel was the wife of the wicked king of Israel, Ahab, and she caused Ahab to commit idolatry and to turn from the pure worship of the true God. If you will remember that the Church of Thyatira represents the Church of the Dark Ages, you will see that no better figure than that of Jezebel could be used. It was during these years that the Vandals, the Huns and the Goths overran Europe and brought with them their own idolatrous pagan worship. The Church, in a spirit of compromise, seeking to win them to professing Christianity, adopted part of their pagan idolatrous religion of these heathen, with the result that there emerged from this age a Church that was partly Christian, partly Judaistic and partly pagan.

God's Judgment Upon Her

This Church of Thyatira, unlike Ephesus, Smyrna and Pergamos, was to continue to the end of the age, and so the Lord says in verse 22 that He will cast her into the Great Tribulation. Revelation 2:22-23 tells of this judgment:

> Behold, I will cast her into . . . great tribulation, except they repent of their deeds. And I will kill her children with death; and all the churches shall know that I am he which searcheth the reins and hearts: and I will give unto every one according to your works.

But to those who are faithful even in the midst of this apostasy the Lord promises His blessing. In verse 25 we read:

> But that which ye have already hold fast till I come.

This is the first time the coming of the Lord is mentioned in the prophecy of the seven churches. Thyatira is the first that will continue even in her wicked state un-

til the coming of the Lord. The wicked worshipers shall
pass through the Tribulation, but the faithful ones have
the promise that they shall rule and reign with Christ
when He comes again.

Sardis—The Reformation Church

The third chapter of Revelation begins with a picture
of the Church of Sardis, the Church of the Reformation.
Remember that in speaking of all these churches we are
referring to professing Christendom. Among this mass
of professing Christendom, of course, are the true believers. Many of the mere professors appear to be genu-
ine believers, but God alone knows which are His own.
Men cannot always distinguish, and it is dangerous to
judge. God has His faithful ones in every age and in
every church of the seven. In Thyatira there were
Christ's faithful followers. In the sixteenth century we
behold the gloom of the Dark Ages lifted, largely because
of the testimony of the faithful remnant of true believers
in Thyatira and the beginning of the Renaissance. The
word "Renaissance" means literally "rebirth." It is
the name given to that great awakening in the fourteenth,
fifteenth and sixteenth centuries, culminating in the six-
teenth-century Reformation in Europe. Many factors
were instrumental in bringing about this deliverance
from the Dark Ages of Thyatira and the birth of the fifth
church of Revelation called "Sardis." The word "Sardis" means "remnant or that which remained." Until
this time great darkness in every sphere prevailed over
the earth, but then certain discoveries and inventions set
the stage for the Reformation and the Church of Sardis,
the Reformation Church. Among these factors were the
discovery of America, the invention of the printing press
and the giving of the Scriptures in printed form to the
laity. Until the invention of the printing press the Scriptures were unkown to the common people. Each copy had

to be individually transcribed and as a result the number
was sharply limited and confined to a few scholars and
the clergy. However, with the discovery and invention of
the printing press in the middle of the sixteenth century
by Johann Gutenberg of Germany, a new light dawned
upon the world of Christendom. The first complete press
was completed in about 1550 and the first complete book
printed from type was the Latin Bible known as the
"Mazarin Bible" or the "Bible of forty-two lines," because there were forty-two lines to a page.

A New Interest in the Bible

With this God-given, God-sent and God-timed invention of printing, a new study of the Bible began, lost
truths were rediscovered, unbiblical errors were exposed
and so the stage was set for the Church of Sardis, the
Church of the Reformation. It swept over Europe under
the leadership of Luther, Erasmus, Zwingli, Le Fevre
and Calvin. Luther's influence extended throughout
Germany and the Scandinavian countries, hence the
prevalence of Lutheranism there. The French, Swiss
and Dutch movements followed the leadership of Calvin
and as such became the Calvinistic group of Reformation
churches, and later Scotland, under John Knox, followed
the teachings of John Calvin.

The Reformation fell short of accomplishing that
which might have been achieved. While it was a protest
and reaction against the rigid ecclesiastical hierarchy of
Thyatira, it went to the other extreme and, being free
from the restraints of the absolute vicar and potentate of
the Church, was split by the abuse of its own liberty and
freedom and became divided into numerous sects and denominations. This is a matter of history. The Church
boasted of its orthodoxy but did nothing about it. It de-
nounced all who disagreed, and confusion instead of soli-
darity resulted, so that soon there were denominations,

sects and groups without number. This spirit of carnality resulted in a dead orthodoxy and the Reformation Church became a great organization with but little evidence of spiritual life. This was the Church of Sardis as described by John in Revelation sixteen hundred years before it was born. Here is the record and we marvel at its historical accuracy:

> And unto the angel of the church in Sardis write; These things saith he that hath the seven Spirits of God, and the seven stars; I know thy works, that thou hast a name that thou livest, and art dead. Be watchful, and strengthen the things which remain, that are ready to die: for I have not found thy works perfect before God. Remember therefore how thou hast received and heard, and hold fast, and repent (Rev. 3:1-3).

God says concerning this confusion of tongues among professing Christendom of the Reformation that they have a name that they live, but are dead. This, of course, is God's estimate of the Church as a whole, but just as in the others there is a remnant of true believers, so also here, and to these the Lord addresses Himself in Revelation 3:4:

> Thou hast a few names even in Sardis which have not defiled their garments; and they shall walk with me in white: for they are worthy.

The Church of Philadelphia

As a result of the carnality, division and worldliness of the Church of Sardis, God rebukes its dead orthodoxy and deals with this remnant and presents next to us the missionary Church of the revival of the nineteenth century. The word "Philadelphia," the sixth church, comes from two words meaning "brotherly love." It is the revival Church. With the nineteenth century came a change. Until the nineteenth century the blessed hope of the premillennial return of the Lord was seldom stressed. The truth was believed by many of God's faithful remnant, but it was seldom preached and was utterly unknown to the masses of church members. A hundred and fifty years ago the truth of the imminent return of the Lord was revived and as a result the true Christians were inspired and fired with their responsibility, and God raised up men full of power and zeal and fire and passion for souls to awaken the dead Church of Sardis to its responsibility. The names of Whitefield, Wesley, Edwards, and, later, Moody, Darby and Spurgeon, are too familiar to need comment here. Revivals swept the continent and spread virtually throughout the world. As a result it was during this century that the great missionary movements were born and the powerful missionary societies were formed. Although missionary work was conducted by the faithful remnant in the Church before the revival of the nineteenth century, it was circumscribed and limited, and was done chiefly by the Moravians. With the coming of the Church of Philadelphia as a protest against the deadness of the denominations of the Church of Sardis, the missionary fire broke out, and the names of Livingstone, Tayler and many others bear testimony to the zeal and love of the revived Church of Philadelphia.

In our next message we shall go into greater detail regarding the Philadelphian church and conclude with the last of the seven churches in Revelation, the Church of Laodicea. From what we have said, you have no doubt inferred that to be a Christian is not merely to belong to a so-called ''Christian'' Church or observe its rituals and ceremonies. Professing Christendom is *not* Christianity. Membership in the organized Church is not enough. Religion is not enough. You must be a member of the one true Church of Jesus Christ, which is His body. Whether you be Jew or Gentile, Catholic or Protestant, Presbyterian or Methodist, makes no difference. If you have received Christ by faith and have been born again, then you are a member of the true Church and a brother or sister to every other believer in every other church. Have *you* been born again, and have *you* been admitted into the body of Christ by faith? Then, though you may be in Thyatira or Philadelphia or even Laodicea, you are among that faithful remnant found everywhere and in every age. Forget these man-made distinctions and accept God's only way of salvation by faith in the Son of God.

CHAPTER FOUR

The End of This Age

And to the angel of the church in Philadelphia write;
these things saith he that is holy, he that is true, he that
hath the key of David, he that openeth, and no man shutteth;
and shutteth, and no man openeth; I know thy works: behold,
I have set before thee an open door, and no man can shut it:
for thou hast a little strength, and hast kept my word, and
hast not denied my name (Rev. 3:7-8).

There is only one true Church in the world. It is
neither Protestant nor Catholic, neither Presbyterian
nor Baptist, but consists of all those, whether white or
colored, rich or poor, Jew or Gentile, who have by faith
in the shed blood of the Lord Jesus Christ become members of that one true Church, which in Scripture is
called the Church of God, the body of Christ, and the
assembly of the first-born whose names are written in
heaven. This is the one true Church, irrespective of
denomination, race, nationality or organization. When
we stand before the Almighty Judge of heaven and of
earth, we will not be asked what church on earth we
belonged to, but the only question will be: "What have
you done with Jesus who is called the Christ?"

This is the Biblical picture of the one true Church, but
the word "church," is used also in another sense to
describe a local body of Christians among whom are
found the true believers. The Bible speaks therefore, of
the Church which is in Corinth, the Church which is in

Ephesus, in Laodicea, or Smyrna. These were groups of
Christians in the various cities. Not all the members of
these local assemblies were members of the one true
church but they were found in these assemblies. When
God wrote to these churches, He took into account only
this remnant of true believers in every church. We must
distinguish between the professing church and the true
church. The professing Church is the organization; the
true Church is the organism among the organization.
As the Lord says, "It is not all Israel that is called
Israel," so it is true that it is not all Christian which is
called Christian. This co-existence in the world and in
the local churches of the true and false, the professors
and the possessors, is taught throughout the Bible. In
the company of Israel who went out of Egypt there were
a mixed multitude, who looked like and acted like and
ate like true Israelites but were not; for they were a
mixed multitude who went along only because they saw
that God was with His people, but they were not of them.
Jesus taught this same truth in His parable of the wheat
and the tares in Matthew 13. The tares of which we read
were so much like the wheat that He forbade the servants to try to separate them, but admonished the la-
borers to wait until the harvest, when the Lord of the
harvest Himself would separate the true from the false.

TRUE IN REVELATION

We have seen the same truth in Revelation 2 and 3.
In the second and third chapters of the book of Revela-
tion are seven letters written by the Head of the
Church, through John, to the seven churches in Asia.

John tells us that this book of Revelation is a prophecy and we have seen that these seven churches give
us in that exact order the seven periods of the history
of the Church from Pentecost until the second coming
of Jesus Christ. The Church of Ephesus is a picture of

the early Apostolic Church. The Church of Smyrna represents the Church of the second and third centuries, the persecuted Church. The Church of Pergamos typifies the worldly Church, beginning with the so-called conversion of Constantine the Great in 312 and extending to about 500 A. D. Then came the ritualistic Church of the Dark Ages with its superstitions, idolatry and legalism, and this was followed by the Church of Sardis, the Church of the Reformation and Counter Reformation in the sixteenth century. In all these periods of Church history there were two kinds of members: true and false. The false, Christ condemned and judged, and with the true He dealt in mercy, and this true remnant runs like a thread through the entire history of the Church. When the Church of Sardis, the Reformation Church, failed to live up to its name, which meant "the remnant," God began to deal again with the faithful remnant within the professing Church and called out the Church of Philadelphia. This, we saw, was the revival missionary Church of the nineteenth century. While space prevents a detailed study, we are trying to give the outline of these chapters rather than an exhaustive exposition, two facts in the letter to the Church of Philadelphia are sufficiently important to warrant more careful attention. In Revelation 3:8 we read;

> I know thy works: behold, I have set before thee an open door, and no man shut it: for thou hast a little strength, and hast kept my word, and hast not denied my name.

That is the first fact. This church has an open door. We have already pointed out that the age covered by the Philadelphian period was the greatest missionary age since the days of the Church of Ephesus, the Apostolic Church. In addition to the open door of missions, God has added in these latter days the open door of the radio, the greatest challenge which God has

given to the Church. Few there are among Christians
who realize fully this tremendous challenge of the open
door of broadcasting, for the Philadelphians, the true
believers in the Church, are all too few, and, therefore
the Lord says to them, "Thou hast a little strength."
They are described, this little minority, who belong to
Philadelphia, as those who have kept His Word and have
not denied His Name. We are living in an age when
Sardis has "gone modern." The Cross, the inspiration
of the Book, the blood of Christ, His deity, His resurrection, and His coming again are denied on every hand,
but there is a remnant who have kept His Word and
have not denied His Name, and to these He gives a
special promise. That brings us to the second verse in
this passage which merits special comment (Rev. 3:10).
The Lord is speaking to Philadelphia:

> Because thou hast kept the word of my patience, I also
> will keep thee from the hour of temptation, which shall come
> upon all the world, to try them that dwell upon the earth.
> Behold, I come quickly: hold that fast which thou hast, that
> no man take thy crown (Rev. 3:10-11).

Here is the first definite promise to the Church that
some will escape the Great Tribulation. It is well to
remember that the last four of these churches mentioned
in Revelation 2 and 3 — Thyatira, Sardis, Philadelphia
and Laodicea—all will continue in the world simul-
taneously until the coming of the Lord. Only of the
Church of Philadelphia is it said that they shall be taken
out and kept from the hour of trial and tribulation which
will come upon the earth after the rapture of the true
Church as described in Revelation 4:1-4. Of the Church
of Thyatira it is said:

> Behold, I will cast her into . . . great tribulation.

Thyatira will pass through the Tribulation, except the
remnant who belong to Philadelphia. The same is true

of Sardis and Laodicea. When we come to Philadelphia and Laodicea we approach the end of the age of the Church, and the coming of the Lord draws near.

LAODICEA

While the Church of Sardis continues in her formalism and dead theology and the Philadelphian Church buys up every opportunity to utilize the open door for the Gospel, the rest of professing Christendom will merge into the last form of organized professing Christendom, pictured in Revelation 3: 14-19 in the Church of Laodicea. It is a sad, sad picture of the close of the age. Let the Scriptures speak:

> And unto the angel of the church of the Laodiceans write; These things saith the Amen, the faithful and true witness, the beginning of the creation of God; I know thy works, that thou are neither cold nor hot: I would thou wert cold or hot. So then because thou art lukewarm, and neither cold nor hot, I will spue thee out of my mouth. Because thou sayest, I am rich, and increased with goods, and have need of nothing; and knowest not that thou art wretched, and miserable, and poor, and blind, and naked: I counsel thee to buy of me gold tried in the fire, that thou mayest be rich; and white raiment, that thou mayest be clothed, and that the shame of thy nakedness do not appear; and anoint thine eyes with eyesalve, that thou mayest see. As many as I love, I rebuke and chasten: be zealous therefore, and repent (Rev. 3:14-19).

This is God's picture of professing Christendom at the end of this age and just before the Lord Jesus returns, as described in the opening verses of the next chapter. She is described as lukewarm, indifferent. Lukewarm water is produced by mixing hot and cold. There is a zeal and a fervor for organization but a coldness and indifference to the Gospel. This church, says God, He will reject. He will spue her out of His mouth. While the Church of Philadelphia will be raptured before the Tribulation, and the Church of Thyatira will be cast into tribulation, the Church of Laodicea will be utterly rejected of the Lord. But even in Laodicea there are those who are the Lord's, and are, while identified with the lukewarm Church, really a part of the Church of Philadelphia.

SPIRITUAL PRIDE

In addition to the charge of lukewarmness the Lord characterized this Church of the latter days as a self-satisfied, proud and self-righteous organization. They knew not that they were poor, miserable, and wretched, blind and naked. Surely we need make but little comment on that which the Lord has so plainly described. One other fact is evident. The Laodicean Church has shut the Saviour out, for after His severe rebuke He says in Revelation 3:20:

> Behold, I stand at the door, and knock: if any man hear my voice, and open the door, I will come in to him, and will sup with him, and he with me.

The Lord Jesus, the One who in the Church of Ephesus was walking in the midst of the churches, who was the center and the object of all their devotion and service, now stands outside the door and still offers to the individual sinner His forgiveness and perfect salvation. Rejected by the masses, He still calls to the individual, "If any man hear my voice." Surely this is the picture of the end of the age religiously. There is no wholesale revival anywhere. True to the prophecies concerning the last days and in complete harmony with the predictions concerning the age of professing Christendom, the age is closing in apostasy and lukewarmness. Wickedness, immorality, crime, war and hatred are increasing apace in the world, while religiously there is an apathy and an indifference, a letting down of the bars, a denial of the faith and the cardinal truths of the Bible. The man

who still preaches the truth for which our forefathers
left their native country to find a place where freedom
of worship might be enjoyed without interference or
persecution is now considered a bigot. We have developed
the spirit of compromise and a modern theology that
has lost its lifeblood.

THE END OF THE AGE

These conditions should not alarm and confuse us, for
they are to us the evidence of the coming again of the
Head of the Church, the Lord Jesus. The closing of the
door in Laodicea is the signal for the opening of the
door in heaven and the coming of the Lord Jesus Christ.
Notice, therefore, that Revelation 3 ends with a closed
door at which Jesus stands and knocks, but that Revelation 4 begins with an open door through which Jesus
will return. Note this carefully. With the story of
Laodicea in the closing part of Revelation 3 the Church
Age ends, and it is the signal for the coming of the Lord.
Therefore we read in chapter 4:1 as follows:

> After this I looked, and, and, behold, a door was opened in
> heaven: and the first voice which I heard was as it were of
> a trumpet talking with me; which said, come up hither, and
> I will shew thee things which must be hereafter.

John, a member of and a representative of the true
Church, is called from the scene on earth to his place in
heaven. This represents the Rapture, the catching away
of the Church at the close of this dispensation, at the end
of Laodicea. Notice the time when this shall occur:
"after this!" We ask of course, "after what?" After
the Church of Laodicea; after the time when the Church
has become lukewarm and the doors have been shut to
the message of Jesus Christ. That happened during the
past few years. All over the world men have shut the
door to the Lord Jesus—because of the results of war,

because of hatred for the Gospel, because of powerful agents who would banish all Gospel preaching. Whatever the cause, we have seen doors closed all over the world. Missionaries are restricted or forbidden, and in many places even radio time is not available for the Gospel of the grace of God.

What does this mean? Simply that God's program is running on time. We have nearly reached the end of the Laodicean period of Church history, the end of the final period, and the imminent event on the program of God is the coming again of His Son Jesus Christ to snatch away His bride, and then to return to set up His everlasting kingdom of permanent peace and righteousness. In succeeding messages we shall study some of these events which must come to pass after this Church Age is closed. May the Lord use these messages to prepare us for the soon return of Him who said:

> I will come again, and receive you unto myself, that where I am, there ye may be also (John 14:3).

CHAPTER FIVE

The Translation of the Church in Revelation

> Behold, he cometh with clouds; and every eye shall see him, and they also which pierced him: and all kindreds of the earth shall wail because of him. Even so, Amen (Rev. 1:7).

The surest thing in all the world is the coming again of the Lord Jesus Christ. Surer than death is the coming of the Lord, for my Bible tells me that there will be a generation of believers who will never see death when the Lord returns, for they will be caught away and changed in a moment. Paul says in I Corinthians 15:51:

> Behold, I shew you a mystery; We shall not all sleep, but we shall all be changed.

In I Thessalonians 4 he says:

> For the Lord himself shall descend from heaven with a shout, with the voice of the archangel, and with the trump of God: and the dead in Christ shall rise first: then we which are alive and remain shall be caught up together with them in the clouds, to meet the Lord in the air (I Thess. 4:16-17).

Yes, the strongest certainty in all the world is the coming again of the Lord Jesus Christ. It is surer than the sunrise, although the sun has never failed to rise, there is a day coming, when Christ returns, that the sun will fail to shine, for our Saviour Himself tells us in Matthew 24:29-30 that this will happen:

Immediately after the tribulation of those days shall the
sun be darkened, and the moon shall not give her light, and
the stars shall fall from heaven, and the powers of the
heavens shall be shaken . . . and they shall see the Son of
man coming in the clouds of heaven with power and great
glory.

Yes, Jesus Christ is coming again. Though long delayed and scoffed at by infidels, "the day of the Lord
will come." Unfortunately, comparatively few Christians
believe this. I mean, of course, *nominal* Christianity.
All true believers believe in the second coming of Christ.
One canot believe the Bible without believing in His
second advent. Without the second coming of Christ
the Bible is a book of fables, God becomes a liar, Jesus
Christ an impostor, His first coming to die on the Cross
a failure and a miscarriage of divine justice, and every
child of God in all ages who has been crying for His
return is a simpleton and a fool, following a will-o-the-
wisp of an independable book.

But He is coming again! Every prophecy bearing on
this truth has been fulfilled, and current events are
shaping themselves in perfect harmony with the Scriptural outline of the last days. Many Christians profess
to believe it, but do not live as though they believed it.
All the creeds of every Christian group contain the confession of faith in His return, and yet every generation
places the event in the far-distant future as something
that does not immediately apply to them or affect them.

In the messages to follow this we will speak of
the blessed hope of Christ's return as revealed in the
book of Revelation, the last book of the Bible. In this
chapter I wish to present an introduction to the coming
messages and will seek to accomplish one aim: to remind
you that His coming again is a fact, which the entire
Bible teaches, and that it was the hope of believers in
all ages. Consider Acts 1:9-11:

> And when he had spoken these things, while they beheld, he was taken up; and a cloud received him out of their sight. And while they looked steadfastly toward heaven as he went up, behold, two men stood by them in white apparel; which also said, Ye men of Galilee, why stand ye gazing up into heaven? this same Jesus, which is taken from you into heaven, shall so come in like manner as ye have seen him go into heaven.

Yes, Jesus Christ *is* coming again. He said so when the hearts of the disciples were troubled by the announcement of His death and His departure. It was then that He comforted them with the words:

> Let not your heart be troubled: ye believe in God, believe also in Me. In my Father's house are many mansions: if it were not so, I would have told you. I go to prepare a place for you. And if I go and prepare a place for you, I will come again, and receive you unto myself; that where I am, there ye may be also (John 14:1-3).

Yes, Jesus Christ is coming again. The fact may be denied by the scoffers and infidels and ignored by the worldly and carnal Christians, but He is coming. Peter tells us plainly and unmistakably,

> Where is the promise of his coming? for since the fathers fell asleep, all things continue as they were from the beginning of the creation (II Peter 3:4).

This is what the scoffers say about this blessed truth. Then Peter calls their attention to the Flood and reminds them that no one believed Noah when he foretold the coming of the Deluge, but it came, and so Peter adds in 2 Peter 3:10:

> But the day of the Lord will come as a thief in the night; in the which the heavens shall pass away with a great noise, and the elements shall melt with fervent heat, the earth also.

THE FIRST PROMISE IN THE BIBLE

In spite of the denials the Lord is coming back again, says Peter. The first promise in the Bible after Adam

fell has to do with both the First and Second Comings
of Christ. You will recall that after man had sinned and
God had called him as he hid among the trees of the
garden, He, after pronouncing a curse upon Adam and
Eve and all the creation under him, turned to the serpent
who represented Satan, the deceiver, and the one who
had tempted our first parents to fall. While cursing the
serpent, God gave the promise of the coming Redeemer.
Many believe that the promise of the coming Saviour
in Genesis 3:15 was spoken to Adam, but in reality it
was spoken to the serpent. Here it is:

> And I will put enmity between thee (the serpent) and
> the woman, and between thy seed and her seed; it shall
> bruise thy head, and thou shalt bruise his heel (Gen. 3:15).

One Half Fulfilled

This promise has been only partly fulfilled, when
Jesus came the first time. It was then that Satan succeeded in bruising the heel of the Redeemer, but the
second part of the promise, the bruising of the serpent's
head, still lies in the future, and—we believe—the near
future. At Calvary the Lord Jesus crushed the serpent's
head potentially, but the actual carrying out of the
final crushing was not at Calvary. That awaits His
glorious triumphant coming again. This is evident from
Paul's words in Romans 16:20. Remember that Paul
wrote Romans some thirty years after the Cross, and yet
he says in this passage:

> And the God of peace shall bruise Satan under your feet
> shortly.

You see, then, that Genesis 3:15 is more than a promise
of a coming Redeemer. It includes two comings: the
first, when the Saviour would apparently be defeated,
and the second, His ultimate triumph. Notice that there
are two conflicts spoken of here: the first, in which the

seed of the woman, shall crush the head of the serpent, Satan. The first conflict occurred nineteen hundred years ago when Jesus hung on the Cross and Satan bruised His heel. But that was not the end. That same Jesus is coming again and will crush the serpent's head and put an end to his reign forever.

Mother Eve's Hope

When the first child born into the world lay in the first mother's arms, she claimed that promise and called his name Cain. In your Bible you read that when Eve gave birth to her first-born she called his name Cain because she said, "I have gotten a man from the Lord."

The words translated thus are in the original as follows: "Cainithi Jehovah." That means "I have begotten a man even Jehovah." As Eve looked upon that little bundle of life, the first baby, and recognized her seed, she supposed him to be the promised seed and cried out "I have begotten a man even Jehovah Himself." But she thought he was the promised one, but she was mistaken. That seed was not to come for another four thousand years, but the hope continued during all those years. Enoch looked for the coming of the Lord in power. That man who is the great type of the Rapture in the Old Testament, we are told in Jude, prophesied concerning our Lord's coming as follows:

> Behold, the Lord cometh with ten thousands of His saints, to execute judgment upon all, and to convince all that are ungodly among them of all their ungodly deeds which they have ungodly committed, and of all their hard speeches which ungodly sinners have spoken against him (Jude 15-15).

Job, who lived before Abraham or shortly after, looked for the coming of the Lord and declared:

> For I know that my Redeemer liveth, and that he shall stand at the latter day upon the earth: and though after worms destroy this body, yet in my flesh shall I see God (Job 19:25-26).

David looked for the coming again of the Lord in glory, and said in Psalm 2:4-6:

> He that sitteth in the heavens shall laugh: the Lord shall have them in derision. Then shall he speak unto them in his wrath, and vex them in his sore displeasure. Yet have I set my king upon my holy hill of Zion.

Isaiah looked for His glorious coming and cried:

> For unto us a child is born, unto us a son is given: and the government shall be upon his shoulder . . . Of the increase of his government and peace there shall be no end, upon the throne of David, and upon His kingdom, to order it, and to establish it with judgment and with justice from henceforth even for ever (Isa. 9:6-7).

Space fails us to mention how Joel, Amos, Micah, Naham, Habakkuk, Jeremiah, Zephaniah and Zechariah took for their theme that glorious day still future when wars should cease, and Christ should "have dominion over land and sea" and "earth's remotest regions" should His empire be.

After four thousand years He came. The Jews thought that when the Messiah came He would immediately establish the Kingdom. The secret of this present age of His rejection by Israel and the calling out of a bride to reign with Him at His second coming was unknown to them. When the Saviour came as a man of sorrows instead of a triumphant King and went to the Cross instead of the throne, they could not understand, and they rejected Him. No wonder, for all their Old Testament prophesies had told far more about His glorious reign (still future) than concerning His death and the crucifixion. When He began to reveal to the disciples that He must die, they were greatly confused. They had looked for a triumphant king who would sweep His enemies away before Him and set up the kingdom; naturally, when He set His face to the Cross, they asked the question, "What about all the hundreds of Old Testament prophecies concerning Your glorious reign? Are they all untrue? Will they not be fulfilled, and have we been mistaken?'' Then the Lord reassured them by saying that although He was going to die and leave them and go back to heaven, He was coming back again and then all His promises concerning His reign on the earth and the restoration of Palestine and Israel would be fulfilled to the minutest detail. Then begins a new series of revelations concerning His Second Coming. We read His promise in John:

If I go away . . . I will come again.

During the days just before Christ went to the Cross He spent almost His entire time with His disciples in talking, not about His passion and death, but His coming again. (See Matthew 24-25; Mark 11-13; Luke 21). The primary fact of which Jesus spoke during that period was His coming again and the last days. After His resurrection during the forty days with His disciples He spoke of the things pertaining to the Kingdom of God. His first message to the disciples after He left was: ''This same Jesus is coming again.''

This Second Coming is the theme of all the apostles in the Epistles. The first two epistles in point of time are the First and Second letters of Paul to the Thessalonians. Read them and study the truth he wanted these young Christians to grasp. Paul looked to that glorious day and declared in his Epistle to the Romans:

The whole creation groaneth and travaileth in pain together until now (Rom. 8:22).
For the earnest expectation of the creature waiteth for the manifestation of the sons of God (Rom. 8:19).

In Corinthians he says:

Behold, I shew you a mystery; We shall not all sleep, but we shall all be changed.

In the first letter to the Corinthians he urges:

Judge nothing before the time, until the Lord come.

In the Second Epistle to the Corinthians he warns:

> For we must all appear before the judgment seat of Christ.

In Colossians, Ephesians, Philippians and in his letters to Timothy, Paul speaks of the Coming Again of the Lord. In Titus he says:

> For the grace of God that bringeth salvation hath appeared to all men, teaching us that, denying ungodliness and worldly lusts, we should live soberly, righteously, and godly, in this present world; looking for that blessed hope, and the glorious appearing of the great God and our Saviour Jesus Christ (Titus 2:11-13).

Peter tells us:

> The day of the Lord will come as a thief in the night (II Peter 3:10).

John tells us:

> Beloved, now are we the sons of God, and it doth not yet appear what we shall be: but we know that, when He shall appear, we shall be like Him; for we shall see Him as He is (I John 3:2).

Jude says:

> Behold, the Lord cometh with ten thousands of His saints, to execute judgment (Jude 14-15).

The entire last book of the Bible is occupied with the coming again of the Lord Jesus and the events accompanying that glorious event. In the first chapter John cries:

> Behold, He cometh with clouds; and every age shall see Him.

Then as if to seal the matter so that none shall have excuse to doubt the reality of Christ's return, the Bible closes with these words:

> He which testifieth these things saith, Surely I come quickly. Amen. Even so, come, Lord Jesus. The grace of our Lord Jesus Christ be with you all. Amen (Rev. 22:20-21).

The last promise in the Bible is "He is coming again." The last promise of the Lord Jesus is: "I come quickly."

The last prayer in the Bible is: "Even so, come, Lord Jesus." Can anyone with an open Bible doubt the reality, the literalness, the certainty of the second coming of Christ? In our next message we want to study some of the indications and signs which the Lord gives us by which we may know when His coming is near. All of these are today for the first time in human history in the process of literal fulfillment. I want you to see that there can be no question about the greatest of all events. The truthfulness of Christ depends upon His literal Coming Again. The truth of the Bible stands or falls with Jesus' Coming. If Jesus is not coming personally and literally, then throw your Bible away, for it is a dangerous, unreliable and vicious book. Then the world is doomed, the Church is deceived, all preachers who preach the Coming of Christ are either deceived or tragically dishonest and the only hope for a dying world is gone.

The first promise in the Word is concerning His coming. The last promise in the Old Testament (Malachi 4) is concerning His coming. The first announcement given by the angel in the New Testament to Mary was:

> The Lord shall give unto Him the throne of His father David: and He shall reign over the house of Jacob for ever; and of His kingdom there shall be no end.

Yes, Jesus Christ is Coming Again. The very same Jesus Who was born in a stable, died on a cross and ascended into heaven, is Coming Again, and everyone will have to meet Him either in glory or in judgment. One of these days the last church bell will ring, the last sermon will be preached and the last broadcast sent forth before His coming again. My friend, are you ready to meet Him who said:

> Marvel not at this: for the hour is coming, in the which all that are in the graves shall hear His voice.
> And shall come forth; they that have done good, unto the resurrection of life; and they that have done evil, unto the resurrection of damnation (John 5:28-29).

CHAPTER SIX

They That Look for Him

> After this I looked, and, behold, a door was opened in heaven: and the first voice which I heard was as it were a trumpet talking with me; which said, Come up hither, and I will shew thee things which must be hereafter. And immediately I was in the spirit: and, behold, a throne was set in heaven, and one sat on the throne. And he that sat was to look upon like a jasper and a sardine stone: and there was a rainbow round about the throne, in sight like unto an emerald (Rev. 4:1-3).

The fourth chapter of the book of the Revelation opens with the words ''after this.'' It marks, as we have mentioned, the third division of the book of the unveiling of Jesus Christ, and the revelation of the things which must come to pass.

The book of Revelation teaches us that professing Christendom will deteriorate and degenerate, in harmony with all the prophecies of the Bible. The world will not be converted in this dispensation and the great masses of men and women will not be saved, but will be content with a religion of good works and ceremonies, a bloodless religion of compromise and condemnation. Unless we recognize this program as outlined by the Lord we have no explanation for the present state of affairs in the world, with its death, destruction, suspicion, wickedness, crime and immorality, its denials of the blood and the Book. Never has there been as much violence and crime as have today. The home is broken; society is mad; religion has been substituted for faith in Christ and

His atoning blood. Juvenile delinquency is alarmingly prevalent. Divorce, with its blighting effects upon the children, the family and the community is increasing and the Church has been afraid to voice its Scriptural denunciation of this festering evil.

Conditions Will Become Increasingly Worse

In spite of the rosy promises of the idealistic dreamers who prate that the world will be converted through a social gospel, and the talk of a golden age and lasting peace, the Bible declares that there will be increasing corruption and wickedness until Jesus comes. That is apparent in the seven churches of the Revelation. Today, in the age typified by the Church of Laodicea, Christ is locked out, and infidelity, evolution and the new psychology have been given His place. We find the same teaching in Matthew 13 in the seven parables of our Lord Jesus. First is the parable of the sower, corresponding to the Ephesian Church, the great age of missionary sowing. Then we read the parable of the tares and the wheat, corresponding to the Church of Smyrna, when the first seeds of evil were sown among the true wheat and resulted in the age of persecution. Then follows the parable of the mustard seed, typifying the abnormal, unnatural growth of the nominal Church, represented by Pergamos, the "state-subsidized" Church of Constantine's days. Then follows the parable of the leaven, which speaks of the age of corruption, typified by Thyatira, when the leaven of evil doctrine and practices are introduced into the Church with its superstitions and paganism, for in the Bible leaven always symbolizes evil, never good. Next we find the parable of the treasure hid in the field, corresponding to Sardis, the Reformation Church, with its discoveries of hidden truth and treasure, and especially the rediscovery of God's plan and purpose for the nation of Israel, His

peculiar treasure. Then follows the parable of the
pearl of great price, the Philadelphian church, the true
Church of the Lord Jesus. The last parable in Matthew
13 is that of the dragnet, a picture of the judgment at
the end of the age when God will separate the just from
the unjust and the wicked from the saved. Laodicea
and its final denial of Christ, will be followed by the
coming of the Lord.

We are living today in the Laodicean Age. Lukewarmness and indifference are evident on every hand.
Christ has been denied His central place, where once He
walked in the midst of the golden candlesticks; in His
place we have dance halls, poolrooms, theaters, banquet
halls and recreation rooms. The Church has been mod-
ernized and streamlined and the old-fashioned gospel
preaching of sin, judgment and salvation by the blood
has all but ceased in many places. All these things
might well discourage us if we believed the Modernistic
program of the postmillenarians. If the Bible taught
that conditions would become better and better as the
age wore on, we would abandon all hope after nineteen
hundred years, in which we observe the contrary. But
God has made His program plain. Not only in the teaching of the Revelation and Matthew, but throughout the
Scriptures, this belief is declared to be erroneous. Jesus
said that the world would become as it was in the days before the Flood and in the days of Sodom and Gomorrah.
Jesus, in describing the latter days in Matthew 24, Luke
22, and Mark 13-14, leaves no doubt in our minds but
that as we approach the end of the age, conditions will
become unspeakably violent and wicked. What, then,
shall we do? Give up? Become discouraged? Ah, no!
Instead, we are greatly encouraged to know that the
Bible is right, and that the program is running according to schedule. Jesus says:

When ye see these things come to pass, look up for your
redemption draweth nigh.

These events point us to the coming again of Christ.
As Laodicea runs to its end we look eagerly for the re-
turn of our Lord who has promised that after Laodicea,
He will return. This is implied in Revelation 4:1:

After this I looked and behold a door was opened in
heaven.

Again we ask, "After what?" After the things described in the closing verses of the preceding chapter
(Revelation 3). Here we read that the last period of
the professing church would be characterized by lukewarmness. Christ would be pushed aside, stand outside
the door and then only to invite the individual to let
Him come in. But in this Laodicean age there are still
the true believers, the Church of Philadelphia, and they
are represented by John in the first verses of the fourth
chapter: John says, "After this I looked and behold a
door was opened in heaven." When that door opened,
John heard a voice, the voice of the King and the Head
of the true Church, and it said, "Come up hither." John,
who here represents the true believers, is invited to
"come up hither," and immediately he was caught away
in spirit into heaven and saw His Lord.

The Rapture of the Church

We have in this passage the Rapture of the Church,
the catching away in that dark Laodicean Age of those
who had not been carried away by the world's false
hopes of a man-made millennium and Utopia. The time
is at hand, and although we would not attempt to set
any dates for the coming of the Lord, for we know that
no man knows the day nor the hour of His appearing,
we are confident that the day is near at hand. Of one
fact we are absolutely confident: today, this moment,

we are nearer the coming of the Lord than we have
ever been before. One of these days, He will come.

"After This"

John, having beheld the last phase of professing
Christendom, typified by Laodica, says, "after this I
looked." The next event on God's program we confi-
dently believe to be the Rapture of the church. In our
succeeding messages we shall discuss the details of this
blessed hope as described in Revelation 4. We trust
that you will familiarize yourself with this important
chapter in Revelation, for every word is freighted with
comfort and instruction and teaching. Having seen *when*
the Lord will come (at the close of the Laodicean period), John tells us also for whom He will come.

"After This I Looked"

John was looking up when the door was opened in
heaven to catch him away. He does not say that a door
was opened and then he looked, but he looked, and, then
the door was opened. Significant words these, for the
Rapture is for those who *look* for His return. In Hebrews 9:27-28 we read:

> And as it is appointed unto men once to die, but after this
> the judgment: so Christ was once offered to bear the sins of
> many; and unto them that look for him shall he appear the
> second time without sin unto salvation.

"Unto Them That Look For Him"

You may criticize this statement, but according to
these words, only those who are looking for the coming
of the Lord will be caught away when He returns for
His own. Some of you may ask, "Do you then believe
in a partial Rapture? Do you believe that only some
believers will be caught away?" No, indeed, I do not
believe in a partial Rapture, but I believe that all born-

again believers will be caught away to meet the Lord before the Tribulation. What about those believers who are not looking for Him? Speaking frankly, I admit that I cannot conceive of a believer who is not looking for the return of His Saviour. Anyone who has seen himself as a lost sinner, on the way to eternal hell, and has found salvation and peace at the Cross of Christ, should not only be looking for but longing and crying for His return. The true believer's heart longs for the day when we shall see the Man who died for us, who gave His life, shed His blood, carried our sins, bore our curse and saved us from eternal perdition. I repeat, I cannot conceive of a true born-again believer who is not looking for the return of the Lord. It is, therefore, not difficult to accept the words of Hebrews: "Unto them that look for him shall he appear the second time" or John's words in Revelation 4: "After this I looked, and, behold, a door was opened in heaven." Are *you* looking for His return? If you profess to be a Christian and are not looking for His return, I will not judge you, but I must warn you. How can you think of Calvary and what it meant for you and not think of seeing Him who saved you from eternal doom? If I were not looking for His coming, I would doubt my salvation.

THE SOLUTION TO EVERY PROBLEM

The more should we be looking for His return in these dark days of gloom and apostasy. Man's program has little interest for the believer in the light of the program of God outlined in the Bible. It may well be that before the Lord comes He will permit to come to pass upon this earth afflictions so terrible that every Christian will be forced to look for Him, because He alone remains. But this is sure: "Unto them that look for him shall he appear the second time without sin unto salvation." Christian friend, if you are not looking for Him it is time to "examine" yourself and to see whether you "be in the faith."

May the Lord cause any unsaved who perchance may read these words to fly to Christ and flee from the wrath to come!

CHAPTER SEVEN

Three Doors in Revelation

> After this I looked, and, behold, a door was opened in heaven: and the first voice which I heard was as it were a trumpet talking with me; which said, Come up hither, and I will shew thee things which must be hereafter. And immediately I was in the spirit: and, behold, a throne was set in heaven, and one sat on the throne (Rev. 4:1-2).

This brief passage from Revelation is one of the shortest yet one of the clearest pictures in Scripture of the Rapture of the Church at the end of this dispensation and just before the coming of the day of the earth's greatest sorrow and tribulation. The Bible teaches that this age will end in apostasy and wickedness, to be followed by a brief but intense period of sorrow on the earth such as it has never experienced in all its history. All the tribulations, wars, famines, earthquakes and scourges of the past will pale into insignificance in the light of this brief period of awful judgments promised for this earth at the close of this present age, now almost run out.

Before that awful day breaks the Lord is going to call the true believers up into heaven and only after they are gone will this terrible day come. That is the teaching of Revelation and of the entire Bible. In chapter 1 of Revelation we have seen the glorious picture of the Lord Jesus Christ in the glory of His Second Coming. In Revelation 2 and 3 we saw the history of the professing Church portrayed under the figure of the seven

61

churches. The age will end not in a great revival, but in a great apostasy. We are not looking for revival, but for His return. If in the meantime, while He tarries, a revival does come, then praise God for it, but there is nothing in the Scriptures which encourages us to believe that there is to be another great awakening; rather, the Bible teaches that conditions will become worse and worse, and then suddenly the Lord will come.

"After This I Looked"

That is why Revelation 4 opens with the words "after this I looked." When Laodicea had run its course, and John looked up, the door was opened in heaven and the voice of Christ cried, "Come up hither", John, representing the True Church, was caught away, and after these events we have the description of the tribulation period in the remainder of the book of the Revelation.

Some people find it difficult to believe that Christendom will end in apostasy and defection, since they have always believed the popular delusion of Modernism and postmillennialism that the world will gradually become better and better until all men are converted and the age of peace is ushered in. It is not strange, then, that many of you find it difficult to accept the interpretation which we are attempting to present. These facts may clarify the issue:

1. The church is not an organization, but a body. Christendom is not Christianity. The true church of Jesus Christ is not a denomination or a group of denominations, but an organism consisting of all born-again believers. Although the organization fails, the program of the calling out of the true body, the organism of the Church, goes forth uninterrupted.

2. In every age we find declension and increasing departure of Christendom from the truth, but always there

is a small group who are the true body, a remnant, who
protest, and constitute the true church.

3. All the statements of beliefs and creeds throughout the history of the church are proof of the constant
deterioration of the organized Church. Again and
again the Church has had to formulate creeds, that is,
put in condensed form what it believes and teaches, as a
protest against the errors which sought to undermine it.
Every creed was an answer to some error which threat-
ened the truth.

4. The failure of the age does not mean that God's
program has failed. The age of innocence was not a
failure, but a demonstration of the righteousness of God.
The age of law was not a failure, but served its purpose
in preparing us for the truth of Grace. The failure of
man to set up a Utopian world and a perfect Church
is only in preparation for God's purpose in setting up
the Millennial kingdom of His Son and the perfection
of the true church, the body of Christ.

We need today to re-emphasize the fact that until
Christ comes there can be no improvement and no lasting peace. In the face of six thousand years of human
failure, men ought to be ready to admit that more than
human efforts are needed to change the heart of man
and bring in the age of peace.

While the mass of men never receive Christ, there is a
remnant with whom God deals. It was thus before the
Flood: Noah and his family. It was thus after the
Flood: Abraham and his descendants. It was thus with
Israel. While the nation of Israel as a whole had for-
saken God, there was still a remnant of seven thousand
in Elijah's day who had not bowed the knee to Baal.
Paul tells us in Romans that today there is still among
Israel, "a remnant according to the election of grace."
Amid the apostasy, Modernism and skepticism of this
day, with their denial of the deity and virgin birth of

Christ, the power of His blood and His literal coming again, thank God there is also a remnant who still believe and hold to and preach these doctrines, and will not bow the knee to Baal. The rest of the world is rushing on to judgment, and one of these days the time of greatest trouble the world has seen will come.

When it comes, what of this faithful remnant in every age, those who have believed God? Millions of them have died, and scattered over the world their wasting ashes lie, whereas other millions of true believers are alive. What will happen to these? Will they, too, go into that period of tribulation? The Bible gives the answer. Before that terrible day comes, the dead in Christ shall arise and the living believers shall be changed, and together with the resurrected dead shall be caught away into heaven, far, far away from all anguish and the horror of the world's tribulation.

REVELATION 4

That is the teaching of Revelation 4. In our previous message we saw that those who looked for Him will be caught away. That is what John says:

> After this I looked, and, behold, a door was opened in heaven.

A door is an opening through which we pass from one room to another, from one place to another. Scripture tells us that there is one door into heaven. The Lord Jesus said:

> I am the door: by me if any man enter in, he shall be saved.

Jesus is the door, and so John saw Jesus opening Heaven and inviting him to come up and out of the world before the storms described in Revelation 6 to 19 were to break upon the earth. Jesus is the Door. He is the way into heaven and the way out of the world.

The door shuts in and it shuts out. Those who come by faith He shuts in — in the place of salvation and safety. Those who reject Him He shuts out in darkness and the gloom of eternal perdition. But the door will also swing at His second coming. In Revelation 4:1 we read that John saw the door opened, but at the same time it was the shutting of the door for the unbelievers. A door was opened in Heaven. John saw the church after Laodicea, caught away through Christ, caught away from the awful tribulation.

Four Doors

There are four doors mentioned in Revelation, or, rather, the word "door" is used four times. The first occurs in Christ's letter to the Philadelphian Church (Rev. 3:8).

> I know thy works: behold, I have set before thee an open door, and no man can shut it.

This is the open door of the Gospel. Before the age of the Philadelphian Church the Bible was largely a closed book. The common people knew little of it. The world as a whole was closed to the Gospel. But with the perfection of printing, rapid transportation, and the discovery of the telegraph and the telephone, countries and areas hitherto unreached were thrown open to the Gospel. It was the open door of the missionary era. Recently God has flung wide open the greatest door of opportunity for the Gospel: the radio. The world lies before us through the open door of radio broadcasting.

The second door is mentioned in Revelation 3:20. Christ is speaking concerning the Church of Laodicea, the last form of professing Christendom before He returns, and He says:

> Behold, I stand at the door, and knock.

While the open door of missions and the radio challenges us to go "into all the world" with the Gospel, Christ, outside the door, stands at the heart of every individual, knocking and asking to be admitted. It is the closed door of the human heart, closed by sin. It is the closed door of Revelation, closed door of the heart of man, and yet while man is forgetting God and despising the Gospel and rejecting His Son, He continues His offer of the Gospel. While the great masses reject Him, there are, however, some, the remnant, who will open the door.

The third door in Revelation is mentioned in this same verse: Revelation 3:20. Christ is still outside the door. His call to the masses goes unheeded, but He is still being received by the individual, one here and a few there, and so He says:

> If any man hear my voice, and open the door, I will come in to him, and will sup with him, and he with me.

That work is going on now. While they are sitting beside their radios, some are opening the door and welcoming the Saviour. When the last one has opened the door, when the last soul which must be brought in to complete the body of Christ, then another door is to be opened in Heaven and that door is described in Revelation 4:1:

> After this I looked, and, behold, a door was opened in heaven.

At the close of this age, when the last soul has said "Yes" to Jesus, He will return, He who Himself is the Door, and will appear to His own to take them out before the day of God's wrath breaks upon the world. This was the promise in Revelation 3:10 to the Church of Philadelphia, and He keeps His word,

> Because thou has kept the word of my patience, I also will keep thee from the hour of temptation.

"Because thou has kept the word of my patience," we read. Patience for what? Patience for His coming again. In other words, to them that look for Him shall He appear the second time without sin unto salvation.

Before we close this message we want to call your attention to one other matter of interest and instruction in regard to this door. Notice, "a door was opened in heaven." There are three places in the book of Revelation where we read that Heaven was opened. The first, of course, is this. A door is opened to admit the Church into heaven before the tribulation. There is a second instance which occurs in the middle of the Tribulation period. It is described in Revelation 11:19:

> And the temple of God was opened in heaven, and there was seen in his temple the ark of his testament.

This opening is for Israel, God's ancient covenant people. The Church will be raptured before the Tribulation. Israel must pass through the Tribulation. In chapter 11 we have reached the first half of this terrible period, and the last half, called the Great Tribulation, is about to commence. It will be the worst time of travail and suffering Israel has experienced, and is therefore called by the prophet "the day of Jacob's trouble." To encourage the faithful remnant of Israel in this awful period, God will open heaven once again and they will see their Temple and in that Temple the Ark of the Covenant. To encourage His suffering people of Israel He will open heaven. The Temple reminds them of the glory of Solomon's day as a picture of their future glory, and the Ark of the Covenant reminds them of the blood and the Mercy Seat and God's faithfulness in keeping His covenant promises concerning the restoration of the nation of Israel and the rehabilitation in the land of Palestine and their everlasting blessing. They will need this encouragement to hold fast in that awful day of Israel's tribulation.

THE THIRD OPENING IN HEAVEN

We read also in Revelation 19 that heaven was opened. Heaven will be opened at the beginning of the Tribulation. Here is the passage which tells of the third opening, in the middle of the Tribulation, and at the end of the Tribulation. Here is the passage which tells of the third opening in heaven:

> And I saw heaven opened, and behold a white horse; and he that sat upon him was called Faithful and True, and in righteousness he doth judge and make war (Rev. 19:11).

It is clear that the description concerns the Lord Jesus Christ's coming in the glory of His return. The Church will be caught into Heaven before the day of sorrow. Israel will be encouraged by an open Heaven in the midst of her sorrow, and the whole world is to face the opened Heaven as He comes to judge and destroy those who have rejected Him. Paul says there are three classes of people on earth today. In I Corinthians 10:32 he declares:

> Give none offence, neither to the Jews, nor to the Gentiles, nor to the church of God.

The three types are: Jews, Gentiles and Christians. The Christians will be caught away to Heaven at the Rapture. Israel will be redeemed to Jehovah by the vision of their Messiah and Lord in the Tribulation. The Gentiles, the unbelievers, will meet the wrath of God when Heaven is opened for the last time. Are *you* ready? You can be today. Whether you be Jew or Gentile, bond or free, white or black, moral or wicked, the moment you take Christ as Saviour you become a Christian to whom He says:

> Because thou hast kept the word of my patience, I also will keep thee from the hour of temptation, which shall come upon all the world, to try them that dwell upon the earth.

CHAPTER EIGHT

A Vision of the High Priest

> . . . behold, a throne was set in heaven, and one sat on the throne. And he that sat was to look upon like a jasper and a sardine stone: and there was a rainbow round about the throne, in sight like unto an emerald (Rev. 4:2-3).

The Lord Jesus Christ—The same Jesus who was born of a virgin, crucified on the Cross of Calvary and who arose and ascended into heaven more than nineteen hundred years ago is coming back to this earth. The Scriptures assert this fact and Christians everywhere have always believed in the Second Coming of Jesus Christ. But all believers do not agree regarding the detals of His coming or the time of His return. It does seem strange, with the revelation concerning the return of Christ and the clearness of His promises, that there should be many and varied interpretations among sincere and Christ-loving believers.

However, one of the clearest facts in the Scriptures is this: there are two comings of the Lord Jesus, still future: His coming *for* His Church and His coming *with* the Church. The first is called the Rapture; the second is called the Revelation. The first, the Rapture, will occur *before* the Tribulation and the second, the Revelation, will occur immediately *after* the Tribulation. Jesus Himself taught in Matthew 24 this great fact:

> Immediately after the tribulation of those days shall the sun be darkened, and the moon shall not give her light, and the stars shall fall from heaven, and the powers of the

> heavens shall be shaken: And then shall appear the sign of
> the Son of man in heaven: and then shall all the tribes of the
> earth mourn, and they shall see the Son of Man coming in
> the clouds of heaven with power and great glory (Matt.
> 24:29-30).

These are Jesus' own words, and they describe His coming again, publicly, immediately after the tribulation. There is also a secret coming of Christ mentioned frequently in the Scriptures. In these passages He is described as coming secretly like a thief, and He will be noticed only by those who will be waiting for Him. This is called the Rapture and will take place *before* the tribulation days. Jesus says to John in Revelation 16:

> Behold, I come as a thief. Blessed is he that watcheth,
> and keepeth his garments, lest he walk naked, and they see
> his shame (Rev. 16:15).

The Second Coming of Christ was known to the Old Testament saints and the subject of His second coming occupies the bulk of Old Testament prophecies: As early as the days of Enoch, before the Flood, God had already revealed to His saints the truth concerning the second coming of Christ. Jude tells us in Jude 14:

> And Enoch, also, the seventh from Adam, prophesied of
> these, saying, Behold, the Lord cometh with ten thousands
> of his saints to execute judgment upon all, and to convince
> all that are ungodly among them of all their ungodly deeds.

Notice that Enoch, who lived before the Flood, prophesied the coming of the Lord with His saints. If they are to come *with* Him they must first go *to* Him. Concerning this other aspect of the coming of Christ *for* His saints, however, the Old Testament prophet knew nothing. It was prophesied in type but the revelation concerning the coming of Christ *for* His Church was not known until *after* Pentecost. There was no Church in the Old Testament, and consequently we find no direct revelation concerning the Rapture of the Church.

For the teaching concerning the rapture, therefore,

we turn to the New Testament. Many passages could be quoted, but one in particular will make the matter clear. In I Corinthians 15 we read:

> Behold, I shew you a mystery; we shall not all sleep, but we shall all be changed, in a moment, in the twinkling of an eye, at the last trump: for the trumpet shall sound, and the dead shall be raised incorruptible, and we shall be changed (I Cor. 15:51).

The Lord's coming *with* His saints was no mystery; it was clearly revealed as early as the days of Enoch, but here Paul speaks of the mystery of the Lord's coming *for* His saints, a distinct and different event from His coming *with* His saints.

We have emphasized the two distinct aspects of the Lord's return because we believe that until we distinguish between His coming *for* the Church *before* the Tribulation and His coming *with* the Church *after* the Tribulation we shall never be able rightly to divide the Word of Truth and understand the Bible's teachings concerning the last days and the coming of the Lord. Moreover, we cannot rightly interpret the first few verses of Revelation 4. In Revelation 4:1-3, we have one of the most beautiful pictures in all Scripture of Christ's coming *for* the Church. There are two Comings of the Lord mentioned in Revelation. One is described in Chapter 4, where John, representing the Church, is caught up to meet the Lord. Then follow Chapters 6 to 19 in which we have a graphic description of the days that will follow the catching away of the Church, called in Scripture "the tribulation," a period of several years of intense judgment and suffering. At the end of that period the Lord will come publicly with His Church. Here is the record:

> And I saw heaven opened, and behold a white horse; and he that sat upon him was called Faithful and True, and in righteousness he doth judge and make war. His eyes were as a flame of fire, and on his head were many crowns; and he

had a name written, that no man knew, but he himself. And
he was clothed with a vesture dipped in blood: and his name
is called The Word of God (Rev. 19:11-13).

John in his Gospel record tells us that Jesus Christ
is the Word. Notice the next verse (Rev. 19:14).

And the armies which were in heaven followed him upon
white horses, clothed in fine linen, white and clean.

This reference speaks of the saints who were caught
up before. We know they were not angels, but saints,
for they were clothed in white linen and Revelation 19:8
tells us that the white linen is the garment of the bride
of the Lamb.

I am sure that if you remember this fact you will be
able easily to find the correct interpretation of Revelation 4:1-4:

After this I looked, and, behold, a door was opened in
heaven: and the first voice which I heard was as it were of
a trumpet talking with me: which said, Come up hither, and
I will shew thee things which must be hereafter. And immediately I was in the spirit: and, behold, a throne was set
in heaven, and one sat on the throne (Rev. 4:1).

Notice first that when the door opens in heaven, John
hears a voice and the voice is like the sound of a trumpet.
That immediately identifies the scene. In I Thessalonians we read:

For the Lord himself shall descend from the heaven with
a shout, with the voice of the archangel, and with the trump
of God . . . (I Thess. 4:16).

The voice that wakes the dead and the trump that
assembles the saints is the voice of Him who made the
worlds and who breaks the bands of death. It is the
voice of Him who, when the earth lay in the cold, bleak,
barren stillness of death, said, "Let there be light," and
there was light, the voice of Him who cried at the grave
of Lazarus, "Come forth." Death knew the voice of the

Master and corruption recognized the Author of life and fled in dismay as the dead man came forth. It is the same voice that cried on Calvary, "It is finished," and we are told by Matthew that "the earth did quake . . . and the graves were opened."

Paul tells us that the trumpet shall sound and the "dead shall be raised incorruptible." Notice also the rapidity of the event. John says, "Immediately I was in the spirit, and behold a throne was set in heaven." This corresponds with I Corinthians 15:51-52:

> We shall not all sleep, but we shall all be changed, in a moment, in the twinkling of an eye.

A LOOK INTO HEAVEN

After the description of the door opened in heaven and the catching away of John we get a glimpse of what we shall see when the event here prophesied takes place and we are caught up to meet the Lord in the air. John saw first the One sitting on a throne—The One he longed most to see, the One for whom he had longed, the One upon whose bosom he had laid his head. John immediately recognized Him as the Lord and then follows the description of this glorified Lord. John had seen Him hanging on the Cross, but now he beheld Him seated the same upon a throne. How his heart must have rejoiced! What indescribable joy we will experience when you and I who love the Lord glimpse for the first time His glorious face. Surely "rapture" is the term which best expresses this Blessed Hope!

"JASPER AND SARDINE"

John sees something about the throne which immediately identifies the sitter upon that throne. In Revelation 4:3 we read:

> And he that sat was to look upon like a jasper and a sardine stone.

Three stones are mentioned in this passage: the jasper, sardine and the emerald. Since we believe with all our hearts in the literal and verbal inspiration of every word in Scripture, these terms have a definite function in identifying the one who sits on the throne and His peculiar mission and office. The Jasper spoken of in Scripture was a clear, brilliant, transparent stone. The Sardius, on the other hand, was a blood-red precious stone much like a ruby. These two stones are mentioned by John in his description of the One whom he saw sitting on the throne after he was raptured and caught up into heaven. We do not read that the throne was of jasper and of sardine, but He that sat upon the throne "was to look upon like a jasper and a sardine stone." To understand the meaning of this statement we must turn to another passage of Scripture in which these precious stones are mentioned.

The High Priest's Breastplate

We read in Exodus 28 that Moses gave to the children of Israel the pattern of the Tabernacle and the order of the Sanctuary. After giving the instructions for the building of the Tabernacle, he issued minute orders concerning the garments of the High Priest. Among these garments was a breastplate of curiously wrought cloth and in it were twelve precious stones corresponding to the names of the twelve tribes of the children of Israel, beginning with the oldest, Reuben, and ending with the youngest son, Benjamin. The record is exceedingly interesting as found in Exodus 28:15-21:

> And thou shalt make the breastplate of judgment with cunning work; after the work of the ephod thou shalt make it . . . and thou shalt set in it settings of stones, even four rows of stones: the first row shall be a sardius, a topaz, and a carbuncle: this shall be the first row.

We read the following in verse 20:

> And the fourth row a beryl, and an onyx, and a jasper: they shall be set in gold in their inclosings. And the stones shall be with the names of the children of Israel, twelve, according to their names, like the engravings of a signet; every one with his name shall they be according to the twelve tribes.

After a detailed description of how every part of this breastplate was to be made and bound to the ephod or robe of the priest, the Lord gives us the meaning of this mysterious provision in Exodus 28:29:

> And Aaron shall bear the names of the children of Israel in the breastplate of judgment upon his heart, when he goeth in unto the holy place, for a memorial before the Lord continually.

Here, then, is the picture. The High Priest in the Old Testament Tabernacle carried on his robe, over his heart, the breastplate of judgment. In it were twelve precious stones arranged in four rows. The first stone was a sardius, the blood-red stone, which had the name of the first-born, Reuben, engraved upon it. The last stone in the last row was a jasper, a clear transparent stone with the name of Benjamin engraved upon it. Between these were the stones and names of all the other tribes. Not one was missing. Everywhere the priest went in the Holy Place, he bore these stones upon his heart as he interceded for Israel and averted judgment by the constant application of the blood from the Altar of Burnt Offering. This was a picture of safety and security. The children of Israel were sinful, defiled and unworthy, but the High Priest ministered daily and continually for their cleansing while he carried their names, each individually, upon his heart.

OUR HIGH PRIEST TODAY

We know from the New Testament, and especially
from the book of Hebrews, that Aaron in his priestly
office was a type of the Lord Jesus Christ in His priestly intercession for us after His ascension into heaven.
All these symbols in the Old Testament were shadows of
better things to come.

JESUS IN REVELATION

Jesus was the One whom John saw sitting upon the
throne. In Revelation 4 He is described as a jasper
and a sardine. The jasper was the clear stone, the
sardius, the bloody stone. Exodus 28 mentions the sardius first, the blood-red stone of Reuben. Revelation
4, however, speaks of the jasper first, the clear white
stone of Benjamin. There is a definite reason for this
reversing of the first and last stones. The sardius was
the red stone. It spoke of sacrifice and blood. It pointed to the Cross at the first coming of Jesus. The name
"Reuben" also pointed to this. The term is derived
from two Hebrew words, meaning "behold the son."
It pointed to the one of whom John said, "Behold
the lamb of God, which taketh away the sin of the
world." It tells us that He was the first-born of
every creature and the first begotten Son of God. The
jasper, the last stone in the Old Testament breastplate,
represented Benjamin. It was a clear stone speaking
of victory. On it was Benjamin's name which is a
combination of two Hebrew words ben and jamin, "the
son of my right hand," or, better still, "the son of my
power." The first and last stones pointed forward to
the first and second comings of the Great Priest, the
Lord Jesus.

THE ORDER REVERSED

In Revelation 4, however, the order is reversed. John sees Him first as the jasper and then as the sardius. The reason is simple. In the Old Testament the saints looked forward to the Cross and therefore saw the sardius, the red stone, first, and beyond that, the jasper, the stone representing His power and rule at His second coming. However, when John had the experiences of which Revelation 4 tells us, He was on this side of the Cross and the rapture, and therefore, looking back, he saw first of all the jasper stone and beyond that the red stone of the Cross and sacrifice.

Jesus has not changed. He that keepeth Israel never slumbers nor sleeps; today that same Jesus is at the right hand of God ever living to make intercession for us. When we shall see Him we shall be like Him. We are told that there was a rainbow round about the throne in sight like an emerald. The emerald was Judah's stone and was green, denoting eternal freshness and endurance. It was the wedding stone of ancient oriental times. In our next message we will deal with the meaning of the emerald rainbow, but before closing this chapter let me ask you, are you ready to meet the Sardius Lamb of God who died for you, who is coming again as the Jasper King and today offers to be your faithful High Priest and amid all the trials of life. Is He your daily Intercessor, Comforter and Keeper? Receive Him now and be ready to meet Him, for He said:

I will come again, and receive you unto myself.

CHAPTER NINE

The Promise of the Rainbow

When John the Apostle was caught up and translated into heaven to meet his Lord, as recorded in Revelation 4, a most impressive and wonderful sight met his eyes. He came face to face with his Lord and Saviour. Although he was surrounded by all the glories of heaven, one Person engaged all his attention. This One was like a jasper and a sardius in appearance and sat upon a beautiful throne surrounded by an emerald rainbow.

This is a picture of what the Church will see when she is caught up to meet her Lord in the Rapture. John was caught up after the church of Laodicea had run its course. One of these days we shall experience what John saw. After this present Church Age closes, as predicted in the second and third chapters of Revelation under the figures of the seven churches, we shall be translated together with the dead in Christ who shall be raised first. This is the unbroken and incontrovertible testimony of Scripture. Paul says:

> The Lord Himself shall descend from heaven with a shout, with the voice of the archangel, and with the trump of God: and the dead in Christ shall rise first: then we which are alive and remain shall be caught up together with them in the clouds, to meet the Lord in the air (I Thess. 4:16-17).

In First Corinthians he tells us:

> Behold, I shew you a mystery; We shall not all sleep, but we shall all be changed, in a moment, in the twinkling of an

78

eye, at the last trump: for the trumpet shall sound, and the
dead shall be raised incorruptible, and we shall be changed
(I Cor. 15:51-52).

THE RAPTURE

This event we call the Rapture of the Church at the
end of this present age. The truth regarding it is taught
directly and in figure throughout the Bible. One of the
most beautiful descriptions of this event is found in
Revelation 4 in which John is pictured as standing at
the end of the Church Age as described in the second
and third chapters of Revelation, and while he is looking heavenward, because everything on earth has gone
to ruin, suddenly a door is opened in heaven and John
hears the voice of his Lord bidding him to come up hither.
Then we read:

> And immediately I was in the spirit: and behold, a throne
> was set in heaven, and one sat on the throne. And he that
> sat was to look upon like a jasper and a sardine stone: and
> there was a rainbow round about the throne, in sight like
> unto an emerald (Rev. 4:2-3).

We have mentioned in our previous messages the
significance of the Rainbow round about the throne.
However, let me call your attention to the statement that
when John was caught up into heaven we read these
words, "Immediately I was in the spirit." John was
not actually caught up into heaven bodily, for all this
was part of John's vision. This expression "in the
spirit" may mean that he experienced the sensation of
being caught away in his spirit, or it may indicate that
John's spirit for the moment left his body and his
spirit alone was caught away into heaven to behold
His glorified Lord. The latter appears to be the correct
interpretation. John's body was not yet glorified, and
no man can behold the beauty and majesty of our
glorified Lord in an unredeemed and mortal body.

This explains the reason for the fact that after the resurrection of Jesus the eyes of the disciples were held lest the blazing beauty of Christ's resurrection body should blind them. When John saw Jesus he fell at His feet as one dead. When Paul caught a glimpse of the glorified Lord he was struck blind for three days and had weak eyes throughout the remainder of his life. But John's rapture was a picture of our rapture when Jesus comes, and when that occurs we shall be caught away not in the spirit but in the body as well. Our bodies will be glorified spiritual bodies. The moment Jesus comes, the dead will be raised incorruptible and we will be changed into bodies of immortality. In Philippians 3:20-21 we read:

> For our conversation is in heaven; from whence also we look for the Saviour, the Lord Jesus Christ: who shall change our vile body, that it may be fashioned like unto His glorious body, according to the working whereby He is able even to subdue all things unto Himself.

John was caught away in the vision of the spirit, but we shall be caught away Body, Soul and Spirit. Then John saw the king upon His throne and round about the throne was a rainbow like an emerald. To understand the meaning of the rainbow-crowned throne and its teaching we must compare Scripture with Scripture, and we refer you first of all to the first Biblical mention of the rainbow as found in Genesis 9.

THE LAW OF FIRST MENTION

We have many times cited "the Law of First Mention." It is one of the many rules which we have found exceedingly valuable in arriving at the correct interpretation of Scripture. Briefly stated, the law is this. The first time a word, incident or phrase occurs in the Bible it gives us the key to its meaning elsewhere in Scripture. So it is with the Rainbow. Turning to the passage which mentions the bow for the first time, we find that God gives us the meaning of the rainbow so that we shall be able to know its significance whenever we read of it elsewhere. The rainbow is mentioned only a few times in Scripture, including the first and the last books: Genesis and Revelation. We see its significance in the first reference in Genesis 9 and thereby find the interpretation of the rainbow-surrounded throne described in Revelation 4.

THE BOW IN THE CLOUD

First of all let us consider the first rainbow of Noah's day. God had sent a great Flood upon the earth which had destroyed all but eight souls: — Noah and his family. The Flood was a terrible judgment, and after Noah emerged from the Ark he built an altar, slew a sacrifice and presented the blood (Gen. 8:20). We read in Genesis 8:21-22 that when God beheld this sacrifice (a type of Calvary), He made a promise:

> And the Lord smelled a sweet savour; and the Lord said in His heart, I will not again curse the ground any more for man's sake; for the imagination of man's heart is evil from his youth; neither will I again smite any more everything living, as I have done. While the earth remaineth, seedtime and harvest, and cold and heat, and summer and winter, and day and night shall not cease.

Notice first of all that God's covenant, God's promise, was on the basis of a sacrifice of blood. It was when He saw the blood and smelled the sweet savour of the sacrifice brought in faith that God bound Himself with a covenant that He would never again destroy the earth with a flood. He promised, moreover, that there would always be seedtime and harvest. There would always be food for all His creatures. That promise God has kept. From that day to this there has been an abundance of food for all God's creatures at all times. True, there have been famines, but they have been local, and always due to faulty distribution of the world's supply. While one nation starved, another was wasting its surplus, plowing under its corn, wheat and cotton, and processing meat. That which was wasted would have supplied all who lacked. God has not failed. There has always been sufficient food, but man has destroyed God's abundant supply. All these millenniums since Noah's day "seedtime and harvest" have not failed, day and night have never failed to follow each other.

THE TOKEN OF THE COVENANT

As a token of this covenant, God placed the rainbow in the cloud as a reminder of His faithfulness so that whenever that bow appeared we should remember that God is keeping faith and covenant with the earth. Here is the record of the Token of the Covenant:

> And God said, This is the token of the covenant which I make between me and you and every living creature that is with you, for perpetual generations: I do set my bow in the cloud, and it shall be for a token of a covenant between me and the earth. And it shall come to pass, when I bring a cloud over the earth, that the bow shall be seen in the cloud: And I will remember my covenant, which is between me and you and every living creature of all flesh; and the waters shall no more become a flood to destroy all flesh.
>
> And the bow shall be in the cloud; and I will look upon it, that I may remember the everlasting covenant between God and every living creature of all flesh that is upon the earth (Gen. 9:12-16).

We have quoted the passage in full that you may have it clearly in mind as we seek to discover the meaning of the Rainbow about the throne of Christ at His second coming.

THE FIRST RAINBOW IN HISTORY

Before Noah's day there was no Rainbow because there was no rain. There is no record of rainfall before the flood, but we are told that the earth was watered by a mist or dew that arose *from* the earth (Gen. 2:6). That is probably why the antediluvians of Noah's day refused to believe him when he predicted that waters would fall from above. It had not happened in the past and they could not conceive of such an event. Then the rains came and the storm broke, but after the storm had passed, the sun again pierced the clouds, and God set the bow in the cloud as His promise that He would not again destroy the earth with a flood. This is God's covenant with the earth, as well as with Noah. Scientifically, a rainbow is produced by the refraction of light through the droplets of water. The curved surfaces of the raindrops refract the light rays, breaking them into the seven visible colors of the rainbow called the solar spectrum. A storm and a sun are required to make a rainbow. But the rainbow always appears after the storm is over. The rainbow is the symbol of receding judgment; it indicates that the storm is past. That is precisely what the coming of the Lord means, and that is why John sees a rainbow about the throne. Earth's redemption has come, Israel's redemption has come, the Church's storm is over, and the new day dawns.

Jesus' Teaching Regarding the Storm

A very illuminating passage, given in the words of Jesus, will illumine this truth. It is found in Matthew 24:27:

> For as the lightning cometh out of the east, and shineth even unto the west; so shall also the coming of the Son of man be.

Note carefully this apparently contradictory statement: "As the lightning cometh out of the *east*. Electrical storms come from the west or, less frequently, from the south. The lightning, therefore, of an approaching

storm comes from that direction. But Jesus says, "As
the lightning cometh out of the east," which indicates
that the storm is past. You have no doubt watched
after a storm how the lightning played among the clouds.
It was in the east. The rainbow revealed itself after
the storm. It was so in the first instance in Genesis.
The Rainbow came *after* the Flood, the storm, was
over. So, too, in Revelation 4 we read that John is
caught up, raptured into heaven, and sees the One on
the throne, the Covenant-keeping Saviour, surrounded
by a rainbow, to assure us that the dark night of man's
awful failure is at an end and a new day is upon us.
Every time we see a rainbow after a storm we are reminded that no matter how dark the days may become,
He has not forgotten His promise. He said, "I will come
again," and He will come.

THE WORLD'S ONLY HOPE

For this glad day every spiritual Christian is longing,
and for it the whole creation groaneth. Where John
stood in prophetic vision nineteen hundred years ago we
stand today in historical actuality. We have reached
the final period of this dark age and the next event on
the program of God is the return of the Lord Jesus
Christ. When we shall see Him we shall see Him on
the throne, and we shall behold the symbol of His never-
failing covenant: the Rainbow in the Cloud. This will
mean that all life's struggles are over. It will mean
reunion with believing loved ones gone before. It will
mean that after a few years of tribulation the creatures
of the earth, too, will be delivered from the bondage of
corruption. It will mean the dawning of Israel's new
day when, after the day of Jacob's trouble, she shall
be delivered and be replanted in the land of Palestine and
her wandering shall be over forever.

Let us consider also this thought concerning the rainbow. We have already indicated that it heralds the end of judgment. The bow points upward and its convex side points heavenward, but there is no string to the bow and it has no arrow. The arrow of judgment is past for the believer, and instead the bow provides the arch from earth to heaven.

Finally, let us remember that all this is on the basis of the blood and the acceptable sacrifice. It was when Noah brought his sacrifice and shed the blood of the clean animals upon his altar that God made His covenant with creation. That still holds true today. If you would be one of those who will meet the King when He comes, you, too, must come by the way of the Cross and through the blood of the Lamb of God slain upon Calvary for *your* sins. Receive Him today and be on the rainbow side of the storm of God's Eternal wrath.

This is your only hope. Scripture says that all creation groans for His coming. How much more we who have this marvelous revelation of the certainty of His coming!

Why speak ye not a word of the coming of the King?
Why speak ye not of Jesus and His reign?
Why talk about a kingdom and of its glories sing,
And nothing of His Coming back again?

O hark, creations groans—how can they be assuaged,
How can our bodies know redemptive joy,
When will the war be over in which we are engaged,
Except He come the lawless to destroy?

Come quickly, Blessed Lord, our hearts a welcome hold,
We long to see creation's second birth;
The Promise of Thy coming to some is growing old,
Oh, hasten Thy returning back to earth.

And he that sat was to look upon like a jasper and a sardine stone: and there was a rainbow round about the throne, in sight like unto an emerald.

The emerald was the stone of Judah, the first stone in the second row of the Priest's breastplate. Judah was the tribe out of which the King was to come, and the name "Judah" means "praise." How we do praise Him today for the blessed hope of His return. Are *you* ready?

CHAPTER TEN

The Seven-Sealed Book

(THE KEY TO REVELATION)

And I saw in the right hand of him that sat on the throne a book written within and on the backside, sealed with seven seals. And I saw a strong angel proclaiming with a loud voice, Who is worthy to open the book, and to loose the seals thereof? And no man in heaven, nor in earth, neither under the earth, was able to open the book, neither to look thereon. And I wept much, because no man was found worthy to open and to read the book, neither to look thereon. And one of the elders saith unto me, Weep not: behold, the Lion of the tribe of Juda, the Root of David, hath prevailed to open the book, and to loose the seven seals thereof. And I beheld, and, lo, in the midst of the throne and of the four beasts, and in the midst of the elders, stood a Lamb as it had been slain, having seven horns and seven eyes, which are the seven Spirits of God sent forth into all the earth. And he came and took the book out of the right hand of Him that sat upon the throne (Rev. 5:1-7).

We have quoted the first seven verses of Revelation 5 because of their tremendous importance in rightly understanding the remainder of the book of the Revelation of Jesus Christ. Someone has aptly said, ''The little seven-sealed book in the hand of the one on the throne mentioned in Revelation 5 contains the secret of the chapters which follow and is the key which opens the entire book of the Revelation.'' The right interpretation of the mysterious little book or scroll will give you the correct understanding of the rest of the book. A mistake here,

and you will be wrong all the rest of the way. In the following messages, therefore, we shall try to set before you
the plain Bible teaching concerning the scroll in the hand
of Christ mentioned in this chapter and the meaning of
the seven seals with which it was sealed, as explained
later in the book.

THE SETTING OF THE SCENE

Most of you are familiar with the setting of this
chapter. In Revelation 1, we have the vision of the
glorified Christ in the majesty of His second coming. In
chapters 2 and 3 we have a history of professing Christendom prewritten under the figure of the seven churches
from Ephesus to Laodicea. When Laodicea has run its
course, it is then that John, representing the true Church,
is caught away and raptured (Rev. 4:1-3). He is caught
away into heaven and sees, first of all, Christ on the
throne in all His glory and majesty, followed by heaven's
song of praise and adoration by the entire hosts of glory,
the elders, representing the saints of all ages and the
four beasts, or living creatures, representing the angelic
hosts. Chapter 5 is a continuation of chapter 4. It begins
with the conjunction "and" and, therefore, links it with
the closing verse of Revelation 4.

THE SCENE IN HEAVEN

The scene is in heaven where John was caught up to
meet the Lord and where he saw Christ on the throne.
At first John sees nothing but Him, the Saviour, and is
completely occupied by his rapturous vision of his Lord
and his God. But now John notices something else, of
which he had not been aware. He sees another sitting
on the throne and in the hand of this one is a little book.
The word "book" should be "scroll," a roll of parchment sealed with seven seals. Everything comes to a
standstill in heaven while diligent search is made to find

someone who can break the seals and open the book. Until that man is found there can be no further revelation. Everything hinges upon the finding of one who is worthy to open the book. In this little book is contained the revelation and the account of all that is to follow upon the breaking of the seven seals, the blowing of the seven trumpets and the pouring out of the seven final vials, or bowls, of the wrath of God.

THE BOOK OF REDEMPTION

For the interpretion of the book we must go back to Israel's history in the Old Testament. In the giving of the numerous laws and regulations there was a law which dealt with the redemption of three things. God provided that a wife, a slave and a possession might be redeemed. In the case of a wife, if her husband died before leaving offspring, in order that his name might not disappear from the earth the dead husband's brother was to take the widow as his wife (if he were able) and to perpetuate the name of his departed brother. There was also the law of redemption of a slave. If a man, because of his neglect or misfortune, fell into debt and was legally tried and unable to pay, he was to serve his master to whom he owed this debt as a servant, but the law provided that after six years he could again go free. If in the meantime, however, a near of kin, some close relative, chose to redeem him and were able to meet the payment, he could redeem his poor brother and release him before the six years ended. This marvelous provision is described in Leviticus 25 among the laws of redemption.

THE LAND REDEEMED

Provision was also made for a third redemption: the redemption of land which had been lost by its owner. In Leviticus 25:23-25 we read:

> The land shall not be sold for ever: for the land is mine;
> for ye are strangers and sojourners with me. And in all the
> land of your possession ye shall grant a redemption for the
> land.
>
> If thy brother be waxen poor, and hath sold away some
> of his possession, and if any of his kin come to redeem it,
> then shall he redeem that which his brother sold.

Now this was the method of redemption. When a man
had fallen into debt and lost his property or land, he was
taken before the judges and a document was prepared
which stated that the land had passed from the debtor
into the possession of the one to whom he owed the debt.
But this was not a permanent transfer. When the Year
of Jubilee came, the land was to be returned to the
original owner. In the meantime, however, it could be
redeemed and returned to him. This could be done in
two ways. Either the man himself could pay the redemption price, which was unlikely, for he was now a
servant, or it could be purchased back by a near relative,
an uncle or a closer kin. The papers, therefore, were
written on two scrolls of parchment. On both of these
were written the terms of the redemption of the lost
possession. One scroll was left open in the court of the
Temple or Tabernacle for all to read, but the other was
rolled up, sealed with seven seals and placed in the
Temple to be brought out only when a kinsman redeemer
gave evidence that he was willing and able to redeem
it. He would go to the court of the Tabernacle, read the
terms of redemption as found in the open public scroll,
and then go to the priest or judge and demand that the
sealed document be brought forth and the debtor be
freed and his property returned. If this kinsman, this
relative, were able to show that he was able to pay the
redemption price and could meet all the conditions of
the law, the sealed scroll was produced and he publicly
tore open the seals and invalidated the mortgage and
the man could return to his purchased possession.

ONE SCROLL SUBSTITUTED

As time passed the practice of using one scroll instead of two was adopted. Instead of two scrolls, one public and the other sealed, these were combined into one. One scroll or parchment was used, and the terms of the redemption of the mortgage was written on both sides, within and without. When the scroll was rolled into a tube and sealed with the seven seals, the inside corresponded to the secret record and the outside containing the terms for the public and especially for any kinsman redeemer who might want to know the terms for redeeming the lost possession. That is the picture in Revelation 5. There we see the judge of all the earth sitting on His throne and in His hand is this scroll written on the outside and the backside or inside and sealed with seven seals. It is, therefore, a book of redemption. This is evident also from Revelation 5:9-10:

> And they sung a new song, saying, Thou art worthy to take the book, and to open the seals thereof: for thou wast slain, and has redeemed us to God by thy blood out of every kindred, and tongue, and people and nation; and hast made us unto our God kings and priests; and we shall reign on the earth.

The song is of redemption and is in anticipation of the reign of the saints of God over the earth.

WHO MUST BE REDEEMED?

To understand correctly the meaning of the little book we must determine whose redemption terms it contained. In the old Levitical law the scroll had to do with the redemption of land. We have already seen that three things could be redeemed: a servant, a wife and land. At this point in Revelation (chapter 5) the first two have been accomplished. The Church, the bride of Christ, was caught up in the Rapture spoken of in

Revelation 4 and we, His servants, have been fully
redeemed, having received our resurrection bodies at the
Rapture of the Church. But the earth and the creatures
of the earth, both vegetable and animal, are still under
the curse. The earth itself is still groaning under the
curse of man's sin. These also must be redeemed, for
Christ is a perfect Redeemer, and every realm which
came under the curse of Adam's sin must also be delivered by the redemption of the Last Adam.

Adam's Federal Headship

When Adam fell he did not fall alone, but fell as the
head of the entire terrestrial creation. Through his sin
the curse fell upon all that which had been placed under
him. Adam was created to be a king, and a king is
responsible for his subjects. He is the head of the nation.
If, through an act of his, he plunges his nation into war,
all his subjects are plunged into war with him, whether
right or wrong. This was true also of Adam when he
fell. He fell as the head and so the curse of sin fell on
all over which he reigned. First, the whole race fell in
Adam, and today, all are born sinners and children of
wrath because of this headship. This is a fact which
cannot be denied. Through Adam's sin death passed
upon all men. Then, too, the ground, the inanimate soil
of the earth came under Adam's curse, for God said in
Genesis 3:17-18:

> Cursed is the ground for thy sake; in sorrow shalt thou
> eat of it all the days of thy life; thorns also and thistles
> shall it bring forth to thee; and thou shalt eat the herb of
> the field.

Not only was the ground cursed and deserts, wastes
and barren land appeared under the curse of God, but
the vegetable creation was under the curse, and thorns,
thistles and weeds sprang up as a result of the perversion

of their nature brought by the curse. Not only were the mineral and the vegetable realm affected, but the animals, too, were cursed.

Listen to the Word of the Lord as He addresses the serpent, who at this time was the highest of God's creatures under man. He was a beautiful animal, walking upright like a man and having the power of speech and ability to converse with man. The serpent in the garden was not a crawling, ugly, slimy reptile. If he had been, he would never have come close enough to Mother Eve to make her listen to even one word. Instead, the Bible says that he was "more subtle than any beast of the field." The term "subtle" is here used to denote attractiveness and appeal. Moreover, the curse upon the serpent was this:

Upon thy belly shalt thou go, and dust shall be thy meat.

If God cursed the serpent by causing him to crawl on his belly, then surely before the curse he did not thus crawl. This serpent, therefore, who probably was a very beautiful animal which walked upright, came under the curse of Adam as the representative of all other animals. He was classified among the cattle, that is, among clean animals. Consider God's curse upon the animal creation through the serpent:

And the Lord God said unto the serpent, Because thou hast done this, thou art cursed above all cattle, and above every beast of the field; upon thy belly shalt thou go, and dust shalt thou eat all the days of thy life.

You see that Adam by his sin lost everything. He lost dominion over the earth. The soil, the vegetation and all the animals came under the curse and the sentence of death, and Paul declares in Romans 8:22:

For we know that the whole creation groaneth and travaileth in pain together until now.

Christ came to redeem what Adam lost, and He is a
perfect and a complete Redeemer. He is the Second Man
and the Last Adam, and He will bring deliverance to
every realm that came under Adam's curse. He will
redeem the earth, and the desert shall blossom like the
rose. He will redeem the vegetable creation, and "the
parched ground shall become a pool, and the thirsty
land springs of water." (Isa. 35:7).

> The wolf also shall dwell with the lamb, and the leopard
> shall lie down with the kid; and the calf and the young lion
> and the fatling together; and a little child shall lead them.
> And the cow and the bear shall feed; their young ones shall
> lie down together: and the lion shall eat straw like the ox.
> And the sucking child shall play on the hole of the asp,
> and the weaned child shall put his hand on the cockatrice'
> den. They shall not hurt nor destroy in all my holy moun-
> tain: for the earth shall be full of the knowledge of the
> Lord, as the waters cover the sea (Isa. 11:6-9).

THE REDEMPTION OF CREATION

Adam lost his dominion over the earth and must
battle the forces of nature and fight weeds, thistles,
insects, caterpillars, storms, droughts and floods. The
animals prey one upon the other, and death and groaning and destruction are everywhere.

Adam lost his inheritance, but God has provided for
a plan of redemption whereby that which Adam lost
may be redeemed. All this is contained in the little book
in the right hand of Him that sitteth upon the throne,
of whom we read in Revelation 5. The seven-sealed book
contains the terms on which Adam's lost estate may be
redeemed by the Lion of the Tribe of Judah, the Lamb
with seven horns and seven eyes, even the last Adam,
the Lord Jesus Christ. In our next chapter we shall

study the requirements of the Redeemer and the glorious age of His kingdom when the earth shall be redeemed and at rest and when:

> Jesus shall reign where'er the sun
> Doth his successive journeys run;
> His kingdom reach from shore to shore,
> Till moons shall wax and wane no more.

CHAPTER ELEVEN

The Kinsman Redeemer

When John the Apostle was caught away into heaven, as we read in the fourth chapter of Revelation, an experience which pictured the Rapture of the church, he saw first of all the Lord Jesus Christ upon the throne of His glory. After gazing upon His majesty and glory, he turns his attention to another scene. He sees God upon the throne, and in His hand is a little book or scroll written within and without, and a search is made for one who is worthy to open the book and to break the seals thereof. Everything waits for the opening of the little book. There can be no more progress, no more revelation until this scroll has been opened and read.

In our previous message we stated that the correct understanding of the remainder of the Book of the Revelation depends upon the correct interpretation of Revelation 5. The little book in the hand of the One upon the throne contains the account of what is to follow after the Rapture of the true Church as recorded in Revelation 4:1-3. We saw that it was the book of the redemption of the creation. Revelation 5 pictures the Church with her Lord; all the saints of this dispensation are fully redeemed and are in their resurrection bodies. They are being prepared at the judgment seat of Christ to reign with Christ upon the earth after the Tribulation. But the earth is still under the curse and must be redeemed before it can be a fit habitation for the King

and His people. Therefore, before John proceeds with
an account of this tribulation period, he must see first
the One who is to open the seven-sealed book. When an
Israelite had lost his possession it could be redeemed
only by a kinsman redeemer who met the conditions
for its redemption.

ADAM LOST HIS INHERITANCE

Adam, by his fall, forfeited his right to be a king over
the earth and came under the curse. The earth refused
to yield her increase normally and man today must
wrest from it its treasures by force. Satan today is the
god of this age. He holds claim to the earth by reason
of Adam's sin, but the earth is destined to belong to the
saints, for Jesus Himself said, "The meek . . . shall
inherit the earth." This earth, the mineral, vegetable
and animal realms now lying under the curse, must be
redeemed. The terms of this redemption are contained
in the seven-sealed book, and a search is made for one
who could and would redeem the earth by meeting the
conditions set forth in the little book.

THREE CONDITIONS OF REDEMPTION

In the Book of Leviticus we are told that one who
would redeem a possession lost by a brother must meet
three definite conditions:

1. He must be a near relative of the one who had lost
   the inheritance.
2. He must be willing to act as a Redeemer.
3. He must be able to pay the price of redemption.

Bear these three requirements clearly in mind. If
such a relative were found, he could go to the priest, who
was also the judge, and demand that the scroll laid up in
the Tabernacle be brought forth, and if he was able to
meet the three conditions he was permitted to redeem
the lost estate and return it to its previous possessor.

We find an example of this recorded in Jeremiah 32. In the days of Jeremiah Israel was about to go into captivity because of her sin and lose the inheritance in the land of Palestine, but Jeremiah had confidence in the promise of God that the land would be redeemed and that Israel would return again to the land of her possession. Therefore he posted his intention to redeem the inheritance which was to be lost:

> And Jeremiah said, The word of the Lord came unto me, saying, Behold, Hanameel the son of Shallum thine uncle shall come unto thee, saying, Buy thee my field that is in Anathoth: for the right of redemption is thine to buy it. So Hanameel mine uncle's son came to me in the court of the prison according to the word of the Lord, and said unto me, Buy my field, I pray thee, that is in Anathoth, which is in the country of Benjamin: for the right of inheritance is thine, and the redemption is thine; buy it for thyself. Then I knew that this was the word of the Lord.
>
> And I bought the field of Hanameel my uncle's son, that was in Anathoth, and weighed him the money, even seventeen shekels of silver. . . So I took the evidence of the purchase, both that which was sealed according to the law and custom, and that which was open. . . And I charged Baruch before them, saying, Thus saith the Lord of hosts, the God of Israel; Take these evidences, this evidence of the purchase, both which is sealed, and this evidence which is open; and put them in an earthen vessel, that they may continue many days. For thus saith the Lord of hosts, the God of Israel; Houses and fields and vineyards shall be possessed again in this land (Jer. 32:6-15).

Israel was bound for captivity, but Jeremiah's nephew had lost a possession. Thinking it was lost permanently because of Israel's captivity, he asked his Uncle Jeremiah, to redeem it, and Jeremiah believed that God would bring Israel back again into the land, and so he redeemed the possession so that when Israel returned, his nephew or his heirs could claim possession. Therefore he inquired concerning the redemption price. It was seventeen shekels of silver. He paid the money and then took the scroll, both that which was sealed and hidden and that which was open and public, and gave orders to keep it until the captivity was ended and then it would be returned to its owner. Notice that Jeremiah met the scriptural conditions of the Redeemer:

1. He was a relative, an uncle of the one who lost the possession.
2. He was willing to function as a redeemer, for he obeyed the Lord.
3. He was able. He had the silver to redeem the possession.

The Seven-Sealed Book in Revelation

I trust that these facts will aid you in interpreting the seven-sealed book in the hand of the One on the throne of whom we read in Revelation 5. God holds the scroll containing the price and condition for redeeming the earth and returning it to those who had lost it because of sin. The entire creation lies under the curse. Soon the redeemed saints are ready to come with Christ to reign upon the earth, but someone must be found worthy, fit and able to meet the redemption terms. Evidently it is not easy to find such a one. A search is made through heaven and earth and Hades and no man is found. The question of the strong angel "Who is worthy to open the book?" is answered thus:

> And no man in heaven, nor in earth, neither under the earth was able to open the book, neither to look thereon. And I wept much, because no man was found worthy to open and to read the book, neither to look thereon.

John says that he wept *much*. Little wonder! He knew that everything depended upon the finding of a Redeemer and the opening of the seven-sealed book. If none was found, all the prophecies of the Old Testament concerning the reign of Christ on earth and the restoration of creation and the deliverance of the creatures from the bondage of corruption, as well as the restoration of the nation of Israel to the land of Palestine, would and could never be fulfilled. God's Word would be untrue. This would mean that God had promised to do something which He was not able to accomplish. John wept much because no redeemer was found worthy to open the book, to break the seal and to meet the conditions for redeeming the earth from the curse and restoring it to its Edenic fruitfulness and blessing.

The Lion Of Judah

While John weeps in despair, one of the elders speaks words of encouragement:

> Weep not: behold, the Lion of the tribe of Juda, the Root of David, hath prevailed to open the book, and to loose the seven seals thereof (Rev. 5:5).

His attention is called to the one and only Redeemer. There can be no mistaking who this One is. He is described as the Lion of the Tribe of Judah and the Root of David. It is the Lord Jesus Christ, the Redeemer. He is the Man of many titles, and these two are most instructive and enlightening. In Genesis it had been prophesied that out of Judah the Redeemer, the Lion of the Tribe of Judah, should come. He is further called the Root of David. What a marvelous and wonderful statement of both the humanity and the Deity of Jesus Christ! As a man He is the offspring of Judah. As God and the eternal Creator He is the root, the origin, the creator of David. In Revelation 22:16 we have a similar statement which forever settles the identity of the One John saw who was worthy to open the seven-sealed book. These are Jesus' own words:

> I Jesus have sent mine angel to testify unto you these things in the churches. I am the root and the offspring of David, and the bright and morning star (Rev. 22:16).

The Lord Jesus Christ is both the root and the offspring of David. This is mentioned to indicate that He was worthy to open the book and break the seals. You will recall that we cited three qualifications which the Redeemer must possess:

1. He must be fit, by being related.
2. He must be willing.
3. He must be able.

Two of these conditions are mentioned. He was fit to be a kinsman redeemer because He was the offspring of David. As a man, Jesus was a descendant of David and therefore a human being and near relative of humanity, but as the root of David He was God, Omnipotent God, and therefore fully able to be the Redeemer and to pay the infinite price of redemption from the curse of sin. As we shall see, He was also willing.

The Deity of Jesus Christ

Infidels have asserted again and again that Jesus Christ was not Deity but a mere human like ourselves. They hurl the charge that we build the doctrine of His deity on one vague evidence in Isaiah 7:14:

> Behold, a virgin shall conceive, and bear a son.

They maintain that this is the only Biblical reference to His virgin birth and deity, but to those who have been spiritually born from above and given spiritual eyes of understanding the entire Bible abounds in direct statements concerning His deity and supernatural birth. The first promise in the Bible after the record of man's fall is a declaration of the virgin birth and deity of the Redeemer. He is called "the seed of the woman," rather than "the man". He alone is called the seed of the woman, and in the last chapter of the Bible we are told that He is both the root and the offspring of David. Between these two verses, one at the beginning of Genesis and the other at the close of Revelation, we have scores of other references which present the same truth. Isaiah says:

> Uuto us a child is born, unto us a son is given (Isa. 9:6).

As a human being He was born a child; as the Son of God He was given to us as the Eternal One. We read in the Gospel of John:

> In the beginning was the Word, and the Word was with God, and the Word was God. The same was in the beginning with God. All things were made by him; and without him was not any thing made that was made (John 1:1-3).

Here the Redeemer is called God, but John also records His humanity, for he says in verse 14:

> And the Word was made flesh, and dwelt among us.

Both God and Man

We cannot understand the fact but we believe that Christ was both perfect God and perfect man. This was imperative if He was to be the Redeemer who was to open the book and deliver the earth from the bondage of sin and corruption. It is this One who John sees step forward and, taking the book out of the Hand of the One on the throne, declare that He is fit, willing and able to meet the conditions of redemption, because He is related to us as a human being and able to pay the price because He is Omnipotent God.

The Lamb

As the elder says to John, "Behold, the Lion of the tribe of Juda," he looks up and sees not a Lion, but a Lamb. He is told to behold a Lion and he sees a Lamb.

John is soon put at rest when the Lamb as it had been slain steps forward to take the book and to open the seals. The Lion and the Lamb are the same Person—the Lord Jesus in his first and second comings. When He came the first time He came as the "Lamb of God, which taketh away the sin of the world." He came as a suffering Saviour to die for us and to pay the price of redemption. Then He was rejected and slain, but He is coming again, as a Lion, not as a Lamb—as a Lion to roar and destroy and avenge His enemies, to punish all those who have rejected Him as the Lamb of God.

THE INESCAPABLE CHRIST

Jesus Christ is the inescapable Christ. All men will meet Him either as God's Lamb who died for their sins or as the Judge when He comes to punish the sinner because he has rejected Him. Christ is to you either the Lamb or the Lion. If you come to Him as a lost and guilty sinner and receive by faith the sacrifice He accomplished on Calvary and allow Him to apply the blood of the Lamb to your soul, then you will become a child of God. If you reject this offer, some day, as surely as He came the first time, He will come again as a roaring Lion, to judge you and cast all the wicked into the lake of fire and brimstone. What is Christ to *you* today? Is He your Saviour? If not, will you receive Him now by faith? Trust Him and believe His promise that "whosoever believeth that Jesus is the Christ is born of God."

Trust Him now before He comes as your Judge to plunge you into perdition because you have rejected God's Lamb and the blood of His sacrifice.

CHAPTER TWELVE

Redeeming Earth's Mortgage

And I saw in the right hand of him that sat on the throne a book written within and on the backside, sealed with seven seals. And I saw a strong angel proclaiming with a loud voice, Who is worthy to open the book, and to loose the seals thereof? And no man in heaven, nor in earth, neither under the earth, was able to open the book, neither to look thereon. And I wept much, because no man was found worthy to open and to read the book, neither to look thereon. And one of the elders saith unto me, Weep not: behold, the Lion of the tribe of Juda, the Root of David, hath prevailed to open the book, and to loose the seven seals thereof. And I beheld, and, lo, in the midst of the throne and of the four beasts, and in the midst of the elders, stood a Lamb as it had been slain, having seven horns and seven eyes, which are the seven Spirits of God sent forth into all the earth. And he came and took the book out of the right hand of him that sat upon the throne (Rev. 5:1-7).

The little book in the hand of Him upon the throne contains the terms for the redemption of the earth from the curse and the bondage of sin. Adam had been made a king over the earth and all creation placed under him. Then he sinned and the creation came under the curse because of his sin, but the creation, as well as man, may be redeemed if the conditions are met as contained in the mortgage which sin brought upon it.

The law of the kinsman redeemer operates also in the plan of redemption. The entire creation was under the curse and Adam lost his right to the earth. It must be redeemed. After the Church is caught away and John, representing the Church, is in heaven, the next step is the redemption of the earth. One—and one only—was found who could meet the conditions. He is called the Lion of the Tribe of Judah and the Root of David. We are told also that He is the One who died on Calvary, for He is described as a "Lamb as it had been slain." He is the Lord Jesus Christ Himself.

BOAZ AND RUTH

In the book of Ruth we have a most beautiful picture of the work of the kinsman redeemer. The story of Boaz and Ruth helps us to understand the work of our great Redeemer Christ, as He opens the seven-sealed book of which Revelation tells us. I assume that all of you are familiar with the story of Ruth, but let us rehearse briefly this interesting romance.

There was in Bethlehem a happy family consisting of a father, a mother and two sons. The father's name was Elimelech, the mother's Naomi and the two boys were named Mahlon and Chilion. For a time they were happy and then a famine came upon the land, and this family moved from Bethlehem and traveled to Moab across the Jordan in search of food.

While they were in the land as strangers, the father, Elimelech, died, leaving Naomi a widow. Then one of the boys married a Gentile Moabitess by the name of Orpah and the other married Ruth. Some time after— we do not know how long—both the sons of Naomi died and left her with two daughters-in-law, Orpah and Ruth. Then the famine in the land of Bethlehem subsided and Naomi prepared to go back to her homeland. Orpah remained in Moab but Ruth refused to leave her mother-in-law and traveled with her to Bethlehem.

THE LOST INHERITANCE

However, when they arrived in Bethlehem they found that their home and land, under the terms of the Levitical law, had been confiscated, probably because of the debts which they were unable to pay. They were penniless and Ruth was compelled to work in the field as a gleaner behind the harvesters. It so happened that she gleaned in the field of one Boaz who immediately became interested in her and inquired regarding her identity. He found she was the daughter-in-law of Naomi, a relative of his. Under the Levitical law we have seen that a lost inheritance could be redeemed by a relative if he were willing, able and fit. To be fit he must be a relative; to be able he must be sufficiently wealthy to pay the redemption price. Boaz determined that the inheritance which Naomi had lost and which belonged to Ruth as well, by virtue of her marriage to Naomi's son, should be redeemed and returned to its former owners.

MEETING THE CONDITIONS

Remember that not everyone could be a kinsman redeemer. Only those who met the conditions could function in this capacity, and so the Holy Spirit gives us in Ruth 2:1 a bit of important and interesting information concerning this man Boaz, who was a type of the Kinsman Redeemer, Jesus, the opener of the seven-sealed book. Consider this brief but important verse:

> And Naomi had a kinsman of her husband's, a mighty man of wealth, of the family of Elimelech; and his name was Boaz.

Notice the facts recorded here by the Holy Spirit. Boaz was first a kinsman, and, second, he was wealthy. These were two conditions which had to be met. Was Boaz willing to act as a kinsman redeemer and thus fulfill the third condition? Chapter 4 of Ruth gives us the answer:

Then went Boaz up to the gate, and sat him down there: and, behold, the kinsman of whom Boaz spake came by; unto whom he said, Ho, such a one! Turn aside, sit down here. And he turned aside, and sat down. And he (Boaz) took ten men of the elders of the city, and said, Sit ye down here. And they sat down. And he said unto the kinsman, Naomi, that is come again out of the country of Moab, selleth a parcel of land, which was our brother Elimelech's: and I thought to advertise thee, saying, Buy it before the inhabitants, and before the elders of my people. If thou wilt redeem it, redeem it: but if thou wilt not redeem it, then tell me, that I may know; for there is none to redeem it beside thee; and I am after thee. And he said, I will redeem it.

Naomi was about to lose her inheritance unless a kinsman redeemer was found. Baoz undertook for Naomi and Ruth and called the nearest of kin whose right it was to redeem the property. Boaz challenged him to redeem it and added, "If you don't, I will." The kinsman promised he would but later found that he was unable to do so. Boaz told him that he must not only redeem the land but redeem Ruth, the widow, as well. There was, you will recall, a law which stated that if a man died his brother was to take his widowed wife and perpetuate the name of his brother. This kinsman, however, was unable to do so, and we read accordingly in Ruth 4:6:

And the kinsman said, I cannot redeem it for myself, lest I mar mine own inheritance: redeem thou my right to thyself; for I cannot redeem it.

Upon this confession Boaz immediately offered to redeem the inheritance as well as the widowed Ruth, so Boaz, in the presence of the witnesses, purchased the possession and restored it to the owners by not only paying the price but marrying the owner. Study the record of the transaction as found in Ruth 4:9-10:

And Boaz said unto the elders, and unto all the people, Ye are witnesses this day, that I have bought all what was

Elimelech's, and all that was Chilion's and Mahlon's, of the hand of Naomi. Moreover Ruth the Moabitess, the wife of Mahlon, have I purchased to be my wife, to raise up the name of the dead upon his inheritance, that the name of the dead be not cut off among his brethren, and from the gate of his place: ye are witnesses this day.

JESUS OUR GOEL REDEEMER

The Lord Jesus Christ is the antitype, the One to whom all this points. Adam had lost his inheritance and broken with God. He was separated from God and had lost his dominion which God gave him over the earth when He created him. A Redeemer must be found. But the nearest of kin could not redeem him. In the case of Naomi and Ruth there was a near kinsman whom Boaz challenged, but he was unable to function as a redeemer because he had an obligation of his own to fulfill. What a picture of man's impotency and inability to save either himself or his brother! We, too, must say, "I cannot redeem it lest I mar mine own inheritance." There is no man who can by any means redeem his own soul, much less the soul of another. Someone else must be found who is willing, who is fit and who is able. In the case of Ruth this man was Boaz. He was fit for he was a kinsman. He was able for he was a man of wealth, and he was perfectly willing, as we have seen. Our Redeemer is the Lion of the Tribe of Judah and the Lamb that was slain.

Man was unable to redeem. Turning again to the passage in Revelation 5 with which we began, we see that a search was made in heaven and earth and under the earth for a man who could redeem man and wrest creation from the grip of the curse of God. No man was found and we read in Revelation 5:4:

I wept much, because no man was found worthy to open and to read the book, neither to look thereon (the book of the mortgage containing the terms of redemption).

Then suddenly one stepped forward who is described as the Lion of the Tribe of Judah and the Root of David and as a Lamb that was slain, and He boldly stretched out His hand and took the book, and the book was delivered to Him, signifying that He had met the conditions to redeem man, the widowed bride, and to redeem the earth, the lost possession. See how this One met all the conditions.

He Was Fit

The Lord Jesus was fit to be man's Redeemer. The first requirement was that the Redeemer must be related to the debtor. Nineteen hundred years ago He came from heaven's glory and became one of us, a human Redeemer, a member of the human family. We are told that He was made like unto us in all things, sin only excepted.

John says that "the Word was made flesh."

Hebrews tells us:

> For verily he took not on him the nature of angels; but he took on him the seed of Abraham. Wherefore in all things it behoved him to be made like unto his brethren, that he might be a merciful and faithful high priest in things pertaining to God, to make reconciliation for the sins of the people (Heb. 2:16-17).

The humanity of Christ, His incarnation, was an absolute and indespensible necessity in the plan of salvation. It was as essential as His deity. Christ became a man, a perfect man, one of us, a member of the human family, in order that He might be a kinsman redeemer.

> One day when heaven was filled with His praises,
> One day when sin was as vile as could be,
> Jesus came down to be born of a virgin—
> Dwelt among men, my Redeemer is He!

He Was Willing to Be a Redeemer

The second requirement was the willingness of a Redeemer to act for his lost brother. The obligation could

not be forced upon him. Like Boaz, Jesus Christ was
willing to be a redeemer:

> Then said I, Lo, I come (in the volume of the book it is
> written of me), to do thy will, O God.

In the garden Jesus testified, ''Not my will, but thine,
be done.''

We read in Hebrews:

> Who for the joy that was set before Him endured the
> cross, despising the shame (Heb. 12:2).

The third requirement was that He must be able, that
is, He must be able to pay the price of redemption. The
Levitical law and the case of Jeremiah and Boaz in-
volved money, silver money, the price of redemption.
Silver in Scripture speaks of blood, and it points forward
to the truth that in the great antitypical redemption of
sinners and the world through Jesus Christ the price is
blood, perfect sinless blood. There was only one who
could pay this price, even the Lamb of God.

> The blood of Jesus Christ his Son cleanseth us from all
> sin (I John 1:7b).

> Forasmuch as ye know that ye were not redeemed with
> corruptible things, as silver and gold . . . but with the
> precious blood of Christ, as of a lamb without blemish and
> without spot (I Peter 1:18-19).

On the throne of which we read in Revelation 5 sits
the King. In His hand is a seven-sealed scroll containing
the terms for the redemption of the world, the entire
creation. The seals must be broken by one who meets
the conditions of the kinsman redeemer, and Jesus Christ
is the only one who can meet these requirements. He
steps forward and takes the book and begins to open
the seals as recorded in the remainder of Revelation.
As He does, the tense silence of heaven is broken and
the hosts of heaven, the elders, burst forth into song.
Listen to them:

> And they sung a new song, saying, Thou art worthy to
> take the book, and to open the seals thereof: for thou wast
> slain, and hast redeemed us to God by thy blood out of every
> kindred, and tongue, and people, and nation; and hast made
> us unto our God kings and priests: and we shall reign on the
> earth (Rev. 5:9-10).

Notice that verse 9 is in the past tense, as the elders
sing of something that is already accomplished. They
have been redeemed. But the last part of the next verse
(Rev. 5:10) is in the future tense: "And we *shall reign*
on the earth."

When the Church was raptured, as we read in Revelation 4:1-3, its redemption was complete, but the earth
on which the redeemed are destined to reign still lies
under the curse and must also be redeemed before it is
fit to be a dwelling place of the glorified saints of God.
The little book in the hand of Him on the throne contains
the terms, which this same Redeemer is able to meet, but
Satan refuses to relinquish his power over the earth,
and so as the Lamb opens the seals and awful judgments
pour forth upon the earth under the seals, trumpets and
vials, until at last the judgment is complete, the devil is
bound and cast into the pit and the Lord returns with His
redeemed bride to reign *on* the earth.

Are You Ready to Reign?

In our next message we shall deal with the redemption
of creation—the soil, the vegetation, fish, birds, animals
and creeping things—when Jesus comes again to reign.
But even before that time comes the Lord will return
for His Church in the Rapture. Are you ready to meet
Him or will you be left behind to pass through the Great
Tribulation and then to be lost forever? You can settle
that matter now. "Believe on the Lord Jesus Christ,
and thou shalt be saved."

CHAPTER THIRTEEN

The Redemption of Creation

In our previous expositions of Revelation 5 we have repeatedly pointed out that the little seven-sealed book in the hand of the king upon the throne was the book of the earth's redemption. The scene is in heaven after the Church has been caught up in the Rapture of which we read in Revelation 4. While the Church is redeemed and with her Lord, the creation and all the creatures on the earth have not as yet been delivered from the curse brought upon them by the sin of man. The Bible tells us that this creation also must be delivered from the curse of sin. Many passages present this much-neglected truth, but Romans 8 alone should be enough to establish this fact:

> For the earnest expectation of the creature waiteth for the manifestation of the sons of God. For the creature was made subject to vanity, not willingly, but by reason of him who hath subjected the same in hope, Because the creature itself also shall be delivered from the bondage of corruption into the glorious liberty of the children of God. For we know that the whole creation groaneth and travaileth in pain together until now (Romans 8:19-22).

There is no mistaking these words of Paul written by inspiration. He tells us plainly that the creation today is groaning and travailing in pain under the curse, but it will be delivered at the manifestation of the sons of God, which will occur when Jesus returns after the

Tribulation to set up His kingdom upon the earth. The Church looks for the coming of the Lord *before* the Tribulation; the creation's redemption will not come until *after* the Tribulation. That is why it is said of us in Romans 8:23 that we are "waiting for the adoption, to wit, the redemption of our body." We know that this will occur at the coming again of Christ at the Rapture. Then, after a brief period of great tribulation, the Lord will return to this earth to set up His Kingdom, and at the manifestation of Christ and the saints, the entire creation will be redeemed.

When Christ died on Calvary He died not only to save us from going to hell but He saved us to reign with Him on the earth. He did even more, however, He died not only for sinners but He died to redeem the entire creation. It, too, must be redeemed from the curse. It is significant that when Christ was crucified on the Cross, He wore a crown of thorns. Applying the law of first mention, we find that the thorns are first mentioned in the Bible in Genesis 3, in connection with the curse of God upon the earth and upon vegetation. The wearing of the crown of thorns, therefore, is related to that first mention of thorns and thistles and reminds us that even the creation shall be delivered from the bondage of corruption. The Bible abounds with statements to confirm this truth. Consider carefully a few of them:

> The wilderness and the solitary place shall be glad for them; and the desert shall rejoice, and blossom as the rose. And the parched ground shall become a pool, and the thirsty land springs of water (Isa. 35:1, 7).

God never made a desert. God pronounced His creation good, and Isaiah tells us that He created the earth not to be a void, but to be inhabited. Deserts are the result of the curse upon the ground, but when the Redeemer comes, the entire earth will become once more

like the Garden of Eden. So productive will the earth be
in that day that the Prophet Amos describes it as
follows:

> Behold, the days come, saith the Lord, that the plowman
> shall overtake the reaper, and the treader of grapes him that
> soweth seed; and the mountains shall drop sweet wine, and
> all the hills shall melt (Amos 9:13).

The curse will be removed. The earth will bring forth
her increase and there will be plenty for all. There will
be no more want, no more poverty, no more rent to pay,
for then ''shall sit every man under his vine and under
his fig tree.''

The Animal Creation

The animal creation shall also share in the deliverance
of the Redeemer who opens the seven-sealed book. Hosea
the prophet in describing that day says in chapter 2:18 of
his prophesy:

> And in that day will I make a covenant for them with the
> beast of the field, and with the fowls of heaven, and with the
> creeping things of the ground.

Ezekiel, describing this same day, says:

> And the tree of the field shall yield her fruit, and the
> earth shall yield her increase, and they shall be safe in their
> land (Ezek. 34:27).

Isaiah declares in his prophesy:

> The wolf and the lamb shall feed together, and the lion
> shall eat straw like the bullock: and dust shall be the ser-
> pent's meat. They shall not hurt nor destroy in all my holy
> mountain, saith the Lord (Isa. 65:25).

We could multiply Scripture references which tell the
story not only of man's redemption but of the entire
realm of creation which fell under the curse of Adam's
sin.

This aspect of redemption is often forgotten by Bible

students. We limit the work of Christ as though it consisted only of delivering men and women from hell and destruction, but Christ died to redeem the earth and the creatures as well as mankind. When Jesus reigns, this earth will be like Paradise before the fall. It is to redeem this creation that the Lamb spoken of in Revelation 5 steps forward and takes the scroll or little book out of the hand of the One who sits upon the throne. It contains the terms for the redemption of this creation. The Lamb, the Lord Jesus, has met the conditions and the scroll is given to Him, but Satan refuses to relinquish his claim upon the earth because of man's sin, even though the price that God demanded has been met. He refuses to give up his power, so Christ, the Lamb and the Lion, will take it from him by right and by force.

He opens the first seal and a white horse of spurious and false peace dashes forth. He tears open the second seal (Rev. 6:4) and a red horse (the color of blood) dashes forth and the earth is plunged into the bloodiest war in all its history. He tears open the third seal and a black horse rides out with famine and death and destruction upon the earth. The fourth seal is broken and there rides forth a pale or livid horse called death; disease and pestilence, together with famine, war and hunger, sweep the earth until a third of its population has perished.

Still the devil and his followers will not acknowledge the rightful King of the earth by virtue of His redemption, so the Lord, the Lamb, opens the fifth seal, and we see the saints under the altar in heaven crying for deliverance. They are those who have been martyred and slain and are the justification for the awful judgments to follow upon the earth. The sixth seal of the little book is opened, and anarchy and revolution are rampant. Earthquakes and terrifying sights in the heavens cause men to

hide in caves and pray for the rocks to cover them and the
hills to hide them from the wrath of the Lamb as He
prepares to open the last seal.

THE SEVENTH SEAL

When He opens the seventh seal, of which we read in
Revelation 8, seven trumpeters step forth and as each
blows his trumpet there is hail, fire and a volcanic erup-
tion which hurls a flaming mountain into the sea and
kills a third of the creatures in the sea. The third trump-
eter sounds and a giant meteor hits the earth, thus destroying a third of the supply of drinking water on the
earth. The fourth trumpet sounds and the sun is darkened in the heavens; the fifth sounds and the bottomless
pit is opened and out of it come supernatural demon-
beings like locusts tormenting the wicked upon the earth
until they cry for death but cannot find it. The sixth
angel sounds his trumpet and we behold the preparations
for the Battle of Armageddon and the marshaling of an
army of two hundred million soldiers for the last great
battle the world will see.

THE SEVENTH TRUMPET

When the seventh trumpet sounds we behold seven
vials of the wrath of God which will fulfill all judgment,
and when the last vial is poured out the end will come and
Christ will return. These seven seals, the seven trumpets,
the seven vials of God's wrath—these occupy only about
seven years between the Rapture of the Church and the
coming again of Christ to the earth. The period is called
the Tribulation Period, and is divided into two parts of
three and one-half years each. The first is called the
Tribulation, during which time the seven seals are opened
and the seven trumpets blown, and the last half is called
the Great Tribulation, and during this period the seven
last vials of God's wrath are poured out upon the earth.

All this is implied in the little seven-sealed book of which we read in Revelation 5. You will see from this what we meant when we told you that the seven-sealed book described in Revelation 5 was the key to the remainder of the book of the Revelation. As Christ opens the seals, the judgments which will purify the earth, redeem Israel and then produce a new earth in which even the creatures are redeemed, will be poured out, until it appears that all humanity will perish from the earth, and then suddenly, after the last vial has been poured out, the Lord will return, as we read in Revelation 19:11. Here is the graphic account:

> And I saw heaven opened, and behold a white horse; and he that sat upon him was called Faithful and True, and in righteousness he doth judge and make war. His eyes were as a flame of fire, and on his head were many crowns; and he had a name written, that no man knew, but he himself. And he was clothed with a vesture dipped in blood: and his name is called The Word of God. . . And out of his mouth goeth a sharp sword, that with it he should smite the nations: and he shall rule them with a rod of iron: and he treadeth the winepress of the fierceness and wrath of Almighty God. And he hath on his vesture and on his thigh a name written, King of Kings, and Lord of Lords (Rev. 19:11-16).

This speaks of the return of the Lord at the end of the Great Tribulation.

THE DEVIL BOUND

Immediately upon the return of Christ with His saints the beast and the false prophet will be cast into the lake of fire. Satan will be bound and cast into the pit, and then will follow a thousand years of peace, blessing and prosperity under the rule of the King of Kings and the Lord of Lords. In chapter 20 of Revelation is the account of the loosing of Satan, the end of the thousand years, his doom, the lake of fire, the final judgment of the

wicked dead at the Great White Throne and a description
of the eternity which lies beyond.

The purpose of God has been accomplished and His
program has been fulfilled. Revelation 2 and 3 tell us
that the present age of professing Christendom will end
with Laodicea. Revelation 4 describes the Rapture of
the Church and chapters 4 and 5 show us what happened
in heaven after John, representing the Church, arrived.
In chapter 5 we read of the little seven-sealed book which
contained all that followed the Rapture of the Church.
Revelation 6 to 19:11 tells of the Tribulation and the
nineteenth chapter speaks of the return of Christ to
reign. Then will follow the Millennium and the final
judgment.

This, in bare outline, is the story of Revelation. If we
study it as we would any other book instead of trying to
make it difficult by spiritualizing it away, we find it
not only easy, but interesting. May I remind you once
again that the book is called "Revelation." Those who
will study it will find in it a revelation of the events
which are about to occur. The Age of the Church is near-
ing its close and the next event is the coming of Christ
for His Church as clearly depicted in Revelation 4. Then
Christ will set up His glorious kingdom upon the earth.

The Hallelujah Chorus

Let us consider what happens when Christ takes the
book and is about to open the first seal:

> And when he had taken the book, the four beasts and four
> and twenty elders fell down before the Lamb, having every
> one of them harps, and golden vials full of odours, which are
> the prayers of saints (Rev. 5:8).

The occupants of heaven know what the opening of
this book means, and when the Lamb steps forward they
burst into praise and song and pour out the prayers of

the saints. For thousands of years the saints have been praying, ''Thy kingdom come. Thy will be done in earth, as it is in heaven,'' and now finally, at long last, their prayers are answered and Christ is about to wrest the power from Satan's grasp.

Then they sing a new song of redemption:

> Thou . . . hast made us unto our God kings and priests: and we shall reign on the earth (Rev. 5:10).

Yes, we shall reign on the earth—reign with Him over and upon the earth which now rejects Him and rejects our testimony concerning Him.

Then the angels take up the song (Revelation 5:11-12), and after the angels have joined the four living creatures and the four and twenty elders, the entire creation joins in the chorus and we read in Revelation 5:13:

> And every creature which is in heaven, and on the earth, and under the earth, and such as are in the sea, and all that are in them, heard I saying, Blessing, and honour, and glory, and power, be unto . . . the Lamb for ever and ever.

Every creature in heaven, the earth, the sea and in the ground joins in the great chorus, for this is the signal for the earth's redemption. Are *you* ready? Creation groans and longs for His return. Do *you?*

CHAPTER FOURTEEN

The Four Horsemen of Revelation 6

After this I beheld, and, lo, a great multitude, which no man could number, of all nations, and kindreds, and people, and tongues, stood before the throne, and before the Lamb, clothed with white robes, and palms in their hands; and cried with a loud voice, saying, Salvation to our God which sitteth upon the throne, and unto the Lamb. . . And one of the elders answered, saying unto me, What are these which are arrayed in white robes? and whence came they? And I said unto him, Sir, thou knowst. And he said to me, These are they which came out of great tribulation, and have washed their robes, and made them white in the blood of the Lamb (Rev. 7:9-10, 13-14).

Scripture tells us that this present age will end in war, destruction and religious apostasy, until the Lord Jesus Christ comes back to take out every true believer from both the living and the believing dead of all ages. When the testimony of the true Church has disappeared there will follow a period, brief but intense, when all the wrath of the devil will be loosed upon the earth. There will be earthquakes, pestilence, disease and wars such as have never been known. So fierce will be the destruction that all flesh would perish were it not for the intervention of the coming of the Lord. This brief period of earth's greatest sorrow is characterized in Scripture by many descriptive names. In the Old Testament the most common name is "the day of the Lord." Whenever the expression "the day of the Lord" appears it refers to this

period between the Rapture of the true Church and the
false church. Remember the phrase "the day of the
Lord" when you are reading the prophecies of the Old
Testament. This period is also called "the day of Jacob's
trouble," because during this time Israel will pass under
the rod of God's final chastening and be converted.
This period of trial is also called "the day of darkness"
and "the day of vengeance of our God." In the New
Testament it is called "the Tribulation" and "the Great
Tribulation."

The Tribulation as Described in Revelation

Although the description of this awful day of the Lord
is mentioned and treated in detail by virtually all the
Old Testament prophets, there is no book in the Bible
which gives so clear and comprehensive a picture of this
day as we see in the book of Revelation. Fourteen of
its twenty-two chapters are occupied with a description
of the day of the Lord. After the prophecy concerning
the history of the Church in chapters 2 and 3, the chapter
which speaks of the Rapture (Rev. 4) and the chapter
which describes what the Church saw in heaven (Rev. 5),
we find the description of the Tribulation Period which
begins with chapter 6 and extends through chapter 19.
The Tribulation will end with the Battle of Armageddon
and the coming of the Lord in glory.

The Division of the Tribulation

The Tribulation Period in Revelation is clearly divided
into parts, each three and one-half years in duration.
The first half of this period is referred to as "the Tribulation" and the last half is called "the Great Tribulation." The first half includes the breaking of the seven
seals and the blowing of the first six trumpets of Revelation of which we read in chapters 6 to 10. Then follow
three chapters describing the chief characters in the

Great Tribulation. In chapter 11 we meet the two witnesses of the Lord, Elijah and Moses, who will prophesy for exactly forty-two months (1,260 days) or three and one-half years. We will deal with this more specifically when we study Revelation 11 and 13. Chapter 12 speaks of the chief character in the book, the Lord Jesus Christ in relation to His people in the Great Tribulation. Chapter 13 discusses the devil's two chief allies in the Great Tribulation, the two beasts of Revelation 13: the beast out of the sea, political head of the Antichristian federation of nations, and the beast out of the land, the religious leader of that day. The first is the head of the restored Roman Empire and the second is the Anti-Christ, the man of sin and the son of perdition.

THE GREAT TRIBULATION

Following these three chapters introducing us to the principal characters in the Great Tribulation, we have a detailed account of that awful period discussed in chapters 14-19, ending with Armageddon and the return of the Lord. We have given you this preview so that you will more easily understand the events described in the chapters we are about to study. Remember that the first half of the Tribulation is described in Revelation 6-10 and the last half in chapters 14-19.

THE FOUR HORSEMEN

The description of the Tribulation Period begins in Revelation 6 with an account of the breaking of the seals on the scroll which the Lord Jesus took from the hand of the one on the throne of whom we read in chapter 5. When the first seal is broken, the Tribulation begins and John sees issuing forth a white horse and a rider. The white horse is the symbol of peace and victory. The rider upon the horse is the Antichrist, the false messiah. He is not to be confused with the white horse and its rider of which we read in Revelation 19:11, who is none other than the Lord Jesus Himself in His glorious triumphant return to bring true peace.

Chapter 6 speaks of the false christ, the Antichrist, who seeks to imitate the true Christ and therefore comes on a white horse. He comes promising peace. For a brief period after the true Church is taken up there will be peace on earth. The nations will federate to end all war. The churches which are left behind will unite under one Laodicean system, since all true believers will be gone. They will, therefore, meet with no opposition from the "fanatical" Premillennial and Fundamental "cranks," for they will all be with the Lord in glory.

A period of false peace, a mock millenium, will ensue, and when the Antichrist upon the white horse has convinced the world that the golden age of peace has come, he will unloose his fury upon the unsuspecting nations and plunge the world into war. This is revealed when the second seal, of which we read in Revelation 6, is opened.

> And when he had opened the second seal, I heard the second beast say, Come and see. And there went out another horse that was red: and power was given to him that sat thereon to take peace from the earth, and that they should kill one another: and there was given unto him a great sword (Rev. 6:3-4).

THE RED HORSE

The brief false peace of the Antichrist is followed by the sudden shattering of this spurious peace and the plunging of the entire world into the greatest war of all time, a war that will culminate in the Battle of Armageddon. The rider upon this red horse is undoubtedly the same as the rider upon the white horse. He now begins to reveal his identity: he is not the Prince of

Peace whom he imitates, but the old enemy of mankind
and God, the devil, incarnated in the man of sin, the
personal Antichrist.

THE BLACK HORSE

When the Lamb opens the third seal we see issuing
forth a black horse. Here is the description:

> And when he had opened the third seal, I heard the third
> beast say, Come and see. And I beheld, and lo, a black
> horse; and he that sat on him had a pair of balances in his
> hand. And I heard a voice in the midst of the four beasts
> say, A measure of wheat for a penny, and three measures
> of barley for a penny; and see thou hurt not the oil and
> the wine (Rev. 6:5-6).

From this description the black horse and its rider
are easily identified. The black horse typifies the scourge
that always accompanies and follows war. It is the black
horse of famine and inflation. The rider has a balance
in his hand which indicates that everything must be
weighed. We have seen this in our own country during
the war when commodities became scarce, prices soared
and everything was sold by weight.

After the Church has been taken out, the short false
peace will be followed by war and the greatest famine
of all history will grip the world. A measure of wheat
will sell for a penny. (A measure of wheat is approximately a quart.) A penny was a day's wages for the
average laborer of those days. This means that the entire daily wage of the working man will be required to
buy one quart of wheat (about two pounds). If the daily
wage is five dollars, it will buy two pounds of wheat,
which will be $150 a bushel. The poor will suffer in-
describably, whereas the rich will be left largely un-
touched until their money is gone. That is the meaning
of the phrase "hurt not the oil and the wine."

Oil and wine are symbols of wealth and only the
wealthy will have sufficient food for a time.

THE PALE HORSE

Following closely behind the black horse of famine comes the pale horse of pestilence and disease, with its resultant death. Here is John's description:

> And when he opened the fourth seal, I heard the voice of the fourth beast say, Come and see. And I looked, and beheld a pale horse: and his name that sat on him was Death, and Hell followed with him. And power was given unto them over the fourth part of the earth, to kill with sword, and with hunger, and with death, and with the beasts of the earth (Rev. 6:7-8).

A fourth of the population will die because of the results of this awful war, famine and pestilence. If the population of the earth is as great as it is now, this will mean that as a result of war, famine and disease, approximately five hundred million persons will die. From these facts you will begin to understand why this period is called "the Tribulation" and why we Christians rejoice in the fact that we shall be taken out before the great and terrible day of the Lord comes.

THE FIFTH SEAL

The fifth seal gives us a glimpse into heaven. Under the altar in heaven (there is a temple in heaven) John sees the souls of those martyred during that intense period described under the opening of the first four seals. There will be people saved during this Tribulation, notably many of the house of Israel, who will be martyred for their faith. Under the fifth seal they are assured that they have not died in vain but that they are to be patient and wait until the indignation of the Lord is past.

THE SIXTH SEAL

With the opening of the sixth seal we note an alarming increase in the tempo and intensity of the judgments falling upon the earth after the removal of the true

Church, the body of Christ. The first four seals concerned war on earth but with the opening of the sixth, judgments from heaven are poured upon the earth. Here is the record:

> And I beheld when he had opened the sixth seal, and, lo, there was a great earthquake; and the sun became black as sackcloth of hair, and the moon became as blood; and the stars of heaven fell unto the earth, even as a fig tree casteth her untimely figs, when she is shaken of a mighty wind. And the heaven departed as a scroll when it is rolled together; and every mountain and island were moved out of their places. And the kings of the earth, and the great men, and the rich men, and the chief captains, and the mighty men, and every bondman, and every free man, hid themselves in the dens and in the rocks of the mountains; and said to the mountains and rocks, Fall on us, and hide us from the face of him that sitteth on the throne, and from the wrath of the Lamb; for the great day of his wrath is come; and who shall be able to stand? (Rev. 6:12-17).

The Atomic Bomb

It is not hard to understand this description when we consider recent developments and the use of the atomic bomb. We believe there are two instances in Revelation which may well describe the use of the atomic bomb by the Antichrist in the Tribulation Period. One is in the passage quoted above and the other, still more graphic and clear, is found in Revelation 16, which describes the pouring of the seventh vail into the air. We shall discuss this further when we reach the sixteenth chapter.

Note that Revelation 6 speaks of "a great earthquake;" remember also that the atomic bomb shook the earth for miles around and almost dislodged the fliers who dropped the death-dealing missile. The sun became darkened by a pillar of smoke which rose twenty-thousand feet, and several nights later the moon still could not be seen through the pall of smoke but appeared to be a blood-red disc. The billowing clouds of smoke made the heavens appear to be rolled away like a scroll. Fear such as had never gripped man seized the Japanese, who capitulated with agonizing speed even though their land had not been invaded and they still had seven million men under arms. They sought shelter in caves, dens and underground shelters and many committed suicide.

This is but a mild description of the havoc wrought by the atomic bomb, but we are led to believe that the passages in Revelation 6 and 16 also describe this instrument of death.

MacArthur's Prophecy

At the surrender of Japan, General Douglas MacArthur spoke from that country as a prophet of the Lord. Among the many striking remarks in his prophecy was this, which undoubtedly refers to the atomic bomb.

> Military alliances, balances of power, leagues of nations, all in turn failed, leaving the only path to be by the crucible of war. The utter destructiveness of war now blots out this alternative. If we do not devise some greater and more equitable system, Armageddon will be at our door.

Where did MacArthur get the word "Armageddon"? The term is found only in the Bible and refers to the last battle of all time. It will be so terrible that except the coming of the Lord intervene there shall no flesh be saved. We know that MacArthur was referring to the inconceivable destructiveness of released atomic energy. MacArthur was a prophet. The last war will be Armageddon. It is described in Revelation. That awful day will spare no one. Men will seek death and cry for the rocks and the mountains to fall upon them.

The Blessed Hope

There is a bright side, too, for there is hope—the blessed hope which God promises to all who will receive

Christ, namely, that they shall not have to pass through the Great Tribulation but shall be caught away before the man of sin, the final world-dictator, releases his fury upon the earth. God's promise to the Church of Philadelphia is:

> Because thou hast kept the word of my patience, I also will keep thee from the hour of temptation, which shall come upon all the world, to try them that dwell upon the earth (Rev. 3:10).

Are You Ready?

The Lord will soon be here to take away His faithful followers and the wicked will be left behind to face the wrath of God. Oh, flee today from the wrath to come!

Believe on the Lord Jesus Christ, and thou shalt be saved.

CHAPTER FIFTEEN

The 144,000 of Revelation 7

And after these things I saw four angels standing on the four corners of the earth, holding the four winds of the earth, that the wind should not blow on the earth, nor on the sea, nor on any tree. And I saw another angel ascending from the east, having the seal of the living God: and he cried with a loud voice to the four angels, to whom it was given to hurt the earth and the sea, saying, Hurt not the earth, neither the sea, nor the trees, till we have sealed the servants of our God in their foreheads. And I heard the number of them which were sealed: and there were sealed an hundred and forty and four thousand of all the tribes of the children of Israel. Of the tribe of Juda were sealed twelve thousand. Of the tribe of Reuben were sealed twelve thousand. Of the tribe of Gad were sealed twelve thousand. Of the tribe of Aser were sealed twelve thousand. Of the tribe of Nepthalim were sealed twelve thousand. Of the tribe of Mannasses were sealed twelve thousand. Of the tribe of Simeon were sealed twelve thousand. Of the tribe of Levi were sealed twelve thousand. Of the tribe of Issachar were sealed twelve thousand. Of the tribe of Zabulon were sealed twelve thousand. Of the tribe of Joseph were sealed twelve thousand. Of the tribe of Benjamin were sealed twelve thousand. After this I beheld, and, lo, a great multitude, which no man could number, of all nations, and kindreds, and people, and tongues, stood before the throne, and before the Lamb, clothed with white robes, and palms in their hands; and cried with a loud voice, saying, Salvation to our God which sitteth upon the throne, and unto the Lamb. And all the angels stood round about the throne, and about the elders and the four beasts, and fell before the throne on their faces, and worshipped God, saying, Amen: Blessing, and glory, and wisdom, and thanksgiving, and honor, and power, and might be unto our God for ever and ever. Amen. And one of the elders answered, saying unto me, What are these which are arrayed in white robes? and whence came they? And I said unto him, Sir, thou knowest. And he said to me, These are they which came out of great tribulation, and have washed their robes, and made them white in the blood of the Lamb. Therefore are they before the throne of God. and serve him day and night in his temple: and he that sitteth on the throne shall dwell among them. They shall hunger no more, neither thirst any more; neither shall the sun light on them, nor any heat. For the Lamb which is in the midst of the throne shall feed them, and shall lead them unto living fountains of waters: and God shall wipe away all tears from their eyes (Rev. 7).

This seventh chapter of Revelation is a continuation of the description of the Tribulation Period. We have repeatedly emphasized the simple structure and outline of the book of Revelation. Far from being a dark book and one difficult to understand, it is what its name implies, a revelation, and clear in its statements of future events in God's program. We repeat, therefore, the simple outline. Chapter 1 gives us a vision of Christ in the glory of His Second Coming. He is the center of the book and we must never lose sight of Him amid the events surrounding Him at His Second Coming. Many people have been so occupied with His *coming,* that they have forgotten *Him.* Prophecy deals not so much with future events as with the future of a Person, the Person of the Lord Jesus. Hence the opening chapter of Revelation is devoted to Him who must from beginning to end hold the central place in our study of this wonderful book of the Revelation of Jesus Christ.

Chapters 2 and 3, as we saw, describe the course of the professing Church in this dispensation ending with Laodicea. In the midst of professing Christendom is the true Church, the body of Christ. At the close of chapter 3 we see the Church lukewarm and indifferent, and the

fourth chapter of Revelation opens with a discussion of
the Rapture, the catching away of the true body of
Christ from professing religious Christendom. The remainder of chapters 4 and all of 5 are a description of
what John (representing the raptured Church) saw in
heaven.

With the beginning of Revelation 6, the scene returns
to earth, and what follows in the remainder of the book
to the return of Christ discussed in chapter 19:11 concerns God's judgments on the earth during the Tribulation while the true Church is with her Lord in heaven.
Chapter 19 speaks of the return of the Lord, followed
by the Millennium, the last judgment and the eternal
state. This, in brief, again is the simple outline of the
book, and if you will keep it clearly before you, you will
find the detailed study of Revelation not only instructive
and interesting but exceedingly easy.

In our messages thus far we have studied the first
six chapters of Revelation and we will consider now the
seventh chapter with which we prefaced this phase of
our study. Six seals have been broken by the Lamb and
we have seen the result. The Antichrist is revealed,
first as the promiser of a false brief peace under the
symbol of the white horse, followed by the red horse of
war, the black horse of famine and the pale horse of
pestilence and death. The fifth seal revealed that amid
all this tribulation there was a faithful remnant who had
been martyred for their faithfulness and who will share
in the kingdom glory. The sixth seal gives a graphic
picture of the awful time of sorrow and death upon the
earth when a fourth of the population will perish in war,
by hunger and pestilence.

The 144,000 Elect

Chapter 7 of Revelation is a pause, a parenthesis,
between the sixth and the seventh seals. When the

seventh seal is to be opened it will usher in judgments
so terrible and destruction so complete that except those
days are shortened no flesh should be saved. This seventh
chapter of Revelation records how God is going to keep
and protect His people in the midst of this Tribulation
and the approaching day of Jacob's trouble. Judgment
will be suspended for a brief period and the Tribulation
will be held in abeyance until these faithful ones have
been sealed. That is the meaning of the opening verses
of Revelation 7:

> And after these things I saw four angels standing on the
> four corners of the earth, holding the four winds of the
> earth, that the wind should not blow on the earth, nor on
> the sea, nor on any tree . . . till we have sealed the servants
> of our God in their foreheads (Rev. 7:1, 3).

Picture the situation. The true Church has been
caught away, as we read in chapter 4. Satan is loose
and the Antichrist is doing his best to defeat God. In
this Tribulation Period his greatest hatred is against
God's ancient people, Israel. During the dispensation
in which you and I live his hatred is directed particularly
against the true Church, but after she is taken out, he will
focus his attention entirely upon the children of Israel.
Satan knows that Israel is God's covenant nation, and
although Israel now rejects His Son Jesus, there is a
day coming when Israel shall be converted and all the
promises of the kingdom and their re-establishment in
the land of Palestine will be fulfilled. Satan seeks to
thwart God's program and so sets out to destroy all
Israel and thus defeat the program of God. He attempted
this through Pharaoh, Nebuchadnezzar, the Assyrians,
the Greeks and the Romans, and, more recently, through
Mussolini and Hitler and a host of other ignorant riot
rabblers and inciters of race hatred. As Satan has failed
to destroy the nation of Israel in the past because of the
intervention of God, so he will fail again. In the past

the Lord raised up Moses, Nehemiah and Mordecai, and
so again in the Tribulation He will protect His faithful
remnant.

THE TWELVE TRIBES OF ISRAEL

How clear is the record in Revelation 7! We are told
that there were sealed of the twelve tribes of Israel
144,000, 12,000 from each tribe. John mentions each
tribe by name and the number from that tribe, from
Judah to Benjamin. Passing strange it is that there
should have been difference of opinion among Bible
students regarding the identity of the 144,000. Yet,
strange to say, many scholars—who should have escaped
such a snare—have misinterpreted the meaning of the
144,000 mentioned in Revelation 7. They have stolen
all the promises of the nation of Israel and left them
only the curses. Theirs is the grievous but common
error of spiritualizing the Scriptures, making the Church
Israel and Zion the Church, and confusing law and grace,
Israel and the body of Christ, and the Church and the
kingdom. As a result of this failure to read and believe
the Bible literally and the insistence upon spiritualizing
the Scriptures, confusion has gripped Christians everywhere. If they would learn to read the Bible as they
read any other book—literally—all confusion would disappear.

VARIOUS INTERPRETATIONS

Many are the human interpretations of the 144,000.
There are first of all those who make themselves Israel.
They say that God will deal no more with literal Israel
and they maintain that the Church now is spiritual Israel.
Consequently they claim for themselves the Abrahamic
covenant and declare that Jerusalem is the Church and
that all the prophecies of the restoration of Israel to the
land of Palestine must be spiritually interpreted as

applying to the Church. This spiritualizing of Scripture, I repeat, is one of the most serious evils which has beset the Church. Begin with this rule in your interpretation of Scripture: God means what He says, and although we find types, symbols and figures of speech in the Bible, as we do in every other book, it is written that simple folk like you and me may understand if we read and believe it as it is written and do not twist the meaning to fit our personal preconceived ideas.

Numerous groups of religious people have in all ages tried to maintain that they were the 144,000, but none of them have been able to establish their identity with one of the twelve tribes. How much easier to read the Bible as it is written and then simply believe it! Here is the record:

> And I heard the number of them which were sealed: and there were sealed an hundred and forty and four thousand of all the tribes of the children of Israel. Of the tribe of Juda were sealed twelve thousand. Of the tribe of Reuben were sealed twelve thousand. Of the tribe of Gad were sealed twelve thousand. Of the tribe of Aser were sealed twelve thousand. Of the tribe of Nepthalim were sealed twelve thousand. Of the tribe of Manasses were sealed twelve thousand. Of the tribe of Simeon were sealed twelve thousand. Of the tribe of Levi were sealed twelve thousand. Of the tribe of Issachar were sealed twelve thousand. Of the tribe of Zabulon were sealed twelve thousand. Of the tribe of Joseph were sealed twelve thousand. Of the tribe of Benjamin were sealed twelve thousand (Rev. 7:4-8).

This passage states—so plainly that a child can understand—that during the Tribulation Period God will remember His covenant with Abraham, Isaac, Jacob, David and Solomon, and all the promises of Israel's restoration in Isaiah, Jeremiah, Ezekiel, Daniel and all the other prophets, and before the Antichrist can destroy the nation of Israel, God is going to save a remnant of twelve thousand from each of the twelve tribes of the sons of Jacob and seal them for Himself—seal them to escape destruction of the Antichrist and seal them to become His witnesses during the Tribulation whereby a great multitude of Gentiles will be saved because of the testimony of this redeemed remnant from the twelve tribes of the nation of Israel.

144,000 MISSIONARIES

These 144,000, all Israelites, the physical descendants of Abraham through Isaac and Jacob, will become God's missionaries during the Tribulation Period. As a result of their preaching and testimony there will be a great number saved from the Gentiles, or, as Revelation 7:9 states:

of all nations, and kindreds, and people, and tongues.

These saved ones, from every nation, will be those who have never heard the Gospel of God's grace. When the Church is raptured, all those who have heard the Word and been invited to Christ and have rejected Him will be left behind to perish in the Tribulation. There will be no "second chance" for them. But the great masses in the world who have never heard the Gospel of God's grace will hear the message in the Tribulation from the lips of these 144,000 Israelites, and as a result a great number will be saved, most of whom will be martyred, and will be raised at the close of the Tribulation Period, as the final gleanings of the First Resurrection. There is no question regarding their identity, for we read:

And one of the elders answered, saying unto me, What are these which are arrayed in white robes? and whence came they? And I said unto him, Sir, thou knowest. And he said to me, These are they which came out of great tribulation, and have washed their robes, and made them white in the blood of the Lamb (Rev. 7:13-14).

In the original, as well as in the Revised Version, the expression reads thus: "These are they which are come out of *the great* tribulation." Here is the picture. After the sixth seal, and before the seventh, God, who knows what lies ahead, seals and saves 144,000 missionaries from Israel who preach the Gospel during the remainder of the Tribulation Period. As a result, a great multitude of Gentiles are saved, who are martyred for their faith and will be added to the glorious company of the Church when Jesus returns, as we read in Revelation 19:11.

They are to be safe, out of the awful day of the Lord and awaiting the coming of Christ in power. In the meantime they are before the throne of God in perfect felicity, the gleanings of the Gospel harvest. How marvelous is the final description of their bliss in the closing verses of the chapter:

> Therefore are they before the throne of God, and serve him day and night in his temple: and he that sitteth on the throne shall dwell among them. They shall hunger no more, neither thirst any more; neither shall the sun light on them, nor any heat. For the Lamb which is in the midst of the throne shall feed them, and shall lead them unto living fountains of waters: and God shall wipe away all tears from their eyes (Rev. 7:15-17).

What a picture of peace, joy and quietness! Contrast this with the chapter which follows when the opening of the seals is resumed and we study the judgments of the seven trumpets when the seventh seal is opened. Here we have a resumption of the awful judgments of the Tribulation, but far, far removed from them are His redeemed saints who because of their faith in the Lord Jesus Christ are in the place of eternal bliss and peace.

We believe that the fulfillment of the prophecies which we are studying is near. Soon the Lord will come to call out His own, and those of you who have heard the message and have been given the invitation but rejected it will have to face the awful day of God with all its terrible judgments. But the day of mercy is still here and the door of grace is still open. The Lord still invites, "Come unto me," and warns you to "flee from the wrath to come." Trust Him *now*.

CHAPTER SIXTEEN

The Trumpet Judgments

And when he had opened the seventh seal, there was silence in heaven about the space of half an hour (Rev. 8:1).

There was silence in heaven for half an hour. That
is no doubt the longest silence which heaven has ever
known, for the celestial realm resounds continually with
the shouts of praise and adoration of the heavenly hosts
as they pay homage and bring glory to God the Father,
God the Son and God the Holy Ghost. The silence is
mentioned because it is unusual for heaven to be silent.

The occasion for this silence was the opening of the
last of the seven seals that sealed the little book of redemption which was in the hand of the One upon the
throne, as we read in Revelation 5. That seven-sealed
book contained the terms of the redemption of the earth,
but it contained also the awful judgments of God upon
those who had spurned His redemption.

As the seals were opened, one by one increasingly
terrible judgments fell upon the earth until six had been
opened. War, famine, pestilence, death, earthquakes,
hailstones and fire had taken a toll of fatalities that
swept a fourth of the people of the earth into judgment
and death. One more seal remained to be opened, and
the hosts of heaven, realizing it was the last and the
most terrible, stood in awe and expectation. They knew
something of what lay ahead, though they may not have

known all, but this they knew: they were about to witness the greatest time of sorrow the world had seen. This expectation accounts for the silence in heaven for half an hour.

Many and varied have been the explanations of this silence but I am sure that you will understand what I mean when I say that this was the silence of awesome expectation. It was as if all things in heaven "held their breath" as they awaited the sounding of the first of the seven trumpets which followed the breaking of the seventh and the last seal of the little book. Expectation and suspense can be so intense that one dares not breathe. We often describe such a situation thus: "It was so quiet you could hear a pin drop."

Suppose that I were to tell you a story of a hair-raising experience and relate to you how a victim was being chased by a madman who had escaped from a prison for the criminally insane. With a knife between his teeth and a gun in each hand sneering and cursing, he pursues the innocent victim of his rage. He is gaining on her, inch by inch, foot by foot. The path leads to the edge of a great precipice which drops hundreds of feet to jagged rocks below. Closer and closer the slayer comes to his victim. His hands reach out to seize her as she reaches the end of the cliff. She hesitates, she wavers for a moment, and then, just as the villain lunges at her . . .

That is suspense. If this were an account of an actual experience, you would be holding your breath when the maiden reached the cliff. There would be silence—the silence of suspense.

This illustration, weak though it is, helps us to understand the silence in heaven. The heavenly hosts have been following the rapid unsealing of the book and have been carried away by the fast-moving events of war, famine, pestilence and death. We saw men hiding in caves and

rocks and crying for the mountains to fall upon them.
But these events occurred during the opening of the
first six seals. The seventh is coming, and it is the most
terrible of all. Consequently, as the Lamb opens this
seventh seal and before the first angel-trumpeter of
judgment sounds his trumpet, all heaven is in suspense
as they await the awful judgments of God. They are
breathless . . . silent for half an hour.

My friend, you, too, would be silent and breathless if
you knew the fearfulness of the holiness and judgments
of God upon sin. Not a sinner reading these words or
reading the Bible would wait another minute, certainly
not a half-hour, to cry to God for mercy and forgiveness
if he understood the full significance of the doom of the
lost as these hosts of heaven must have known as they
breathlessly watched the breaking of the last seal in the
Tribulation Period.

The Seven Trumpets

The awful suspense was occasioned by the events
which were about to take place under the seven trumpets.
You will recall that the entire Tribulation Period consists
of a trio of sevens: seven seals, seven trumpets and
seven vials of wrath. The seventh seal ends in seven
trumpets and the seventh trumpet ends in the seven vials
of final wrath. Generally speaking, the first half of the
Tribulation includes the seven seals and the first six
trumpets which are a part of the seventh seal. The last
half of the Tribulation, called the Great Tribulation,
is discussed in chapters 15-19 under the seven vials.
Between these two are four chapters, 11, 12, 13 and 14,
which are a preview of the coming Great Tribulation and
introduce us to the major characters in the last half of
the Tribulation Period. The sounding of the first six
trumpets concludes the first half of the day of the Lord.

As the seventh seal is opened, seven angels with trumpets make their appearance:

> And I saw the seven angels which stood before God; and to them were given seven trumpets. And another angel came and stood at the altar, having a golden censer; and there was given unto him much incense, that he should offer it with the prayers of all saints upon the golden altar which was before the throne. And the smoke of the incense, which came with the prayers of the saints, ascended up before God out of the angel's hand . . . And the seven angels which had the seven trumpets prepared themselves to sound (Rev. 8:2-4, 6).

Before the first angel blows the trumpet we have the assurance from God that in spite of all the dire judgments which are about to fall, God has not forgotten His people, and their prayers, though long delayed, will be answered by Him. For nineteen hundred years the saints have been praying "Thy kingdom come, Thy will be done," and yet it seems that the man of sin, the Antichrist, will yet prevail. Before the terrible time under the trumpets, God gives the vision in which Christ adds the efficacy of His own blood as the acceptable incense, together with the prayers of all saints, to assure them that come what may, their prayers for the return of Christ and the establishment of the kingdom will be answered.

The First Trumpet

The first angel sounds the trumpet and there falls upon the earth and its wicked inhabitants—

> hail and fire mingled with blood . . . and the third part of the trees was burnt up, and all green grass was burnt up (Rev. 8:7).

This is the judgment which destroys a third of all growing vegetation on the earth.

THE SECOND TRUMPET

And as it were a great mountain burning with fire was cast
into the sea: and the third part of the sea became blood
(Rev. 8:8).

THE THIRD TRUMPET

And the third angel sounded, and there fell a great star
from heaven, burning as it were a lamp, and it fell upon
the third part of the rivers, and upon the fountains of waters:
And the name of the star is called Wormwood: and the third
part of the waters became wormwood; and many men died
of the waters, because they were made bitter (Rev. 8:10-11).

THE FOURTH TRUMPET

And the fourth angel sounded, and the third part of the
sun was smitten, and the third part of the moon, and the
third part of the stars; so as the third part of them was
darkened, and the day shone not for a third part of it, and
the night likewise (Rev. 8:12).

I have refrained from commenting on the four trumpet
judgments because I believe that they should be read
and interpreted literally. The moment we begin to
spiritualize and make the sun and the stars mean something other than the sun and the stars, we err, for then
everyone has his own interpretation. Believe it literally
and you will have no difficulty. When the first angel
sounds, literal hail and fire fall from heaven. When
the second sounds, a literal burning mass falls into the
sea and turns to literal blood. If you doubt that, may I
ask you if you doubt also that Moses turned literal water
into literal blood. We interpret Exodus literally, but
when we study Revelation we declare that the statements
in this book are to be interpreted not literally, but
symbolically and figuratively. Attempts to symbolize
these statements limit the omnipotence of God.

A SAFE RULE

Let me mention a simple rule of interpretation which applies not only to the book of Revelation but to the entire Bible. Always interpret every statement in the Word of God literally as meaning exactly what it says, unless it is definitely stated otherwise or the structure and context are such that you can plainly see that the passage concerns a figure and a symbol. This is the most important rule to follow when interpreting Scripture. When a verse in Scripture states plainly that what follows is a parable, then we need not interpret the passage literally, or when the grammatical structure indicates that a passage is not a literal fact, for example, this statement, "The kingdom of heaven is *like unto* a merchantman," we know it is a parable or a figure. A case in point is found in Revelation 8:8 where we read:

And the second angel sounded, and as it were a great mountain burning with fire was cast into the sea.

This verse does not say that it *was* a mountain but "*as it were* a great mountain," that is, it looked like a mountain. It may have been a meteor or another heavenly body, but if this verse had said that it was a great mountain then I should believe this literally. It is, therefore, not difficult to know when we are to interpret statements literally and when they are figures of speech. Our speech in daily life is filled with figures, metaphors and symbols, but we have no difficulty in knowing what they mean and when we are to interpret literally or figuratively. When we say that an athlete is a "star," we know that the word is a figure and does not refer to a literal star. We know how to distinguish in ordinary conversation between the literal and the figurative, but when we interpret Scripture we become confused. Instead of applying the simple rule, "Always interpret literally unless definitely indicated otherwise," we insist upon making a star mean an emperor, a dignitary or something else. An example is the sounding of the fifth trumpet. We are told in Revelation 9:

> And the fifth angel sounded, and I saw a star fall from heaven into the earth.

The context tells us that the reference is to a figure, not to a literal star, for we read:

> And to him was given the key of the bottomless pit.

This star is a being, a person, for personality is ascribed to him. Revelation 9:2 declares that he opened the bottomless pit and a great swarm of locusts issued forth to torment men upon the earth. Here again the context tells us that in this instance the locusts were not literal insects but fallen demon-beings, for we read concerning them:

> And they had a king over them, which is the angel of the bottomless pit, whose name in the Hebrew tongue is Abaddon.

When the fifth angel sounds, the prison of the bottomless pit is opened and there issue forth supernatural spirit beings to torment men five months. They are described as having faces like men, hair like women, teeth like lions and tails like scorpions. Beyond a doubt these were a class of especially wicked demon-beings who because of their viciousness were not permitted to be at large until now. There is reason to believe that they were the fallen angels, called in Genesis 6 "the sons of God," who corrupted the human race by an unholy union until God was compelled to destroy the whole race except one family who had escaped this demon corruption. Jude refers to them when he says:

> And the angels which kept not their first estate, but left their own habitation, he hath reserved in everlasting chains under darkness unto the judgment of the great day (Jude 6).

We are discussing the great day of judgment to which Jude refers when these wicked demon-beings will be let loose for a limited time, for five months only, to bring judgment upon all the wicked.

What a terible time this will be! I am not trying to exaggerate its horrors but am only trying to tell you what God's Word says concerning that coming day of wrath. It is not my purpose to alarm you, but to warn and, if necessary, to alarm you into seeking shelter underneath the precious blood of the Lord Jesus Christ. We will discuss in succeeding chapters the sixth trumpet judgment and the six principal actors in the last half of the Tribulation period. However, before we close this chapter, let me present to you once more the need of finding shelter in Christ. The time is near. All signs point to the soon return of the Lord, and if you are not ready, I plead with you again.

Believe on the Lord Jesus Christ, and thou shalt be saved, and thy house.

CHAPTER SEVENTEEN

Tasting the Word of God

And I saw another mighty angel come down from heaven, clothed with a cloud: and a rainbow was upon his head, and his face was as it were the sun, and his feet as pillars of fire: and he had in his hand a little book open: and he set his right foot upon the sea, and his left foot on the earth, and cried with a loud voice, as when a lion roareth: and when he had cried, seven thunders uttered their voices. And when the seven thunders had uttered their voices, I was about to write: and I heard a voice from heaven saying unto me, Seal up those things which the seven thunders uttered, and write them not. And the angel which I saw stand upon the sea and upon the earth lifted up his hand to heaven, and sware by him that liveth for ever and ever, who created heaven, and the things that therein are, and the earth, and the things that therein are, and the sea, and the things which are therein, that there should be time no longer: but in the days of the voice of the seventh angel, when he shall begin to sound, the mystery of God should be finished, as he hath declared to his servants the prophets. And the voice which I heard from heaven spake unto me again, and said, Go and take the little book which is open in the hand of the angel which standeth upon the sea and upon the earth. And I went unto the angel, and said unto him, Give me the little book. And he said unto me, Take it, and eat it up; and it shall make thy belly bitter, but it shall be in thy mouth sweet as honey. And I took the little book out of the angel's hand, and ate it up; and it was in my mouth sweet as honey: and as soon as I had eaten it, my belly was bitter.

And he said unto me, Thou must prophesy again before many peoples, and nations, and tongues, and kings (Rev. 10).

Revelation presents a chronological account of the course of time from the birth of the Church until the end of time. The first three chapters describe the course of professing Christendom to the Rapture of the true Church, as recorded in Revelation 4. From chapters 6 to 19:11 we have a description in detail of the period between the Rapture of the Church and the Second Coming of Christ in glory to set up His kingdom on the earth. This period of time is marked by the judgments of God upon the wicked nations and is described under the figures of seven seals, seven trumpets and seven vials of the wrath of God. In our studies so far we have considered the seven seals and the first five trumpet judgments.

With the sounding of the sixth trumpet the first half of the Tribulation Period ends. Two sections comprise the events under the sixth trumpet. At the close of Revelation 9 we hear the sixth angel sound and we see the great army of the end-time which will engage in the Battle of Armageddon, the last and greatest battle of all history at the close of the Tribulation Period and just before the establishment of the messianic millennial kingdom upon the earth.

An Army of 200,000,000

Just before the return of the Lord in glory there will be the greatest concentration of military power the world has ever seen, under the leadership of two fierce dictators: the political head of the federated nation (the first beast of Revelation 13) and the religious dictator, the Antichrist (the second beast of Revelation 13). This army is being prepared in the middle of the Tribulation Period. In Revelation 9:13-21 we have a description of an army of two hundred million horsemen. Whether this is the army that will gather at Armageddon is not entirely clear as the army spoken of in Revelation 9 seems to be a supernatural army of horrible beings, probably demons, who are permitted to plague the unrepentant sinners on the earth for a period of time described as "an hour, and a day . . . and a year." A third of the remaining population of the earth will be killed in little more than a year. This will be the highest casualty report the world has known, but in spite of this awful judgment, men will not repent but, instead, become more bitter and fierce against the very God who was seeking to drive them to repentance by this awful scourge and plague upon the earth. Sad indeed are the closing verses of Revelation 9:

> And the rest of the men which were not killed by these plagues yet repented not of the works of their hands . . . neither repented they of their murders, nor of their sorceries, nor of their fornication, nor of their thefts (Rev. 9:20:21).

THE MIGHTY ANGEL

The next chapter, therefore, is a commentary on the corruptness of the unrepentant human heart in rebellion against God. In the passage at the beginning of this message we saw a mighty angel, clothed with a cloud, a rainbow on his head, his face like the sun and his feet like pillars of fire, come down from heaven carrying a little open book and standing with his feet upon the earth and the sea. There is no question regarding His identity. He is the Lord Jesus Christ, the coming King Himself. The description of Him is the same as that given in chapter 1. He still has the little book which we have seen Him take from the hand of the Father on the throne (Revelation 5). For a while we lost sight of it and were so occupied with the opening of the seals that we forgot the little book containing both the terms of the earth's redemption and the judgment which would fall upon the earth in preparation for this redemption. In Revelation 5 we saw that the book was sealed with seven seals. In this chapter we are told it is open. The seals have been broken and we are being prepared for the final judgment of God in the last half of the Tribulation Period.

The End is Near

One more trumpet remains to be sounded, and with the sounding of that final trumpet the last three and one-half years of the Tribulation will begin. This last three and one-half years covered by the last and seventh trumpet is described for us under the pouring out of the seven bowls or vials of the wrath of God. When these have been poured out, the Great Tribulation will conclude with the Battle of Armageddon and the glorious public return of the Lord Jesus Christ of which we read in Revelation 19:11. The angel mentioned in Revelation 10, holding in his hand the open book with the last seal broken, looks to the end of the terrible judgment, and so we see him place his right foot upon the sea and his left upon the land. This is an act of possession. This is Christ coming to redeem the earth.

In olden times a conqueror placed his foot on the neck of his vanquished enemy and raised his hand in triumph. We have a somewhat similar picture in Revelation 10. The one of whom it speaks roars like a lion, indicating his power; and after he has cried and roared like a lion, there is the sudden voice of seven thunders. Thunder speaks of God's judgment and power, and here, too, the seven thunders speak of the judgments which are still to follow under the last trumpet. What the thunders said we do not know, for John was expressly told not to write about what he heard, and so we shall not speculate.

No More Delay

As Christ sets His feet on the land and sea, indicating that He is about to take possession, and raises His hand in victory, He speaks:

> And the angel which I saw stand upon the sea and upon the earth lifted up his hand to heaven, and sware by him that liveth for ever and ever, who created heaven, and the things that therein are, and the earth, and the things that therein are, and the sea, and the things which are therein, that there should be time no longer (Rev. 10:5-6).

The expression "that there should be time no longer" is an inaccurate translation of the original and conveys the wrong idea. The literal translation, as you may see by referring to the marginal note in your Bible or by consulting the Revised Version, is this: "That there should be no more delay." The next verse gives the explanation:

> But in the days of the voice of the seventh angel, when he shall begin to sound, the mystery of God should be finished, as he hath declared to his servants the prophets (Rev. 10:7).

This, then, is what Christ says in the midst of the Tribulation. There is only one more trumpet judgment. It covers the last phase of the Tribulation and during those last three and one-half years the entire program of God will be completed and the glorious millennial kingdom set up. Notice that "in the days of the voice of the seventh angel" when he begins to sound, there will be no more delay, but, as we shall see, the program of God in judgment will gain in momentum and intensity and reach completion without pause.

This last part of the Tribulation is described in chapters 15 to 19. In the intervening chapters we are introduced to the six principal characters in the last half of the Tribulation, the Great Tribulation. Presently we will study these, the two witnesses described in Revelation 11, the woman clothed with the sun and her man-child, the dragon, and the two beasts discussed in Revelation 13. A thorough reading of these chapters before we study them will prove profitable indeed.

EATING THE LITTLE BOOK

There remains an interesting fact in Revelation 10: the eating of the little book in the hand of the angel. You recall that we first saw the little book in Revelation 5. It was sealed with seven seals; now it is opened and we know what it contained: the good news of the redemption of the creation and the bad news of the judgment of the wicked. The entire book is open now and we know what it tells us. John, as he looks, is given a strange command:

> And the voice which I heard from heaven spake unto me again, and said, Go and take the little book which is open in the hand of the angel which standeth upon the sea and upon the earth. And I went unto the angel, and said unto him, Give me the little book. And he said unto me, Take it, and eat it up; and it shall make thy belly bitter, but it shall be in thy mouth sweet as honey. And I took the little book out of the angel's hand, and ate it up; and it was in my mouth sweet as honey: and as soon as I had eaten it, my belly was bitter.
>
> And he said unto me, Thou must prophesy again before many peoples, and nations, and tongues, and kings (Rev. 10:8-11).

Many and varied have been the interpretations of this passage. I believe, however, that we will find the explanation simple if we remember what the little book is. It is the book which contains the glad news of creation's coming deliverance but also the doom of the wicked. Ezekiel 2, I believe, will aid us in interpreting the passage correctly. Ezekiel is commanded to preach to the nation of Israel the word of the Lord. This word, as in every other instance, was a two-edged sword. It was both a message of salvation and a message of damnation. The Gospel sword always has these two edges, a fact which is too often forgotten. We are told today not to preach judgment and hell brimstone, but,

rather, the love of God, His mercy and His goodness.
The people of Isaiah's day made a similar request. They
said:

> Prophesy not unto us right things, speak unto us smooth
> things, prophesy deceits (Isa. 30:10).

Jesus emphasizes the two-edged nature of the Gospel
when he says:

> He that believeth on him is not condemned: but he that
> believeth not is condemned already, because he hath not
> believed in the name of the only begotten Son of God (John
> 3:18).

God is love, but He is also justice. He is merciful,
but He is also righteous. He loves the sinner, but He
hates sin. The Gospel is pleasant to the saint but a
terrible prediction of judgment to the unbeliever. The
message is both bitter and sweet—bitter when we realize
that it increases the damnation of the unbeliever who
hears the Gospel, but deliberately rejects it. The Word
of God not only promises heaven to the believer, but
threatens hell to the unbeliever. It is a two-edged sword.
It cuts two ways. It is both sweet and bitter.

Sweet in the Mouth

That is undoubtedly the meaning here when John eats
the little book. It is sweet in the mouth and bitter in the
belly. Ezekiel 2, referring to the same book, declares:

> But thou, son of man, hear what I say unto thee; Be not
> thou rebellious like that rebellious house: open thy mouth,
> and eat that I give thee. And when I looked, behold, an
> hand was sent unto me; and, lo, a roll of a book was therein;
> and he spread it before me; and it was written within and
> without: and there was written therein lamentations, and
> mourning, and woe (Ezek. 2: 8-10).

John's responsibility as well as Ezekiel's was tremendous, and no less important is the responsibility of every

preacher whom God calls to preach the Gospel. His duty is not to preach what he likes or what the people like, but he must preach what God commands him to preach. That includes the message of salvation to those who believe and the judgment to those who reject—the sweet message of hope and the bitter message of condemnation and judgment. Woe to the minister, the servant of the Lord, who because of fear of man "cuts the corners" and omits part of God's message. God will hold us accountable, for He says in Ezekiel 33:7:

> So thou, O son of man, I have set thee a watchman unto the house of Israel; therefore thou shalt hear the word at my mouth, and warn them from me. When I say unto the wicked, O wicked man, thou shalt surely die; if thou dost not speak to warn the wicked from his way, that wicked man shall die in his iniquity; but his blood will I require at thine hand. Nevertheless, if thou warn the wicked of his way to turn from it; if he do not turn from his way, he shall die in his iniquity; but thou hast delivered thy soul (Ezek. 33:7-9).

When I left the practice of medicine and began to preach the Gospel I promised God that I would preach anything God showed me in His Word, no matter what the cost might be. I did not know the cost then or I might have wavered, but when I had to pay the price for preaching what I believed, I found God's grace sufficient for me. The cost was high. My refusal to compromise to please men has cost me friends, position, earthly honor and the applause of men, but I thank God I can stand before Him and say, "To the best of my ability I have preached all I found in the Word, without fear or favor," and His "Well done, thou good and faithful servant," will compensate a thousand times for the bitterness, privation, heartache and persecution I have experienced at the hand of "religious" men.

Reader, I bring again the message—the full message— of the Gospel: salvation for you if you believe; damnation if you reject; joy now and peace and heaven hereafter if you believe; sorrow now and fear and hell at the end of the road if you refuse to receive the only One who can save, even the Lord Jesus Christ.

This is the book—sweet in the mouth, but bitter also. To those who believe, it is sweetness—honey from the rock. To those who reject, it is bitterness and, finally, perdition. Receive Him today. Believe on the Lord Jesus Christ.

> For God sent not his Son into the world to condemn the world; but that the world through him might be saved. He that believeth on him is not condemned: but he that believeth not is condemned already, because he hath not believed in the name of the only begotten Son of God. And this is the condemnation, that light is come into the world, and men loved darkness rather than light, because their deeds were evil (John 3:17-19).

CHAPTER EIGHTEEN

The Two Witnesses

And there was given me a reed like unto a rod: and the angel stood, saying, Rise, and measure the temple of God, and the altar, and them that worship therein. But the court which is without the temple leave out, and measure it not; for it is given unto the Gentiles: and the holy city shall they tread under foot forty and two months. And I will give power unto my two witnesses, and they shall prophesy a thousand two hundred and threescore days, clothed in sackcloth. These are the two olive trees, and the two candlesticks standing before the God of the earth. And if any man will hurt them, fire proceedeth out their mouth, and devoureth their enemies: and if any man will hurt them, he must in this manner be killed. These have power to shut heaven, that it rain not in the days of their prophesy: and have power over waters to turn them to blood, and to smite the earth with all plagues, as often as they will. And when they shall have finished their testimony, the beast that ascendeth out of the bottomless pit shall make war against them, and shall overcome them, and kill them. And their dead bodies shall lie in the street of the great city, which spiritually is called Sodom and Egypt, where also our Lord was crucified. And they of the people and kindreds and tongues and nations shall see their dead bodies three days and an half, and shall not suffer their dead bodies to be put in graves. And they that dwell upon the earth shall rejoice over them, and make merry, and shall send gifts one to another; because these two prophets tormented them that dwell on the earth. And after three days an half the Spirit of life from God entered into them, and they stood upon their feet; and great fear fell upon them which saw them. And they heard a great voice from heaven saying unto them;

Come up hither. And they ascended up to heaven in a cloud;
and their enemies beheld them (Rev. 11:1-12).

The eleventh chapter of Revelation introduces a new
section of this prophetic book . Four chapters are placed
between the descriptions of the first and the last halves
of the Tribulation Period. We have repeatedly pointed
out that after the Church has run its course in this dispensation, as we learn from the seven churches discussed
in Revelation 2 and 3, and the Church is raptured, as
chapter 4 tells us, we find a description in Revelation
6 to 19 of the terrible day of the Lord, called in the
Bible "the Tribulation," "the day of vengeance of our
God," "the day of the Lord" and "the day of Jacob's
trouble." It is a period of time corresponding to the
unfulfilled seventieth week of Daniel, lasting seven
years and ending with the last great battle of history
and the coming of Christ and the setting up of His
glorious kingdom of peace and righteousness. The day
of the Lord, the Tribulation, will begin at the Rapture
of the Church and will end with the visible personal
return of Christ to the earth *with* His Church to reign
for one thousand years.

In previous chapters we have been studying the first
half of this period, concluding with chapter 10. Then
follow four chapters which are parenthetical. They
function as an introduction to and in anticipation of
the last half of the Tribulation Period called "the Great
Tribulation." The Lord Jesus in revealing to John,
and through John to us, the events which will occur
on the earth after the true Church is gone ,pauses at
the end of the description of the first half of the Tribulation to introduce us to the principal characters in the
last half of this period. These will occupy our attention
until we consider the time of the end, and in these four
parenthetical chapters we are given a detailed description so that we may the better identify the characters

when we study the awful events that will close this period.

In the drama to follow in the Great Tribulation there are seven chief actors. Chapter 11 tells of two witnesses for the Lord. Chapter 12 speaks of a woman, a man-child and a dragon. In chapter 13 we find a description of Satan's two witnesses, the "beast out of the sea" and "the beast out of the land." Read these three chapters carefully, for they provide the setting of the awful final conflict described in the remainder of Revelation, ending with the victory of the man-child and the blessing of the woman clothed with the sun.

Revelation 11 opens with a scene in the city of Jerusalem. For centuries it has been under the dominion of Gentile powers, but now John is told to take a reed or measuring rod and to measure the Temple and the altar. Evidently the Temple has by this time been rebuilt in Jerusalem under the false promise of the false Messiah before he shows his true identity and turns viciously upon those whom he has promised to defend and befriend. He is told not to measure the court, for it was given unto the Gentiles to be trodden underfoot for another three and one-half years. It is wise to remember this fact, for we shall encounter it several times. The time is given as forty-two months, the length of the last half of the Tribulation. In this chapter the period is said to be forty-two months. Elsewhere John declares it to be 1,260 days, and it is also spoken of as "a time, and times, and half a time." It gives the exact limit of the day of the Lord from this point and corresponds to the last half of Daniel's seventieth week.

THE TWO WITNESSES

The Lord Jesus is setting the stage for the end. He claims possession by surveying the city where He is to reign over the house of Israel. Then John is told of the two witnesses who shall prophesy during this period of three and one-half years. Many and varied have been the opinions of Bible students regarding the identity of these two witnesses. The majority maintain that they are Enoch and Elijah. These base their entire decision on the fact that the writer of Hebrews declares:

> And as it is appointed unto men once to die, but after this is the judgment: so Christ was once offered to bear the sins of many; and unto them that look for him shall he appear the second time without sin unto salvation (Heb. 9:27-28).

The statement "It is appointed unto men once to die" leads them to conclude that since Enoch and Elijah were the only two men in Scripture who never died, they must be the two witnesses of whom Revelation 11 speaks. May I remind you, however, that Hebrews 9:27 is not applicable to *all men individually*; the word "men" is used here in the generic sense, as applying to the race. It is appointed unto man once to die, but *all* men will not have to die. There will be a generation of believers who never will die. Those who are alive at the Rapture will never die, for Jesus said:

> He that believeth in me, though he were dead, yet shall he live: and whosoever liveth and believeth in me shall never die (John 11:25b-26a).

Paul tells us in I Thessalonians 4, the classic chapter which tells of the Rapture of the Church:

> The dead in Christ shall rise first: Then we which are alive and remain shall be caught up together with them in the clouds, to meet the Lord in the air.

In I Corinthians 15:51-52b we read:

> Behold, I shew you a mystery; We shall not all sleep, but we shall all be changed, in a moment, in the twinkling of an eye, at the last trump.

From these passages you will see that the statement "it is appointed unto men once to die" cannot refer to every individual but speaks of the race in general. Similarly, in Romans 11:25 we read, "And all Israel shall be saved;" this, however, does not mean that every individual Israelite shall be saved, but, rather, *all* Israel as a nation.

MOSES AND ELIJAH

We realize that by refusing to identify the second witness as Enoch that we are going contrary to the most generally accepted interpretation. Nevertheless, I believe that the evidence in harmony with the remainder of Revelation proves that not Enoch but Moses was the other witness. There is no question about Elijah. We are definitely told in the Old Testament, as well as by the Lord Himself in the New, that Elijah will come again before the second coming of Christ. Moreover, the prophet of fire is identified in Revelation 11:5 by the miracles he performs:

> And if any man will hurt them, fire proeedeth out of their mouths, and devoureth their enemies: and if any man will hurt them, he must in this manner be killed. These have power to shut heaven, that it rain not in the days of their prophecy: and have power over waters to turn them to blood, and to smite the earth with all plagues, as often as they will (Rev. 11:5-6).

These miracles are characteristic of Elijah, who called fire down from heaven and shut the heavens so that it did not rain for three and one-half years in Ahab's day. By the same reasoning, however, the miracles described in this same chapter point us directly to Moses as the other witness. The signs and miracles are the signs and miracles which Moses performed when he delivered the children of Israel from Egyptian bondage. Turning water to blood and smiting the earth with all manner of plagues are miracles which lead one to believe that Moses was the second witness. Moreover, Moses is associated in the Gospel with Elijah in the kingdom glory. On the Mount of Transfiguration not Enoch and Elijah, but Moses and Elijah, were with our Lord. Israel at the first coming of Christ was looking for three men.

Christ — Elijah — Moses

They were looking for the Messiah, for Elijah and for that prophet. Moses and Elijah stand on two great mountain peaks of the history of Israel. It was Moses who came when it seemed as if Israel must perish under the cruel anti-Semitic program of Pharaoh (the type of the Antichrist) and delivered them by a mighty hand and through the grievous plagues he called down upon the enemies of God's people. Moses became the deliverer of Israel from material physical bondage and led them out of the land of Egypt on the way to victory in Canaan. He appeared in one of the darkest moments of Israel's history and delivered them by mighty signs and wonders. Elijah, on the other hand, appeared in the darkest day of Israel's spiritual bondage. The nation had departed from the Lord, under Jezebel and her husband, Ahab, and God sent Elijah, the prophet of fire, and delivered Israel from spiritual bondage as Moses had delivered them from physical bondage. These two men, then, represent the salvation of the Lord from physical and spiritual bondage.

The Day of Jacob's Trouble

How fitting that these two men should reappear in the last great day of Jacob's trouble, in the middle of the Tribulation Period, once more and finally to deliver God's ancient people from both the physical and spiritual bondage which grips them in this darkest day of Israel's travail. For three and one-half years (forty-two months) these two witnesses of the Lord bear testimony. It is undoubtedly, in part at least, the result of their testimony that the 144,000 of the twelve tribes of Israel are converted and become the world's great missionaries, with the resultant conversion of a great multitude of Gentile believers.

Their Death and Resurrection

After three and one-half years of witnessing, with the result that the remnant of Israel is saved and prepared to go into the kingdom, they will be murdered by the beast that comes forth out of the bottomless pit. We shall identify this beast in one of our subsequent chapters. Both these witnesses are killed and their bodies allowed to lie on the street of Jerusalem, where Christ their Lord had been crucified, for three and one-half days, so that all may behold the victory which the enemies of God have apparently won over His two witnesses . . . But the seeming victory really spells defeat, for after the three days, the bodies of the two witnesses, Moses and Elijah, are resurrected and the same call which John heard in Revelation 4, "Come up hither," also summons them into heaven to join those who already had been raised at the Rapture of the Church *before* the Tribulation. We shall have occasion to show that this Rapture of the two witnesses after three and one-half years at the close of the Tribulation is synchronous with the Rapture and resurrection of all the Tribulation saints at this time.

THREE STAGES

The resurrection of saints has three distinct phases, according to Paul's statement in I Corinthians 15:

Christ the firstfruits; afterward they that are Christ's at his coming. Then cometh the end (or the end ones).

In Israel the Feast of the Harvest consisted of these three parts: the firstfruits, when a handful of the first-fruits was brought to the priest; the harvest itself, of which these firstfruits were the earnest; the gleanings, ears which had been trodden underfoot and left at the main harvest. These were gathered and added to the others, and together constituted the complete harvest.

The first resurrection is similar. In Matthew 27 we read of a company of Old Testament saints who were raised on the day Christ arose (Matt. 27:52). These were the firstfruits. When Christ comes, the remainder of the believing dead will be raised, and after the Trib-ulation the gleanings of the harvest (the martyred Tribulation saints together with these two witnesses) will be raised, raptured and added to the body of Christ before the Lord returns with His saints to judge the earth.

Thus the Lord vindicates His faithful witnesses, and He is the same today. The preacher who boldly and fearlessly denounces evil and witnesses wholeheartedly for Christ is not popular. The popular preacher today is he who "goes along with the crowd" and preaches a bloodless Gospel, a powerless Cross, a popular religion which allows people to continue in their sins. But the preacher who, like Moses and Elijah, dares to denounce the apostasy and decay in morals even among Chris-tians (nominal), and who raises his voice against the sins of this day and the immorality, the worldliness and the salaciousness of this present age, is likely to be hated and persecuted.

Today many believe that we must not speak of judgment, hell and eternal punishment. He who does so is considered old-fashioned, antiquated, out of date. But God has not changed, and the Gospel has not changed. God is still just. Sin is still sin, and if ever there was a time when we needed to preach the reality and the awfulness of sin, it is today. Such preaching, I repeat, is not popular, and those who would be faithful to the Lord may have to pay the price, but God will vindicate them. Soon our Lord will come. The all-important question, then, will not be, ''How popular have we been with men? What did the world think of us? Were we successful?'' The only questions of importance then will be: ''Have we been faithful in the proclamation of the Gospel of God's grace? Have we taken His command seriously?''

Go ye into all the world, and preach the gospel to every creature.

CHAPTER NINETEEN

War in Heaven

And there was war in heaven: Michael and his angels fought against the dragon; and the dragon fought and his angels, and prevailed not; neither was their place found any more in heaven. And the great dragon was cast out, that old serpent, called the Devil, and Satan, which deceiveth the whole world; he was cast out into the earth, and the angels were cast out with him. And I heard a loud voice saying in heaven, Now is come salvation, and strength, and the kingdom of our God, and the power of his Christ: for the accuser of our brethren is cast down, which accused them before our God day and night (Rev. 12: 7-10).

The history of the world is the history of wars and of conquests. If we removed from our history books the chapters which tell of wars among the nations, the volumes would be thin indeed. The history of the Bible is also the history of war and conflict. From the first book, Genesis, to the last, Revelation, we find a record of a mighty conflict between two forces, the forces of righteousness and the forces of evil, between God and Satan, between the seed of the woman and the seed of the serpent. The conflict has been raging for almost six thousand years, and we believe we are near the final battle which will result in victory for the seed of the woman and utter defeat and judgment for the enemy of God and of all mankind: Satan.

It Began in Genesis 3

This warfare, in which all the wars and battles of the world are only resultant skirmishes, began at the dawn of human history, immediately after man had broken with his God and given allegiance to the enemy of God, the devil. This war was declared by God. The Almighty declared the first war in history, and David says of Him, "The Lord is a man of war." After man had sinned and God had pronounced the curse and sentence upon the sinner, He turned to the serpent, and through the serpent to the devil, and said:

> And I will put enmity between thee and the woman, and between thy seed and her seed; it shall bruise thy head, and thou shalt bruise his heel (Gen. 3:15).

This was the beginning of the conflict, the battle of the ages, in which Satan seeks to thwart the purpose of God, set up a false kingdom upon the earth, prepare a false church upon the earth and persecute the true believers on the Lord Jesus Christ. It is well to recognize that behind all the wars of men and of nations is the great spiritual battle between sin and righteousness, between the seed of the woman and the seed of the serpent, as described in Genesis 3:15.

The End of the War

As the beginning of this war is described in the first book of the Bible, so, quite properly, the description of the final outcome and end of the conflict is described in the last book of the Bible, the book of Revelation, which is a description of the end-time. It opens, as we have seen, with a picture of the final conqueror, the Lord Jesus Christ, of whom we read in Revelation 1. Chapters 2 and 3 speak of the Lord's dealings in this dispensation, in which He calls out a bride for Himself to reign with Him when He comes again as victor. Revelation 4 tells

of the Rapture of the true Church in anticipation and
preparation for her reign with Him in the Kingdom
Age. Chapters 6 to 10 of Revelation present a description of the first half of the Tribulation Period in which
He purifies the earth by judgment and prepares His
ancient people Israel for the coming Kingdom Age. The
last half of the Tribulation, called The Great Tribulation,
is described in Revelation 16 to 19:11. Between these
two sections of Revelation are chapters 11 to 15, which,
as we have pointed out, are a preview of the Great
Tribulation, and introduce us to the chief actors in this
amazing drama of the end of the age. In the previous
chapter we studied the two witnesses, Moses and Elijah,
mentioned in Revelation 11. We will consider now
Revelation 12. Among the principal charactors in this
chapter are a woman, a man-child and a dragon. Here
is the record:

> And there appeared a great wonder in heaven; a woman
> clothed with the sun, and the moon under her feet, and
> upon her head a crown of twelve stars: and she being with
> child cried, travailing in birth, and pained to be delivered.
> And there appeared another wonder in heaven; and behold
> a great red dragon, having seven heads and ten horns, and
> seven crowns upon his heads. And his tail drew the third
> part of the stars of heaven, and did cast them to the earth:
> and the dragon stood before the woman which was ready
> to be delivered, for to devour her child as soon as it was
> born. And she brought forth a man child, who was to rule
> all nations with a rod of iron: and her child was caught
> up unto God, and to his throne. And the woman fled into
> the wilderness, where she hath a place prepared of God,
> that they should feed her there a thousand two hundred
> and threescore days (Rev. 12:1-6).

Before describing the sorrows of the Great Tribulation to follow, God gives us in this chapter a picture of
the great battle, this age-long war between Satan and
Christ, revealed through a sign which John witnessed.

He saw a woman who was to bring forth a man-child.
There was also a dragon who hated the man-child even
before it was born, because he knew it was the promised
seed who was to crush his head. But God miraculously
spared the man-child and caused him to ascend into
heaven, and while he was there, the dragon persecuted
the woman who gave birth to the child, but was unable
to destroy her because God miraculously spared her. The
interpretation of the passage is simple if we allow the
Scripture to speak for itself.

Who Are These Actors?

The scene in Revelation 12 is called "a great wonder."
This implies a miracle, and leads us to believe that there
was something supernatural about this woman, her
child and her deliverance from the power of the dragon.
Let us attempt to identify these actors. The woman is
said to be clothed with the sun, and the moon is under
her feet. Upon her head is a crown of twelve stars.

The woman is none other than the nation of Israel.
You will recall that Joseph in his dream saw the sun,
the moon and the stars bowing down to him. This was
a prophetic picture which pointed to Joseph's exalta-
tion after he had been sold by his brethren, and, secondly,
to the nation of Israel, for Joseph is a type of both the
Lord Jesus and the nation of Israel. As Joseph was
sold into the hands of the Gentiles, so, too, the nation
of Israel has been sold into captivity and scattered
throughout the world. While there she is persecuted
by Satan through his ancient and his modern Pharaohs
who, inspired by race hatred, seek to exterminate the
seed of Israel from the earth. Israel is the woman who
brought forth the man-child that was destined to rule
the nations with a rod of iron. Only of her can it be said
that she was clothed with the sun, for Malachi tells us,
in speaking of Israel's Redeemer, that "the Sun of

righteousness shall arise with healing in his wings."
Only of Israel can it be said that she brought forth the
Redeemer, for the writer of Hebrews reminds us that—

> Verily he took not on him the nature of angels; but he
> took on him the seed of Abraham (Heb. 2:16).

Neither can it be said of any other that she had a
place prepared for her in the wilderness to be nourished
for three and one-half years. Those who would make
the woman the Church will find it difficult to harmonize
this fact with their interpretation.

WHO IS THE MAN-CHILD?

The second character is as easily identified as the
woman. We are told that the woman (Israel) brought
forth a man-child, and the description enables us to
recognize him immediately:

> And she brought forth a man child, who was to rule all
> nations with a rod of iron: and her child was caught up
> unto God, and to his throne (Rev. 12:5).

The man-child has a primary interpretation and a
secondary application. By primary interpretation the
child is none other than the Lord Jesus Christ. He is
the object of Satan's hatred, and the devil seeks to destroy Him. He sought to destroy Christ before He was
born when by a decree of Caesar he compelled Mary to
make the long and hazardous trip to the city of Bethlehem from Nazareth at the very time she was to give
birth to the child. This plan failed, and then Satan
sought to destroy Him by murdering all the children
of two years and under in Bethlehem through King
Herod. Again and again he sought to destroy Christ at
the hands of the wicked Pharisees but His time had not
yet come. Finally he succeeded in bringing Him to the
Cross, and there it seemed as if the dragon was finally
victorious, for the child, destined to rule the nations

with a rod of iron, died the ignominious death of the
Cross. What rejoicing there must have been in the pit,
what celebrating among the hosts of the demons, as the
Son of God gave up the ghost! But God intervened, and
He was raised from the dead and caught up into heaven
to be seated at the right hand of God until He returns
to make His enemies His footstool and completely defeats the dragon, Satan. In Psalm 2 we are told definitely that Christ shall rule the nations with a rod of
iron.

A Secondary Application

By application, the Church of Christ, which is His
body, is also in view, for what happened to our Head
happens to every member of His body. Christians, too,
are hated by the dragon. Of believers also it is said in
Revelation 2:27 that they shall rule the nations with a
rod of iron. The Church, too, shall be caught away into
heaven before Satan is able to destroy her completely.
When she is gone, Satan will devote his attention to
the nation of Israel and usher in the day of Jacob's
trouble.

However, before he looses all his fury upon the nation,
he will be cast out of the heavens. Scripture seems to
teach that Satan has limited access to heaven. This
need not be the heaven where God dwells, but, rather, the
first and second heavens. The atmosphere is called
"heaven" in Scripture, which speaks also of "the starry
heaven." Paul tells us that Satan today is the prince of
the power of the air. The time of his judgment is draw-
ing near, and so we read that he is cast out of the heaven
into the earth for a short season. Here is John's description:

> And there was war in heaven: Michael fought and his
> angels fought against the dragon; and the dragon fought
> and his angels . . . And the great dragon was cast out, that

old serpent, called the Devil, and Satan, which deceiveth
the whole world: he was cast into the earth, and his angels
were cast out with him (Rev. 12:7,9).

This passage speaks of the beginning of the final
battle which is to end the war declared by God in the
Garden of Eden as recorded in Genesis 3:15. It will
end finally in the Battle of Armageddon described in
the closing chapters of Revelation.

THE DAY OF JACOB'S TROUBLE

Satan's attempt to dethrone God and defeat Christ
in the heavens results in his being cast upon the earth,
and immediately he turns his attention to the woman,
Israel, and seeks to destroy her. His success will mean
the defeat of Christ, for he has promised to redeem
Israel in the end-time, make her chief among the nations
and restore the kingdom of David. Hence his hatred for
Israel and his fury in seeking to make God's Word a lie
and God a deity who cannot keep His promise.

GOD'S DELIVERANCE OF ISRAEL

The same God who saved Israel from the bondage of
Egypt, the tyranny of Nebuchadnezzar, the oppression
of the Persians, the iron rule of the Romans, the schem-
ing of Haman and the diabolical scourge of Hitler, will
again save His people. To the woman were given two
great wings like an eagle that she might fly into the
wilderness and be protected during the brief three and
one-half years of Satan's reign on the earth before the
Lord returns to redeem Jacob. There is no need to
speculate regarding the meaning of these two wings of
the eagle mentioned in Revelation 12:14. Some say the
reference is to the fact that the woman, Israel, will
escape by airplane. Others think that the eagle typifies
the United States of America and that this nation is

destined to be the champion of Israel's cause in the end-time.

Frankly, I do not know what the correct interpretation is, for there is much we may not know until the mists have cleared away, but the main outline of God's plan is clear even though many of the details remain obscure. Because there are many details in Revelation which are difficult to explain, many people reject the entire book, the study of which the Lord has promised to reward with a special blessing. This reminds one of the old story of the man who said he could not see the forest because "there were too many trees in the way." The fact that all the details are not easily interpreted should not close our eyes to the clear outline of the main revelation.

A Summary of Revelation 12

Here is the picture presented in Revelation 12. It is God's picture of the end of the great conflict between the Lord and Satan. God has a covenant people, Israel, whom He called out from among the Gentiles. To Abraham He gave His covenant of grace, promising him that of his seed the Messiah should be born and that his descendants would be given the land of Palestine as an everlasting inheritance. All this was promised in Genesis 12:13-15, reaffirmed to Isaac, to Jacob, and to David, and repeated again and again through the prophets. Furthermore, Paul in the New Testament reassures us that "God hath not cast away his people whom he foreknew."

When we study Revelation 13 we shall consider many of the details of the struggle described in chapter 12. Two terrible personages will emerge to introduce a reign of terror upon the earth and especially against Israel—a reign so terrible that except for the intervention of God no flesh would be saved and the nation destined to be the kingdom nation would perish forever. Revelation 12 is inserted before the description of the two beasts mentioned in Revelation 13 that we may know that no matter how dark the days may become under the last seven vials of the wrath of God, the victory for the Son of Man and His saints is absolutely sure. In the beginning of human history that fact had already been stated, for in Genesis 3:15 we read that the serpent shall bruise the heel of the seed, but the seed of the woman shall crush the head of the serpent.

Here is the picture. When Satan knows that his time is short, he will seek to destroy the nation to whom God had promised the kingdom, but the Lord will give her a place of protection, probably in the land of Moab in the ancient city of Petra. (You will find it profitable to consult an encyclopedia for a description of this mysterious and impregnable city.)

Yes, a battle is raging, and you cannot be neutral in this conflict. You are either on the side of Satan or on the side of Christ. If you have not as yet received the Lord Jesus and by faith sworn allegiance to Him and His cause, then you are still in your sins, under the wrath of God and doomed to the same judgment and perdition which will befall your master, Satan, whom you choose to serve. Volunteer in the victorious army of the Lord Jesus Christ! March on to victory with Him, and escape the wrath of God and eternal destruction!

Believe on the Lord Jesus Christ, and thou shalt be saved.

CHAPTER TWENTY

The Last Dictator

> And I stood upon the sand of the sea, and saw a beast rise up out of the sea, having seven heads and ten horns, and upon his horns ten crowns, and upon his heads the name of blasphemy. And the beast which I saw was like unto a leopard, and his feet were as the feet of a bear, and his mouth as the mouth of a lion: and the dragon gave him his power, and his seat, and great authority. And I saw one of his heads as it were wounded to death; and his deadly wound was healed: and all the world wondered after the beast. And they worshipped the dragon which gave power unto the beast: and they worshipped the beast, saying, Who is like unto the beast? Who is able to make war with him? (Rev. 13:1-4).

The number thirteen has from time immemorial been associated with distress and trouble. In Bible numerology the number thirteen indicates rebellion, disaster and judgment. Numbers in the Bible have a definite meaning. The number one is the number of sovereignty, the number of the absolute unity of the Godhead. Two represents division and trouble. Three represents divine completeness. Four is the number of the earth and five, the number of grace. Six is the number of man, and seven is the number of divine perfection. Bear in mind the significance of the number six when we study the Antichrist. Eight is the number of new beginnings, and nine, the number of judgment. Ten is the number of testimony and eleven, the number of apostasy. Twelve is the number of the nation of Israel and thirteen, the number of rebellion. We realize that the chapter divisions in the Bible were not inspired and not in the original manuscripts. However, it is a striking coincidence that Revelation 13 should be the chapter which describes the two greatest rebels of all history: the political beast out of the sea and the religious beast out of the land.

THE TWO BEASTS DESCRIBED IN REVELATION 13

In Revelation 13 we have a detailed description of two great powers who will arise in the Tribulation Period after the Church of Jesus Christ has been raptured. We have already pointed out that chapters 11 to 15 of Revelation are a pause, a parenthesis, in the description of the Tribulation Period, that awful period of suffering and travail on earth which will come after the Church is caught away to heaven and before the return of the Lord Jesus to the earth to set up His millennial kingdom.

During this brief time of the world's greatest sorrow, Satan will make his last great attempt to defeat the program of God by establishing his kingdom upon the earth. He will seek to do this by instituting two great powers, one political and one religious. These two great powers will be two men, called in Revelation 13 "beasts" because of the viciousness and cruelty of their reign. These two men, representing two movements, will seek to set up a world-federation of nations for political reasons and a world-federation of churches for religious reasons.

WHO ARE TO BE THE ACTORS?

There has been much misunderstanding regarding the identity of these two characters described in Revelation 13. However, if we limit ourselves to the Scriptures we will have no difficulty. As far back as the days of Daniel the Lord had already definitely revealed the fact that in the end-time there would be two persons who would head the opposition and animosity of Satan against the Lord and His Christ. You will recall that in Daniel 2 we read that King Nebuchadnezzzar had a dream which none of his soothsayers could recall or interpret. Finally God gave Daniel wisdom to recall the dream and also to give its interpretation. The king had seen a great image with head of gold, chest and arms of silver, belly and thighs of brass and legs and feet of iron and clay.

Daniel tells us that these four parts of the image represent four stages of Gentile world-domination. You will recall that God had called the nation of Israel to be His kingdom nation, but they rebelled against the Lord, who scattered them abroad and committed the government of the world for a time to the Gentiles. When Christ comes, Israel will be converted and they will be again the Lord's kingdom people, but in the meantime the Gentiles will be in power.

The four parts of the image described in Daniel 2, therefore, are the four successive forms of this Gentile power which began with the captivity of Judah and will end at the second coming of Jesus Christ. The four forms of Gentile dominion were Babylon, followed by Medo-Persia, Greece and, finally, the Roman Empire, all of which in turn oppressed God's covenant nation, Israel. The two legs of the image, typifying the iron kingdom of Rome, indicate that the Roman kingdom would be divided into two parts, and, history records the division into the Western and Eastern Roman Empires. The two feet and the ten toes of the image are a picture of the final form of the restored Roman Empire, which today, augmented by the recent World War, is again taking definite form, and when the territories have finally been claimed by the conquerors, we shall see that the old Roman Empire has been revived.

Daniel saw a great stone cut without hands out of a mountain—a stone which smote the image in its feet (that is, in its final form) and ground it to powder. The stone became a great mountain which filled all the earth. Jesus Christ is the stone, and the image represents the age of Gentile world-power, while Israel is in dispersion. At the end of the age Christ, the stone, will come, destroy the oppressors of Israel and set up His kingdom over the whole earth. This is not mere fancy; we are told definitely that this is the interpretation:

> And in the days of these kings shall the God of heaven set up a kingdom, which shall never be destroyed: and the kingdom shall not be left to other people, but it shall break in pieces and consume all these kingdoms, and it shall stand forever. Forasmuch as thou sawest that the stone was cut out of the mountain without hands, and that it brake in pieces the iron, the brass, the clay, the silver, and the gold; the great God hath made known to the king what shall come to pass hereafter: and the dream is certain, and the interpretation thereof sure (Dan. 2:44-45)

Daniel 7 also records a vision which will help us to identify the beasts described in Revelation 13. In this vision Daniel saw four beasts rising in succession. The first was like a lion, the second like a bear, the third like a leopard and the fourth was a monstrosity, a beast which was a combination of the other three and is described by Daniel as follows:

> After this I saw in the night visions, and behold a fourth beast, dreadful and terrible, and strong exceedingly; and it had great iron teeth: it devoured and brake in pieces, and stamped the residue with the feet of it: and it was diverse from all the beasts that were before it; and it had ten horns (Dan. 7:7).

These four beasts mentioned in Daniel 7 are the same as the four parts of Nebuchadnezzar's image of which we read in Daniel 2. In Daniel 7 they are called the kingdoms of Babylon, Persia, Greece and the fourth kingdom. The monstrosity described in Daniel 7 has ten horns just as the image discussed in Daniel 2 had ten toes. The picture is this. Gentile world-power will run its course under Babylon, then Persia, then Greece and, finally, Rome. The Roman Empire was divided into two parts and finally ceased as an organized empire. The beast apparently died and ceased to exist, but the spirit of Babylon and Rome persisted, and in the end-time this kingdom will be revived under a federation of ten nations, represented by the ten toes. This is taking place now. As a result of the battle for spheres of influence in Europe, two great powers will emerge, one in western and the other in northern Europe. These are called the King of the West and the King of the North, so prominent in Bible end-time prophecy. These two, together with the King of the South and the Kings of the East, will be the four great world-powers who will participate in the Battle of Armageddon at the end of the Tribulation Period. We will try to give you the general outline of the events as they are given in Scripture and trust that you will then continue your study.

Let us summarize the teaching of Daniel 2 and 7. According to Daniel, there will be four successive stages of Gentile world-dominion: Babylon, Persia, Greece and, finally, Rome. The Roman Empire will divide into the Western and Eastern Empires and then seemingly disintegrate, during the centuries when democracy will dominate. But the beast that was apparently dead and had the deadly wound will be revived and in the end-time struggle the old revived Roman Empire will play a prominent part. It will consist of two leading nations, indicated by the two feet. These two dominant nations will have associated with them eight lessor powers, represented by the eight toes. These will rebel against the Lord and under the leadership of the great end-time dictator, the first beast, of which we read in Revelation

13, and the personal Antichrist, the second beast, of which the chapter speaks. They will seek also to set up a devilish satanically-governed federation of nations whose main purpose will be to destroy the kingdom people, the nation of Israel, and set up a false Messiah, the Antichrist.

The effort, however, will be cut short by the sudden coming of Jesus Christ, the stone cut without hands from the mountain, who will crush them and establish His long promised and hoped for millennial kingdom of peace and righteousness. This is the teaching, in brief outline, of the visions in Daniel. History has already proved them to be true and authentic in every detail, and only the formation of the ten toes remains. Then the coming of the Great Stone will bring an end to man's reign of failure, terror, confusion and destruction.

THE BEASTS DESCRIBED IN REVELATION 13

If we keep in mind this outline of Daniel we can better understand Revelation 13. The entire chapter is devoted to a description of two great and terrible characters prominent during the Tribulation Period. The first of these beasts mentioned will come out of the sea:

> And I stood upon the sand of the sea, and saw a beast rise up out of the sea, having seven heads and ten horns, and upon his horns ten crowns, and upon his heads the names of blasphemy. And the beast which I saw was like unto a leopard, and his feet were as the feet of a bear, and his mouth as the mouth of a lion: and the dragon gave him his power, and his seat, and great authority (Rev. 13:1-2).

In Revelation the sea symbolizes the nations. This beast is a Gentile. The seven heads represent seven mountains and probably refer to the capital of the ancient Roman Empire, known to historians as "the city of seven hills." Here is what the Holy Spirit says concerning the seven heads:

> And here is the mind which hath wisdom. The seven heads are seven mountains, on which the woman sitteth . . . And the ten horns which thou sawest are ten kings, which have received no kingdom as yet; but receive power as kings one hour with the beast (Rev. 17:9,12).

This is the end-time form of the last beast spoken of in Daniel 7, and corresponds to the feet of iron and of clay. The iron speaks of the tyranny of totalitarianism and the clay represents the weakness of the pseudo-democracy. The revived Roman Empire, which ceased to exist visibly for many centuries but will be mysteriously revived, is therefore described as the "beast that was and is not, and yet shall be." It is described as follows by John in Revelation 13:3:

> And I saw one of his heads as it were wounded to death; and his deadly wound was healed: and all the world wondered after the beast (Rev. 13:3).

DANIEL REVERSED

John saw this beast as a leopard, with feet like a bear and mouth like a lion. You will recall that Daniel saw the same three beasts but in reverse order. He saw first the lion, then the bear and, last, the leopard. Why John reversed this order is apparent. Daniel stood at the beginning of the age of Gentile world-dominion and therefore saw Babylon first, then Persia, Greece and, finally, the kingdom of Rome. John, however, stands at the end, looking back, and therefore sees first the leopard, then the bear and, last, the lion of Babylon. This harmonizes perfectly with the infallible revelation of the whole body of the prophetic Scriptures.

After the Church has been caught away and the saints are with the Lord, Satan will raise up a world-dictator who will succeed in a measure and for a brief time in making the nations and the world believe that the second beast in Revelation (which we will discuss next) is the

Christ, the Messiah, the Saviour of the world, and will convince the multitudes who have rejected Jesus Christ that He was a fraud and an impostor, and the world will largely follow the advice of this first beast, the political dictator and ruler of the earth, and receive the second beast (the Antichrist) as the Messiah.

A MIRACLE-WORKING IMPOSTOR

This deception of the peoples of the earth will be accomplished by a number of mighty signs and miracles which the beast will perform. Here is John's record concerning this:

> And they worshipped the dragon which gave power unto the beast: and they worshipped the beast, saying, Who is like unto the beast? who is able to make war with him? And there was given unto him a mouth speaking great things and blasphemies; and power was given unto him to continue forty and two months. And he opened his mouth in blasphemy against God, to blaspheme his name, and his tabernacle, and them that dwell in heaven. And it was given unto him to make war with the saints, and to overcome them: and power was given him over all kindreds, and tongues, and nations. And all that dwell upon the earth shall worship him, whose names are not written in the book of life of the Lamb slain from the foundation of the world (Rev. 13:4-8).

These verses speak for themselves, but let me repeat that after the Church has gone, a Gentile political dictator will arise. He will be associated with another person, the false christ. The political head will seek to dominate the entire world, and the religious head will seek the control of all religion. Together they will seek to destroy the saints of God and dethrone the Christ of God. Space forbids details concerning how these two will operate, but we will consider some of them in our chapter on the personal Antichrist the mark of the beast and the number of his name.

Before we close this chapter, however, let me call your attention again to Revelation 13:8.

Terrible are the days which lie ahead. The rumblings of the coming judgment can be heard in the distance. The clouds are gathering. Inventions such as the atomic bomb have made men tremble at what lies ahead. There is only one way out and that is through Him who is the door to absolute safety. Those who receive Him and enter through the door by faith are safe. They are described as those whose names "are written in the Lamb's book of life." Is your name written there? Are you ready for His coming? If not, then will you turn to Him and be saved *now?*

> I care not for riches,
> Neither silver nor gold;
> I would make sure of heaven,
> I would enter the fold.
> In the book of the kingdom,
> With its pages so fair,
> Tell me, Jesus, my Saviour,
> Is my name written there?
>
> Lord, my sins they are many,
> Like the sands of the sea,
> But Thy blood, oh, my Saviour,
> Is sufficient for me;
> For Thy promise is written,
> In bright letters that glow,
> "Though your sins be as scarlet,
> I will make them like snow."
>
> Yes, my name's written there,
> On the page bright and fair,
> In the Lamb's book of life,
> Yes, my name's written there.

CHAPTER TWENTY-ONE

The Antichrist

And I beheld another beast coming up out of the earth; and he had two horns like a lamb, and he spake as a dragon . . . And he doeth great wonders, so that he maketh fire come down from heaven on the earth in the sight of men . . . And he causeth all, both small and great, rich and poor, free and bond, to receive a mark in their hand, or in their foreheads: and that no man might buy or sell, save he that had the mark, or the name of the beast, or the number of his name. Here is wisdom. Let him that hath understanding count the number of the beast: for it is the number of a man; and his number is Six hundred three score and six (Rev. 13:11,13,16-18).

Christ is the incarnation of God Himself and is called the true and faithful witness. The devil, the enemy of Christ and God, will also produce a false witness, who will be an incarnation of Satan, just as Jesus was the incarnation of God. This false Christ, this man of sin, this incarnation of Satan, is called in Scripture the Antichrist, the son of perdition, the deceitful and bloody man and the false prophet. We can trace his slimy trail from Genesis to Revelation, for he is mentioned first in Genesis 3:15 where he is called the "seed of the serpent," just as Christ is called the "seed of the woman."

Throughout the Old Testament we see him in type and shadow. Nimrod, the rebel, mentioned in Genesis 11 and 12, was an early type. Pharaoh, the persecuter of Israel, and Haman, the hater of the Jews, was another type of this coming superman and religious dictator.

Judas Iscariot was Satan's first attempt to produce this superman at the first coming of Jesus, but he failed. In the end-time, just before the second coming of Christ, Satan will make his great and final attempt to set up this superman in opposition to the true Christ of God. As there was a first and a second coming of Christ, so there are two comings of the Antichrist: Judas and the Antichrist.

Was Judas the Antichrist?

There is much evidence that Judas Iscariot was Satan's first attempt to produce a personal Antichrist to destroy the Lord Jesus. Whether you agree with this interpretation or not, I am sure that you will see the striking similarity between the man of sin, the ruler of the earth in the end of the age, and Judas, the false disciple of Jesus. If Judas was not the Antichrist, he certainly was a distinct type. Carefully consider the following Scripture references:

> Those that thou gavest me I have kept, and none of them is lost, but the son of perdition; that the Scripture might be fulfilled (John 17:12).

Notice particularly that Judas is here called by Jesus "the son of perdition."

Notice what Paul says in II Thessalonians 2:3:

> Let no man deceive you by any means: for that day (the day of the Lord) shall not come, except there come a falling away first, and that man of sin be revealed, the son of perdition.

Notice that we have quoted the only two passages in the Word of God in which the name "son of perdition" is used. In the first instance it is applied to Judas Iscariot and in the second it is applied to the man of sin, the Antichrist. Surely, here, is a close association. They are the same. They are called the same.

> Then entered Satan into Judas surnamed Iscariot, being
> of the number of the twelve (Luke 22:3).

This is the only passage which states that Satan entered into a man. We have many passages which tell of demons who took up their abode in men and women, but this speaks of Satan personally as the prince of demons, taking up his temporary abode in Judas. But the argument is made still more conclusive by the statement in the Gospel according to John:

> Jesus answered them, Have not I chosen you twelve, and
> one of you is a devil? (John 6:70).

Judas is called "devil"—not "*a* devil." In the original the verse is translated "one of you is devil (*diabolis*)." The term *diabolis* refers to the devil and Satan. He does not say that Judas is a demon, but *devil*. In another passage, Acts 1:25, we read these words concerning Judas: . . . that he "might go to his own place." When we consider who he was we can understand that it was the devil's own place (the place prepared for the devil and his angels).

Judas, then, will be the Antichrist. The spirit of the Antichrist (when the Spirit of God, which now hindereth, will be taken away) will enter once more into mankind and cause to appear another freak, half man and half devil, who will be the incarnation of the devil. When we remember that the Antichrist will attempt to simulate the true Christ in every detail, we see more and more the subtlety of Satan.

Since the Antichrist will be the imitation of the true Christ, he will claim to come in fulfillment of prophecy. Since the true Christ was to die and rise again according to Scripture, the devil will try to produce an Antichrist who, too, died and was raised again. Judas died and went to his own place. After the true Church is gone, Satan will, as part of his wicked deception, raise Judas from the dead and set him up as the true Christ. Whether you agree with this interpretation or not, it is a fact that the man of sin of the end-time will be an incarnation of the devil in his last great effort to destroy the seed of the woman.

SATAN'S DOOM

For three and one-half years the Antichrist will continue his reign of terror. Note the resemblance of Judas to the description of the man of sin of the end-time. Notice how Judas typifies the Antichrist. The Antichrist will preside over the worship of the false kingdom. Judas was one of Christ's disciples and treasurer of the company, but Satan entered him and he became a devil's son. So, too, the Antichrist will come with a message of peace, but betray his friends.

Judas served with Christ three and one-half years; the reign of the Antichrist will also be three and one-half years. Judas, as an apostle, performed wonders and miracles; so will the Antichrist when he comes. Judas was an idolater; Scripture says that every covetous man is an idolater and the Antichrist will be a great idolater. Judas gave a sign to those who followed him by which they might know Jesus in the garden (Matthew 26:48). The Antichrist will institute the mark of the beast, compelling men to carry this sign on their hands and foreheads or be killed. Surely this similarity is striking, and many more resemblances could de added.

After three and one-half years when the nations of the earth, deceived by Satan, will be gathered together for the great Battle of Armageddon, the heavens will suddenly open (Revelation 19:11) and the true King, the King of kings and the Lord of lords, will descend and destroy those armies, and the beast and the false prophet will be cast into the lake of fire. Satan, who indwelt the man of Sin, will be cast into the pit. After a thousand

years Satan will be loosed for a little season and given
one more opportunity to deceive the nations, to prove
the utter depravity of unregenerate human nature, the
eternal incorrigibility of the devil and the absolute
righteousness and justice of God in condemning the
devil and all his followers to the lake of fire forever. We
read therefore:

> And the devil that deceived them was cast into the lake
> of fire and brimstone, where the beast and the false prophet
> are, and shall be tormented day and night for ever and ever
> (Rev. 20:10).

The description in Revelation 13 is in perfect harmony
with this. In Revelation 13:11 we read that this beast
was from the land and had two horns like a lamb but
spoke as a dragon. The expression "the land" refers
to the ancient land where Christ was born, and where
He died. The horns like a lamb imitate the true Lamb
of God.

See how clever his deception is! He arises in the same
land where the prophets had announced that the Christ
should be born. There is every reason to believe that
this Antichrist will be of the tribe of Dan. The twelfth
verse of Revelation 13 tells us of his league with the
political head of the end-time world-federation of nations. The next verse tells us of his supernatural powers.
Verse 14 describes his deception when in the midst of the
Tribulation he will set up an image of the first beast,
the political dictator, in the holy Temple at Jerusalem.
This refers to the "desolation of abomination" spoken
of in Daniel and again in Matthew 24. Here are Jesus'
prophetic words:

> When ye therefore shall see the abomination of desolation,
> spoken of by Daniel the prophet, stand in the holy place,
> (whoso readeth, let him understand:) then let them which
> be in Judea flee into the mountains: let him which is on the
> house top not come down to take any thing out of his house:

neither let him which is in the field return to take his clothes. And woe unto them that are with child, and to them that give suck in those days! But pray ye that your flight be not in the winter, neither on the sabbath day: for then shall be great tribulation, such as was not since the beginning of the world to this time, no, nor ever shall be (Matt. 24: 15-21).

Let us compare Scripture with Scripture and let the Word of God speak for itself. We must not allow our preconceived and biased interpretations to confuse us. Notice, too, the further deception of the Antichrist. He doeth wonders and causeth fire to come down from heaven as an imitation of Christ's two witnesses in Revelation 11.

The Mark of the Beast

The beast's deception will be greatest when he causes the image of the beast (the abomination of desolation) to become alive and to speak. After he has gained the confidence of the deceived peoples of the world who are left after the rapture, he will inaugurate his satanic program by forming an ultra-exclusive society of his own. Everyone who pledges obedience to the beast will receive a mark in his right hand or on his forehead. This mark will identify him as belonging to the beast's organization. Everyone who refuses this mark will be persecuted and put to death by the dictator. As you know, there will be those who have another mark, the mark of the true Christ, sealed by God in their hands and foreheads. These will be the special object of Satan's hatred, and were it not for the protection of the Lord, all of them would be put to death by the beast.

What this mark of the beast will be we may not know now. Hundreds of answers have been suggested, but I do not believe these are scriptural. Men have tried to identify this Antichrist, and there have been hundreds of guesses concerning his identity, but all of them have been wrong. Anyone throughout the centuries who hated anyone else has branded that enemy as the Antichrist. The Church has been called the Antichrist. Nero, Napoleon, Kaiser Wilhelm, Hitler and Mussolini have also been suggested as possibilities by foolish and misguided souls, who have forgotten that the true identity of the Antichrist will not be known until the Church is gone. This is definitely stated in II Thessalonians 2:3, where we are told that the man of sin will not be revealed until *after* the Church is gone. It is foolish, therefore, to speculate concerning his identity. The same is true of the mark of the beast.

What the mark will be we do not know. There can be no doubt, however, that there are already movements in the world which anticipate this mark of the beast and are preparing the world for it. Recent food and gasoline rationing and union cards are not the mark of the beast, but they are making the world "mark minded." During the recent war we observed many instances when one could not buy or sell unless he had books or tickets. Our point is this: these are preparing us for a system whereby the mark of the beast will be easily imposed upon the people.

> And he causeth all, both small and great, rich and poor, free and bond, to receive a mark in their right hand, or in their foreheads: and that no man might buy or sell, save he that had the mark, or the name of the beast, or the number of his name (Rev. 13:16-17).

The Number of His Name

There are many who believe that the mark will consist of the number 666 tattooed upon the foreheads and hands of the followers of the beast. Be that as it may, the Bible tells us that the number of the beast will be 666. Here again we encounter many and ludicrous guesses, chiefly the result of bigotry and ignorance. The number is 666 and the same verse tells us the meaning. It is the number of man. Place the emphasis in this verse on the word *man*. Six is the number of man. Three is the number of divinity. Here is the interpretation. The Beast will be a man who claims to be God. Three sixes imply that he is a false god and a deceiver, but he is nevertheless merely a man, regardless of his claims. Seven is the number of divine perfection, and 666 is one numeral short of seven. This man of sin will reach the highest peak of power and wisdom, but he will still be merely man. The warning is given undoubtedly for those who will live during the Tribulation. So mighty will be the wonders, so great the wisdom of this super-man, that men will believe that he is God and the Messiah. God warns us, however, "Remember that in spite of the deception, he is still only a man. Do not follow him. Do not believe him." That is the meaning of Revelation 13:18:

> Here is wisdom. Let him that hath understanding count the number of the beast: for it is the number of a man.

As a result of this warning we believe that a great multitude will not be deceived, but will be faithful to the Lord and refuse to bow before the Antichrist and receive his number and his name. The next chapter of Revelation speaks of this great multitude who will refuse to worship the beast because they understand that his number is the number of a man. May God help us to heed His call and be ready for His coming!

CHAPTER TWENTY-TWO

The Beginning of the End

And I looked, and behold a white cloud, and upon the cloud one sat like unto the Son of man, having on his head a golden crown, and in his hand a sharp sickle. And another angel came out of the temple, crying with a loud voice to him that sat on the cloud, Thrust in thy sickle, and reap; for the time is come for thee to reap; for the harvest of the earth is ripe. And he that sat upon the cloud thrust in his sickle on the earth; and the earth was reaped. And another angel came out of the temple which is in heaven, he also having a sharp sickle. And another angel came out from the altar, which had power over fire; and cried with a loud cry to him that had the sharp sickle, saying, Thrust in thy sharp sickle, and gather the clusters of the vine of the earth; for her grapes are fully ripe. And the angel thrust in his sickle into the earth, and gathered the vine of the earth, and cast it into the great winepress of the wrath of God. And the winepress was trodden without the city, and blood came out of the winepress, even unto the horse bridles, by the space of a thousand and six hundred furlongs (Rev. 14:14-20).

The word "Armageddon" has been much in the news during and after the recent World War. It is a Biblical term and has been accepted by the people everywhere as symbolic of the final conflict of the nations. We find in Scripture many descriptions of the day of Armageddon, for that day is more than a symbol. It is an actual future battle, minutely described by the prophets of old and presented in great detail by the writer of the book of Revelation. The passage at the

190

beginning of this message is only one of the several
references to this great and terrible day when the nations shall be gathered about Jerusalem and the Lord
will come in judgment to destroy them. The word
"Armageddon" comes from two Hebrew words meaning "the hills of Megiddo." It is a region in the north
of Palestine among the hills of Megiddo, surrounding
a vast plain called the Valley of Jehoshaphat.

According to Scripture, the last great battle in the
world's history will be fought here just before the return
of Christ to set up His kingdom upon the earth. The two
great leaders in this final battle will be the great dictator
head of the restored Roman Empire and the supernatural false messiah, the Antichrist.

THE BEGINNING OF THE END

In previous chapters we have studied the Rapture of
the Church, discussed in Revelation 4, and the first half
of the Tribulation, of which we read in Revelation 6 to
10. Then we saw God's two witnesses on the earth for
three and one-half years from the middle of the Tribulation to the end. In Revelation 13 we studied Satan's
two witnesses, the beasts out of the sea and out of the
land, and identified them as the end-time world-ruler
and dictator, the last emperor of the revived Roman
Empire, and the great religious superman, the Antichrist. These will be the leaders in that great day of
Armageddon described here and again in Revelation 16.
But before that terrible time comes, the Church will be
taken out and then God will seal a company of Israelites
in the Tribulation and save a great number of Gentiles
as a result of their preaching and testimony.

REVELATION 14

In Revelation 7 we caught a glimpse of that super-
naturally preserved and redeemed company. In Revelation 14 we meet them again:

> And I looked, and, lo, a Lamb stood on the mount Sion,
> and with him an hundred forty and four thousand, having
> his Father's name written in their foreheads (Rev. 14:1).

In chapter 7 these 144,000 are said to be sealed in their
foreheads (Rev. 7:3). Revelation 14 tells us what that
seal was. It was the name of the Lamb's father written
upon their brows. These are the ones who were to preach
the Gospel, with the result that a great multitude of
Gentiles from every tribe and tongue and nation were
saved. The sixth verse of this chapter tells us of the
message they were to bring:

> And I saw another angel fly in the midst of heaven,
> having the everlasting gospel to preach unto them that
> dwell on the earth, and to every nation, and kindred,
> and tongue, and people (Rev. 14:6).

Their message is not only a message of salvation to
those who believe, but it is also a message of judgment
upon those who will not accept the offer of salvation, for
we hear the angel who commits this everlasting Gospel
to the 144,000—

> Saying with a loud voice, Fear God, and give glory to him;
> for the hour of his judgment is come: and worship him that
> made heaven, and earth, and the sea, and the fountains of
> waters (Rev. 14:7).

God's message in the Tribulation is two-fold as pro-
claimed by His servants, the 144,000. It is a message of
salvation to those who believe. It is a message of judgment to those who reject. That is true of the Gospel
in any age and in every age. The true minister of God
has in his possession a two-edged sword. To proclaim
to men and women the free grace of salvation and redemption through simple faith in the Lord Jesus Christ
is only one side of the message we have been committed
to bring to men. There is another and a more unpleasant
side. It is the responsibility of warning those who will

not receive Christ of their swift and sure condemnation and their eternal loss and doom. Men and women do not object to the first part of the message, even though they neglect it and pay no attention to it, but when we preach judgment and punishment for the wicked and proclaim in no uncertain terms the truth concerning hell, then we are dabbling in outmoded superstition and preaching an outgrown gospel of fanaticism, ignorance and ancient bigotry, according to many.

This is why in these latter days there is an increase both in numbers and intensity of cults and new sects whose main purpose, while they apparently preach salvation, is to deny and argue away a literal hell and the Biblical teaching of eternal punishment. They tell us in suave and persuasive tones that God is a God of love and will never condemn His creatures whom He has made. They shrink in unspeakable horror at the thought that a kind and loving God will permit His erring creatures to be punished in a lake of fire, to suffer for their sins and be eternally separated from God in the place called by the kind and lowly Jesus Himself a place of "outer darkness" where there shall be "weeping and gnashing of teeth." Their supersensitive and delicately cultured minds revolt at the grim thought of a God who will cast His creatures away forever.

If these folk are right, then we can throw our Bibles away and especially the book of Revelation, for it is a book of dire judgments upon the wicked. This denial of a literal hell and the truth of God's sure and eternal punishment of sin is the result of two things. First, it is the result of an ignorance of the true nature of sin. Sin is not inconsequential in God's sight. There is no little sin before God. Sin is sin, whether we call it great or small, whether we try to dull its cutting edge by calling it "error" or "mistakes" or "failure." Before God, sin is sin and must be punished as such.

The true nature of sin as God sees it may be learned
from the first record of sin in the Bible. A man and a
woman, Adam and Eve by name, were placed in a
beautiful garden. God required only one thing of them.
They had every privilege, but they were given one
command: they were not to eat of one tree in the garden.
All the other trees were there for them to use freely, but
this one tree was prohibited. You are familiar with the
story. They committed this one sin, and they ate of the
forbidden tree. As a result the death penalty was pronounced upon them and upon the entire human race.
All death, sorrow, disease, tears, suffering and pain
since that day have come as a result of this one sin.

Unbelievers ask, "Do you mean to tell us that God
would condemn an entire race because one man and one
woman committed petty larceny?" Read the record and
see the results. Can you account for the suffering, pain,
death, sorrow, wars, famines, pestilences and destruction
in the world? If there be a loving God, why all this
sorrow? The Bible says it is because sin came into the
world. Have you a more satisfactory answer? Have
you a better explanation to offer than the Bible record?
Have you? If you have not, do not reject this scriptural
answer until you have a better one to take its place.

Men reject the record of God and prattle about a
loving God who will not punish His poor creature
because they do not realize the awfulness of sin. Not the
degree of sin, but the nature of sin is of primary importance. Adam's sin was not petty larceny; it was rebellion—which is quite different. Even in international
and federal life we recognize the gravity of rebellion
and make it punishable by death—the most severe penalty we can inflict. We all agree that this is right and
proper, but when we preach that rebellion against an
Infinite Being must logically be punished by a commen-

surate infinite judgment, then we are accused of making God unjust and cruel.

Once we recognize the true nature of sin, we will have no difficulty in understanding God's judgment upon sin. Again denial of the awfulness of judgment results from ignorance of the nature of the holiness of God. Holiness, like perfection, is an absolute term. There are no degrees of holiness. The word "holiness" is defined as "moral and spiritual perfection." I repeat, there are no degrees of holiness. One is either holy or unholy. The least flaw, therefore, defiles, and God cannot condone the smallest sin.

Sin Is Rebellion

If we understand the nature of sin, therefore, as rebellion against a holy God, we can comprehend the awful judgments pronounced upon the wicked as we read of them in our chapter:

> And the third angel followed them, saying with a loud voice, If any man worship the beast and his image, and receive his mark in his forehead, or in his hand, the same shall drink of the wine of the wrath of God, which is poured out without mixture into the cup of his indignation; and he shall be tormented with fire and brimstone in the presence of the holy angels, and in the presence of the Lamb: and the smoke of their torment ascendeth up for ever and ever: and they have no rest day nor night, who worship the beast and his image, and whosoever receiveth the mark of his name. Here is the patience of the saints: here are they that keep the commandants of God, and the faith of Jesus (Rev. 14:9-12).

The chapter concludes with a picture of judgment upon the nations:

> And another angel came out from the altar, which had power over fire; and cried with a loud cry to him that had the sharp sickle, saying, Thrust in thy sharp sickle, and gather the clusters of the vine of the earth; for her grapes are fully ripe. And the angel thrust in his sickle into the earth, and gathered the vine of the earth, and cast it into

the great winepress of the wrath of God. And the winepress was trodden without the city, and blood came out of the winepress, even unto the horse bridles, by the space of a thousand and six hundred furlongs (Rev. 14:18-20).

This is, as we have indicated, a picture of the coming day of Armageddon and the judgment of the nations at the coming again of the Lord Jesus. The day and the battle are described in added detail in the following chapters of Revelation, but here we have a glimpse of what lies ahead for the wicked. It is described as a harvest of the vintage of the earth. The nations who reject the Lord are described as the vine and its branches, the false vine, the apostate Church of the Antichrist. Jesus said in John 15: "I am the vine, ye are the branches." This is the true Church of Jesus Christ which as we saw in Revelation 4, was raptured and taken out. After she is gone, the empty professing church of the Antichrist with its denial of the true Christ will remain and under the leadership of its false head, the Antichrist, will deceive all the world except the remnant who have heeded the warning.

The Antichrist also has a vine, but it is an apostate vine and its doom and destruction are here graphically described. The reference is also to the wicked nations of the world. They are gathered together to battle against Jerusalem and suddenly the Lord Jesus appears and defeats those nations. So great shall be the slaughter that blood will run in the Valley of Jehoshaphat to a depth of over two feet, even unto the horses' bridles for a distance of sixteen hundred furlongs, or approximately one-hundred-eighty miles. If you doubt this possibility, consult some of the reports of the last war and their descriptions of rivers of blood in Stalingrad, Warsaw and Berlin or the reports which tell us that the sea turned red from the blood of those who died at Tarawa and Saipan.

REVELATION 15

Revelation 15 is a continuation of chapter 14 and its brief eight verses present a picture of the redeemed who have not worshipped the beast and have escaped the judgments of God:

> And I saw as it were a sea of glass mingled with fire: and them that had gotten the victory over the beast, and over his image, and over his mark, and over the number of his name, stand on the sea of glass, having the harps of God. And they sing the song of Moses the servant of God, and the song of the Lamb, saying, Great and marvellous are thy works, Lord God Almighty; just and true are thy ways, thou King of saints. Who shall not fear thee, O Lord, and glorify thy name? for thou only art holy: for all nations shall come and worship before thee; for thy judgments are made manifest (Rev. 15:2-4).

Here, then, we have a description of two groups: the unbelievers who meet the wrath of God and eternal judgment and the saints of God before His throne who acknowledge His justice and truth forever. To which company do you belong? You are either a saint or a sinner. You are either saved or lost. You are either on the way to heaven or on the way to eternal perdition. You may still settle the question. Settle it *now*.

> If thou shalt confess with thy mouth the Lord Jesus, and believe in thine heart that God hath raised him from the dead, thou shalt be saved (Rom. 10:9).
>
> For whosoever shall call upon the name of the Lord shall be saved (Rom. 10:13).

CHAPTER TWENTY-THREE

The Seven Vials

And I saw another sign in heaven, great and marvellous, seven angels having the seven last plagues; for in them is filled up the wrath of God . . . And the seven angels came out of the temple, having the seven plagues . . . And one of the four beasts gave unto the seven angels seven golden vials full of the wrath of God, who liveth for ever and ever (Rev. 15:1,6-7).

And I heard a great voice out of the temple saying to the seven angels, Go your ways, and pour out the vials of the wrath of God upon the earth (Rev. 16:1).

The age in which we live is called in the Scriptures "the dispensation of the grace of God" (Ephesians 3:2). It began at Pentecost with the birth of the Church, the body of Christ, and will end at the Rapture, when Christ will take out of this world the true Church, together with all the dead in Christ. Then will follow a brief period, seven years in duration, called the Tribulation Period, during which the world will experience the severest travail, sorrow, war, destruction and death in its entire history. So trying will this period of travail be that were it not for the sudden intervention of God in the return of Christ, no flesh would be saved. At the end of this awful period Christ will return, subdue His enemies, destroy the wicked and personally set up God's kingdom upon the earth. Then will follow a thousand years of prosperity and peace among the nations, nature and the earth. At the end of the thousand years the wicked dead will be raised, judged and cast together with Satan, their leader, into the lake of fire.

This, in brief, is the outline of the history of the world from Pentecost to the beginning of eternity. We repeat it again and again, for it is the skeleton and the framework of the Old and New Testaments. It is the inspired pattern of prophecy of which every event of history is a part.

We have studied the history of the professing church in Revelation 1-3. Chapter 4 tells us that the Church will be taken out in the rapture and the hollow, professing church of the Antichrist will remain upon the earth. It is called "Mystery Babylon" in Scripture. Chapters 15 to 19 of Revelation describe the last and final phase of this false church on the earth during the last three and one-half years of the Tribulation. This last half of the day of the Lord will be characterized by the seven last plagues of the wrath of God under the figure of seven vials or "bowls" in which the judgments of God will be poured out upon the wicked world and the kingdom of Satan. We shall attempt to give you the main outline of the terrible events predicted by God which will occur during this last phase of God's final judgment before the setting up of the millennial kingdom of Christ.

A Great and Marvelous Sign

Revelation 15 speaks of a great and marvelous sign. John sees seven angels to whom are given seven bowls of the wrath of God to be poured upon the earth, to beat into final submission the enemies of the Lord and His Christ. The key to this great and marvelous mystery is given in the last part of verse 1. John says, "For in them is filled up the wrath of God."

This will be the final stage. It began with the appearance of the four horsemen, of whom we read in chapter 6.

During the first three and one-half years after the true church has been caught away the earth will be plagued by war, pestilence, destruction and death, until almost half the entire population of the world has perished in the brief period of three and one-half years. God says concerning this time of tribulation that there has never been a period like it and there will never be another. How grateful we should be that God has provided a way of escape through faith in the Lord Jesus Christ so that none who receive Him as Saviour need fear the awful days which lie ahead, the shadows of which are already lengthening as a result of the discovery of the modern weapons of destruction, the atomic bomb and the developments in radar and television, which have caused men qualified to speak to tell us frankly that another war will mean the total destruction of this world.

The End Is Near

With the pouring out of the seven vials will come the end of the period of God's judgment. The pouring out of the last vial will be the signal for the return of Christ, of which we read in Revelation 19:11. However, before John describes the awful judgments which will come as one vial after another is poured out, he stops to give us again a picture of those who will be spared all miseries. In Revelation 15:2-4 we read:

> And I saw as it were a sea of glass mingled with fire: and them that had gotten the victory over the beast, and over his image, and over his mark, and over the number of his name, stand on the sea of glass, having the harps of God. And they sing the song of Moses the servant of God, and the song of the Lamb, saying, Great and marvellous are thy works, Lord God Almighty; just and true are thy ways, thou King of saints. Who shall not fear thee, O Lord, and glorify thy name? for thou only art holy: for all nations shall come and worship before thee; for thy judgments are made manifest.

This sea of glass reminds us of another sea of glass mentioned in Revelation 4, but in this chapter we read that the sea of glass is as clear as crystal, whereas Revelation 15 speaks of it as mingled with fire. The reason is evident. Chapter 4 speaks of the Rapture of saints *before* the Tribulation; chapter 15 describes the saints who have come *through* the Tribulation. In Scripture, fire is always the symbol of judgment, and the redeemed spoken of in Revelation 4, who are taken out *before* the judgment, stand on a sea of glass as clear as crystal, but the saints mentioned in Revelation 15 stand upon a sea of glass mingled with fire. These are they that are come out of the Great Tribulation. This is evident, for the second verse of chapter 15 tells us plainly that they—

> had gotten the victory over the beast, and over his image, and over his mark, and over the number of his name.

They sing the song of Moses and the Lamb. The song of Moses was the song which Israel sang after the hosts of Pharaoh perished in the Red Sea, as recorded in Exodus 15. Here again is pictured the nation of Israel in the Great Tribulation, of which their bondage in Egypt under Pharaoh was a type and a shadow. When the nation is once more delivered from their cruel Gentile oppressors and the wrath of the Antichrist, they will sing again the song of deliverance and at that time they will be on the way to Canaan and Palestine, never to be removed.

THE SEVEN VIALS OF GOD'S WRATH

Having introduced us first of all to a company who will not be overcome by the terrible judgments of the seven vials of wrath, John resumes his account of what will occur when the bowls of wrath are poured out. God will not bring His judgments upon the earth until

He has made safe those who belong to Him. This is true also of the Church. He will not permit the Tribulation until after the Church has been caught away. He will not pour out the vials of His final wrath until His ancient people Israel have been made safe. But once His own have been removed, the judgments will fall swiftly and terribly. Let us consider them rapidly:

> And the first went, and poured out his vial upon the earth: and there fell a noisome and grievous sore upon the men which had the mark of the beast, and upon them which worshipped his image (Rev. 16:2).

You will notice in the plagues which follow the pouring out of the vials of God's wrath a striking similarity to another series of awful plagues which fell upon the earth in the earlier era. When Pharaoh persecuted the children of Israel in Egypt and refused to let them go to the land which God had promised them through Abraham, Isaac and Jacob, God sent plagues upon them until Pharaoh and his house had been destroyed. That judgment of plagues was a type and a shadow of those recorded in Revelation 16. The difference is one of scope and intensity. The plagues of Pharaoh's day were limited to the land of Egypt; those described in Revelation will fall upon the entire earth. The plagues during the Tribulation will be more intense and widespread, but in spite of these differences, the plagues in the last seven vials follow closely the pattern of the ten plagues of Egypt. This will become more and more evident as we study the other vials of wrath:

> And the second angel poured out his vial upon the sea; and it became as the blood of a dead man: and every living soul died in the sea (Rev. 16:3).

Again we are reminded of the plagues of blood in the day of Moses, the deliverer of Israel (Exod. 7). You will recall that Revelation 10 speaks of two witnesses who plagued the earth with these same judgments, and we have every reason to believe that these two witnesses, Moses and Elijah, had a part also in the pouring out of these bowls of the wrath of God. Remember that the days of their testimony correspond to the days of the pouring out of the vials of wrath, the last three and one-half years of the Tribulation.

> And the third angel poured out his vial upon the river and fountains of waters; and they became blood. And I heard the angel of the waters say, Thou art righteous, O Lord, which art, and wast, and shalt be, because thou hast judged thus. For they have shed the blood of saints and prophets, and thou hast given them blood to drink; for they are worthy (Rev. 16:4-6).

The pouring out of the third vial results in a judgment similar to the second, but is followed by a vindication of the justice and the righteousness of God. Men find fault with God for sending these terrible judgments upon mankind because they understand neither the awfulness of sin nor the absolute righteousness of God. As long as men minimize sin and fail to realize its basic nature as one of rebellion against an infinite God, they will continue to find fault and not repent. This is clearly evident when the fourth angel pours out his vial upon the sun. Here is the dramatic record:

> And the fourth angel poured out his vial upon the sun; and power was given unto him to scorch men with fire. And men were scorched with great heat, and blasphemed the name of God, which hath power over these plagues: and they repented not to give him glory (Rev. 16:8-9).

One little phrase in the ninth verse manifests the justice of all this: "God, which hath power over these plagues." If we believe that God made the sun, we can believe that God can darken the sun or increase its brillance and heat at will. If we believe that God made the waters, we can believe that He can turn them into blood. Yet when men approach the book of Revelation they seek to argue away the literalness of these plagues and make them symbolic. If one thinks it impossible for water to turn to blood and fire to fall from heaven, then he must disbelieve also the Biblical record of similar events in days gone by. Then we must abandon belief in all miracles and become materialists and infidels. But remember that John says, "God, which hath power over these plagues."

THE FIFTH VIAL OF WRATH

Swiftly following the sign in the sun the fifth angel pours out his vial upon the city of Babylon:

> And the fifth angel poured out his vial upon the seat of the beast; and his kingdom was full of darkness; and they gnawed their tongues for pain (Rev. 16:10).

From preceding chapters you will remember that the beast is the political head of the restored Roman Empire. Some Bible students believe that the city of Rome will become the capital of the world and the seat of the beast, the last great world-dictator, just as Rome was the capital of the ancient Roman Empire. Be that as it may, we see God turning His attention to the very heart of world-opposition. The city is plunged into darkness and men gnaw their tongues in pain. Again we are reminded that all these plagues follow closely the pattern of the plagues in Egypt in the days of Moses.

As the plagues in Moses day came upon Pharaoh and his nation because of their oppression of God's covenant people Israel, so, too, the plagues of which we read in Revelation are God's judgment upon the nations for their treatment of His scattered and persecuted people. Remember that at the rapture the Church will be taken out, and only Israel and the unbelieving Gentiles will be left upon the earth. We are now approaching the end of Gentile world-dominion and at the pouring out of the seventh and last vial, God's plan and purpose in setting up His kingdom will be accomplished. The Great Tribulation will end when the Battle of Armageddon is fought and terminates abruptly with the sudden appearing of Jesus Christ.

When the seventh vial of God's wrath is poured out, we will have reached the Battle of Armageddon. In our next chapter we will consider the pouring out of the last two vials, when the sixth is poured out, the great super-highway will be prepared for the Kings of the East to the bed of the dried-up Euphrates River. When the seventh vial is poured out, God will judge the apostate Antichristian religious system of the Antichrist, and then will occur the Second Coming of the Lord. May I suggest that before reading the next chapters in this book, you study carefully the remainder of Revelation 16 and also chapters 17 and 18.

Today there are movements at work in the world preparing for the events which we have been studying. The spheres of influence are being definitely circumscribed as the King of the North seeks to dominate all of northern and central Europe. The King of the West will come from the countries surrounding the Mediterranean, while the King of the South will push upward from Africa and the Eastern Empire will approach through the bed of the Euphrates River. Recent developments in Europe and Asia lead us to believe that this day is near. The nations are preparing for the last great battle, and if we remember that the rapture will take place at least seven years before the Battle of Armageddon, we are convinced that the Coming of the Lord is near. The most important question, therefore, becomes a personal one: Are *you* ready for His coming?

CHAPTER TWENTY-FOUR

Three Unclean Spirits Like Frogs

And the sixth angel poured out his vial upon the great river Euphrates; and the water thereof was dried up, that the way of the kings of the east might be prepared. And I saw three unclean spirits like frogs come out of the mouth of the dragon, and out of the mouth of the beast, and out of the mouth of the false prophet. For they are the spirits of devils, working miracles, which go forth unto the kings of the earth and of the whole world, to gather them to the battle of that great day of God Almighty. Behold, I come as a thief. Blessed is he that watcheth, and keepeth his garments, lest he walk naked, and they see his shame (Rev. 16:12-15).

"Armageddon" is a word that arouses fear and visions of a fierce battle. The word "Armageddon" has been much in the news since the last war and especially since the development of that terrible weapon of destruction, the atomic bomb. News commentators and military experts speak of Armageddon and the destruction of the world, unless the recent discoveries of science can be utilized as instruments of peace and constructiveness. Lowell Thomas told in one of his broadcasts of an interview with one of the chief scientists responsible for the perfection of the atomic bomb and quoted him as expressing frankly grave fear that the recent discoveries of released atomic energy would wipe out the whole world unless effective preventive measures were taken. General Marshall, in an interview, quoted Gen. H. H. Arnold as follows:

We can direct rockets to targets by electronic devices and new instruments which guide them accurately to sources of heat, light and magnetism. Drawn by their own fuses such rockets will streak unerringly to the heart of big factories, attracted by the heat of the furnaces. They are so sensitive that in the space of a large room they aim themselves toward a man who enters, in reaction to the heat of his body. Within the next few years there will be produced jet-propelled bombers with speeds of 500 to 600 miles per hour, flying to targets 1,500 miles distant at altitudes above 40,000 feet. Development of even greater bombers, to operate in the stratosphere at supersonic speeds and carrying bomb loads of more than 100,000 pounds, already is certain. These aircraft will have sufficient range to attack any spot on the earth and return to a friendly base. At this very moment we are making a single bomb weighing 45,000 pounds to keep pace with the bomber, already under construction, which will carry such a load. Air ordnance engineers have blue-printed a bomb weighing 100,000 pounds. Improvement of our jet fighters may well produce within the next five years an aircraft capable of the speed of sound and of reaching targets 2,000 miles away at altitudes above 50,000 feet. Discovery of the secret of atomic power can be man's greatest benefit or it can destroy him. It is against the latter terrible possibility that this nation must prepare or perish.

These facts are shocking indeed to the average man and woman, but to the student of the Scriptures, they are not new and disturbing. The Bible has clearly predicted the time when "the heavens shall pass away with a great noise, and the elements shall melt with fervent heat, the earth also, and the works that are therein shall be burned up. (II Peter 3:10). Morever, the book of Revelation discusses in detail the last days of this age, which will end in violence and war, and the greater part of the book is devoted to a description of the last great battle of all time ending in Armageddon, when the Lord alone will prevent man from completely exterminating himself. When it seems that all hope is gone, the

Lord will return, stop man's reign of terror, and set up His kingdom of righteousness and peace.

In our study of the book of Revelation we have seen the course of this present age, ending in the apostasy of Laodicea. Then the Lord will come to take His Church out, as we read in Revelation 4, and the Tribulation will begin. This Tribulation is described under the seven seals, the seven trumpets and the seven bowls of God's wrath. In our study we have reached the sixth of these vials of wrath.

Two important events will occur when the sixth angel sounds his trumpet:

1.   The drying up of the Euphrates to produce the greatest natural highway in all the world.
2.   The gathering of the armies of the world for the last great battle, the Battle of Armageddon.

THE EUPHRATES RIVER

The Euphrates River is mentioned in two historical accounts, the account of the Garden of Eden and the account of the city of Babylon. In the region of the Euphrates, where Eden was located, Satan won the first skirmish when he deceived our first parents, Adam and Eve, and plunged the race into judgment and death. In the same region the last battle will be fought—the battle in which Christ shall finally defeat the enemy of man and God, even Satan. The Euphrates was also the site of ancient Babylon, which, as we shall see, represents all that is opposed to God and righteousness. This great River Euphrates, fifteen hundred miles long, ten to thirty feet deep and several miles wide in many places, will be dried up at the pouring out of the sixth vial of the wrath of God. The dry riverbed will become a great highway which will play an important role in bringing together the armies of the world for the last great battle.

The River Euphrates has ever been a formidable natural barrier between the east and the west, but toward the end of the Tribulation the armies of the world will prepare for the last and greatest stand against God and His people. According to Daniel there will be at least four great armies which will meet in the valley of Jehoshaphat to the north of Palestine among the hills of Meggido. These armies are called the King of the North, the King of the South, the Kings of the East and the ten-horned beast mentioned in Daniel and Revelation.

The King of the North will be the empire now occupied by Russia and the countries now known as the Russian sphere of influence. The King of the West will be the revived Roman Empire comprising all the Mediterranean countries. The King of the South will undoubtedly be the African nations and tribes, and the King of the East will be the yellow races. These will meet and fight in the Battle of Armageddon, mentioned in this passage quoted at the beginning of this message and more fully described in Revelation 19.

To make way for the King of the East to reach the battleground the River Euphrates will be dried up to make a natural road by which they can come. I know well that many scoff at the prophecy that the Euphrates River will be dried up, but they are the same who scoff also at the account of the drying up of the Red Sea and in River Jordan. If we believe the account in Exodus and Judges we shall have no difficulty in believing Revelation 16:12. If we interpret the passage literally, we will have no difficulty.

> And the sixth angel poured out his vial upon the great river Euphrates; and the water thereof was dried up, that the way of the kings of the east might be prepared.

THREE UNCLEAN SPIRITS

Mention is made also of another event which occurred when the angel poured out the sixth vial of wrath. John saw three unclean spirits like frogs proceeding out of the mouth of the dragon and out of the mouth of the beast and out of the mouth of the false prophet. Many, strange and ludicrous have been the attempts of men to identify these three unclean spirits. Some have identified them as the spirits of Communism, Fascism and Nazism, and there have been other attempts at interpretation which are even more ridiculous. May I repeat, if we will but interpret the Word literally and let it explain itself, we will have no difficulty. Scripture itself tells us what these spirits are:

> For they are the spirits of devils, working miracles, which go forth unto the kings of the earth and of the whole world, to gather them to the battle of that great day of God Almighty . . . And he gathered them together into a place called in the Hebrew tongue Armageddon (Rev. 16:14,16).

Here is the record, so simple that any child can understand it, and yet wise and august theologians stumble when they attempt to interpret it. The dragon is Satan, the beast is the political dictator of the end-time, and the false prophet is the Antichrist. Out of their mouths proceed three unclean spirits whose responsibility it is to deceive the kings of the earth into fighting the Battle of Armageddon. These evil spirits, called demons, are real creatures. The Bible records frequent instances of demon possession.

Among the fallen angels, as among the angels of God, there are many orders and ranks. We know that Satan is the chief of the demons. There is also Abbadon, the king of the bottomless pit. Jude tells of certain fallen angels so vicious that they are kept in chains of everlasting darkness unto the judgment of that great day. Perhaps some of these ultravicious fallen angels, now kept bound, will then be loosed to deceive the nations to initiate the last desperate rebellion against the Lord. But whoever they are, we are told that they are the spirits of demons with the power to do great signs and miracles to deceive the nations of the earth.

A GLOBAL WAR

We are all familiar with the term "global war," by which we mean, of course, a war which involves the entire globe. But the recent world war was global in effect rather than in actuality, for there were nations who remained neutral. In the last great conflict, however, none will remain neutral, for we read that these spirits go forth—

unto the kings of the earth and of the **whole world.**

This will indeed be a global **war** in its fullest sense of the term. This will be fulfillment of prophecy. In the Garden of Eden the war started, when Satan beguiled the human race and God declared war upon the serpent and his seed. For six thousand years the battle has raged, during which time the heel of the seed of the woman was bruised, but the time will come when the seed of the woman, the Christ of God, will crush the head of the serpent. The armies of the world, deceived by Satan and his foul spirits, will gather in the Battle of Armageddon, on the greatest natural battleground in the world, in the valley of Jehoshaphat to the north of Palestine among the hills of Megiddo. The word "Armageddon" means "the hill of the slaughter." We have seen that the blood will run to the horses' bridles and again in Revelation 19 we are told of the unprecedented slaughter of the armies of Satan when Christ comes to defeat them.

THE SEVENTH VIAL

The sixteenth chapter of Revelation ends with a description of the pouring out of the seventh vial of God's wrath. It gives us a picture of some of the events that will take place when the Battle of Armageddon occurs. Here is the record:

> And the seventh angel poured out his vial into the air; and there came a great voice out of the temple of heaven, from the throne, saying, It is done. And there were voices, and thunders, and lightnings; and there was a great earthquake, such as was not since men were upon the earth, so mighty an earthquake, and so great. And the great city was divided into three parts, and the cities of the nations fell: and great Babylon came in remembrance before God, to give unto her the cup of the wine of the fierceness of his wrath. And every island fled away, and the mountains were not found. And there fell upon men a great hail out of heaven, every stone about the weight of a talent: and men blasphemed God because of the plague of the hail; for the plague thereof was exceeding great (Rev. 16:17-21).

This brings us to a discussion of the Second Coming of Christ of which we read in Revelation 19:11, but between the sixteenth chapter and Revelation 19:11 are three explanatory chapters which deal with Babylon the great and her doom. We will discuss this subject in our next messages.

I want you to see how terrible it will be for men who have rejected Christ to face that fearful day when the air explodes, the earthquakes split the city of Jerusalem into three parts and the wicked apostate Antichristian religious system called Babylon is judged by the God of heaven. So great will be the convolutions of the earth, which will likely be the result of the release of atomic energy, that mountains will disappear, islands will be submerged, hundred-pound hailstones will fall on the earth and God will come to judge the wicked.

But for the true Christian, the believer in Christ, this holds no dread or fear, for he will be removed to a place of peace and safety long before this event occurs upon the earth. Revelation 3:10 assures us of this fact:

> Because thou hast kept the word of my patience, I also will keep thee from the hour of temptation, which shall come upon all the world, to try them that dwell upon the earth.

That is why in the middle of the account of the sixth seal, which we find in Revelation 16, we read this significant verse:

> Behold, I come as a thief. Blessed is he that watcheth, and keepeth his garments, lest he walk naked, and they see his shame (Rev. 16:15).

Here is the promise that *you* may escape these dreadful events of the end-time. "Blessed is he that watcheth." Are *you* watching for the coming of the Lord? If you are not, then you may well fear and tremble. I would, tremble too, if it were not for the blessed hope of Christ's returning to take us away to glory in the Rapture before that terrible day comes. Ominous are the signs today. Those who know tell us that man now has inventions and discoveries which could blow up the earth and destroy all life. A few years ago men scoffed at the book of Revelation with its account of terrible judgments. Today science has made all of them both reasonable and scientific. How necessary it is, therefore, to warn you and cry aloud to all of you, "Flee from the wrath to come!"

CHAPTER TWENTY-FIVE

The Rise and Fall of Babylon

In our studies of Revelation we have nearly reached the end of the Tribulation Period. In chapter 16 we read of Armageddon and the Second Coming of Christ, but the actual coming of Christ and the battle of the ages is described in the last part of Revelation 19. Between Revelation 16 and 19 are three chapters which discuss one great topic, the judgment—the final judgment of God upon the ungodly world-federation of nations in the end-time under the leadership of the last great world-dictator, the beast out of the sea of which we read in Revelation 13, and the judgment of the false Antichristian church of the Antichrist, under the leadership of the beast out of the land, also described in Revelation 13.

We shall not attempt to give a detailed exposition of these three chapters (Revelation 17-19:11), but, rather, present in simple and brief outline the general picture of the beginning of the Antichristian system of religion known as Babylonianism, and its final doom. Babylonianism, begins in Genesis 11 and comes to its end in Revelation 17-19. Let us consider first its beginning in Genesis 11:

> And the whole earth was of one language, and of one speech. And it came to pass, as they journeyed from the east, that they found a plain in the land of Shinar; and they dwelt there. And they said one to another, Go to, let

214

us make brick, and burn them thoroughly. And they had
brick for stone, and slime for morter. And they said, Go
to, let us build us a city and a tower, whose top may reach
unto heaven; and let us make us a name, lest we be scattered
abroad upon the face of the whole earth. And the Lord came
down to see the city and the tower, which the children of
men builded. And the Lord said, Behold, the people is one,
and they have all one language; and this they begin to do:
and now nothing will be restrained from them, which they
have imagined to do. Go to, let us go down, and there confound their language, that they may not understand one
another's speech. So the Lord scattered them abroad from
thence upon the face of all the earth: and they left off to
build the city. Therefore is the name of it called Babel;
because the Lord did there confound the language of all the
earth: and from thence did the Lord scatter them abroad
upon the face of all the earth (Gen. 11:1-9).

This passage is the first record of the building of
the city of Babylon, a city prominent in ancient history
and frequently discussed in the Bible. In Revelation
17 to 19 Babylon is mentioned for the last time.

And after these things I saw another angel come down
from heaven, having great power; and the earth was
lightened with his glory. And he cried mightily with a
strong voice, saying, Babylon the great is fallen, is fallen,
and is become the habitation of devils, and the hold of every
foul spirit, and a cage of every unclean and hateful bird
(Rev. 18:1-2).

I am certain that the words "Babel" and "Babylon"
are of only slight interest to the average person. To
many, the name "Babel" means merely an ancient city
which has long since ceased to be, and Babylon was an
ancient kingdom which flourished for a long time and
then succumbed to another and a stronger nation. However, to the student of Scripture, and especially the student of prophecy, the words "Babel" and "Babylon"
have a much more important meaning, for Babel was not
only a city, but symbolizes a political ideal and a govern-

mental system which has never died but is still at the root of the world's disorders.

It disappeared for a time, but Babylonianism as representing that spirit of the Antichrist which would set up a world-kingdom in opposition to Christ's kingdom and produce a religious world-church as a challenge to the Church of Christ has never died. It is like a forest stream which disappears underground for a while only to gather more moisture and finally burst forth with greater momentum and power. The spirit of Babylonianism goes underground at times but bursts forth periodically in the great revolutions of history, without once changing its basic program or aims.

No less than three entire chapters in the book of Revelation are devoted to the story of the final restoration of ancient Babylon and her ultimate destruction and ruin. Two chief actors appear in these three chapters of Revelation. John sees first a woman garbed in purple and in scarlet, and then he beholds a beast upon which she rides and whom she rules with an iron hand, until finally the beast itself turns upon the woman and utterly destroys and devours her. The colorful description of the woman is given in Revelation 17:1-7:

> And there came one of the seven angels which had the seven vials, and talked with me, saying unto me, Come hither; I will show unto thee the judgment of the great whore that sitteth upon many waters; with whom the kings of the earth have committed fornication, and the inhabitants of the earth have been made drunk with the wine of her fornication. So he carried me away in the spirit into the wilderness: and I saw a woman sit upon a scarlet-coloured beast, full of names of blasphemy, having seven heads and and pearls, having a golden cup in her hand full of abominations and filthiness of her fornication: and upon her forehead ten horns. And the woman was arrayed in purple and scarlet colour, and decked with gold and precious stones was a name written, mystery, Babylon the great, the mother of harlots and abominations of the earth. And I saw the

woman drunken with the blood of the saints, and with the blood of the martyrs of Jesus: and when I saw her, I wondered with great admiration. And the angel said unto me, Wherefore didst thou marvel? I will tell thee the mystery of the woman, and of the beast that carrieth her, which hath the seven heads and ten horns (Rev. 17:1-7).

The description of the beast upon which the woman sits is equally graphic and colorful as recorded in Revelation 17:8-18:

The beast that thou sawest was, and is not; and shall ascend out of the bottomless pit, and go into perdition: and they that dwell on the earth shall wonder, whose names were not written in the book of life from the foundation of the world, when they behold the beast that was, and is not, and yet is. And here is the mind which hath wisdom. The seven heads are seven mountains, on which the woman sitteth . . . And the ten horns which thou sawest are ten kings, which have received no kingdom as yet; but receive power as kings one hour with the beast. These have one mind, and shall give their power and strength unto the beast . . . And the ten horns which thou sawest upon the beast, these shall hate the whore, and shall make her desolate and naked, and shall eat her flesh, and burn her with fire . . . And the woman which thou sawest is that great city, which reigneth over the kings of the earth (Rev. 17:8-9,12,13,16,18,).

THE FIRST BABYLON

To understand these passages relating the final doom of Babylon, we must turn again to the first mention of Babel in the Scriptures. In Genesis 10 and 11 we have a detailed record of the rise of that political religious system known to Bible students as Babylon. We are told that after the Flood the descendants of Noah, forgetting the lesson they should have learned, turned from God and moved to a region to the north of Palestine in the vicinity of the original Garden of Eden. It was called the land of Shinar and was in the region of the

Euphrates River, one of the three principal rivers of
the Garden of Eden.

A certain man, Nimrod by name, seems to have been
the leader of this great movement, and supported by
a great company of followers, he began the building of
a city which was to become one of the seven great
wonders of the world. In this land of Shinar he built a
city and called it Babel. In the midst of the city was
a gigantic temple dedicated to Belus, later called Baal.
At the same time he also built a tower, usually referred
to as the Tower of Babel. From archaeological discoveries and secular history as well as the Bible record we
learn something of the magnificence, the ideals and the
purposes of this mighty project, which was to become
symbolic of Satan's program throughout the ages as
opposed to the program of the Lord and His Church.

THE MAGNIFICENCE OF BABYLON

Many available records tell us of the splendor of
ancient Babylon. The city itself was fourteen miles
square, embracing almost two hundred square miles.
It was surrounded by a wide moat filled with water as
protection against invasion. The wall around the city
was eighty feet thick and two hundred feet high. The
city had a hundred gates of iron and brass, and the
River Euphrates ran through it. In the center of the city
was the famous temple of Belus, the Babylonian god.

THE TOWER OF BABEL

As the city represented the political national strength
and ideals of Babylon, so also there was a tower which
was the symbol and center of Babylon's religious program and worship. This tower rested upon a base of
stone 300 feet square and 110 feet high. Upon this was
built the second stage which was 260 feet square and
60 feet high. The third was slightly smaller and each

decreased in size. The sixth stage was 110 feet square and 20 feet high, and on the top of this sixth platform, 300 feet in the air, was the sanctuary in which was the statue of the Babylonian god. The building of this tower was interrupted by the confusion of tongues but was resumed later under Nebuchadnezzar.

Ruled by Two Despots

This first great city of Babel and kingdom of Babylon was ruled by two persons, a man and a woman. The man ruled politically and was the head of the Babylonian State; the woman ruled religiously and was the head of the pagan system of religion and idolatry. The city and the tower, politics and religion, merged into one great gigantic system of world-unity. Federation was the dream of the first Babylonians and has been the aim and the program since.

The Spirit of Babylon

Babylonianism, then, represents everything which is opposed to God both politically and religiously. God's program calls for a kingdom to be established upon the earth under the personal rule of the Christ. Satan proposes a kingdom of men in the earth under the rulership of the Antichrist of whom Nimrod, the builder of Babel, was the first clear type in the Scriptures. When we study Revelation, which relates the last days of man's rule upon the earth, we see the scarlet beast mentioned in Revelation 18, and the mysterious woman who rides the beast as representing religious Babylon, dominating and dictating to political Babylon.

The Aim of Babylon

The program of Nimrod is clearly described in Genesis 10 and 11. We are told that the beginning of his kingdom was Babel. Then we are told that all the world was of one speech. Men sought a federation of power that would make them secure in the earth for they said:

> Let us build us a city and a tower, whose top may reach unto heaven; and let us make us a name, lest we be scattered abroad upon the face of the whole earth. (Gen. 11:4).

Here is the picture. Satan, in seeking to oppose the plan of God for a Kingdom and a Church, attempted to establish a kingdom and a church of his own. Nimrod was the first who attempted such a program on a grand scale. The name Nimrod means "rebel." He sought a world-federation of religions centered at the Tower of Babel. He sought to establish a world in which one language was spoken, and he called the center of this Babylonian Empire, "Babel." The word "Babel" means literally "the gate to God." That is what man called it. It was a denial of God's way to heaven. The Lord had clearly revealed His way in Genesis 3:21 when He slew an animal, shed its blood and used the skins to clothe the first sinners.

God thus indicated the way of salvation. Man must be saved through the shedding of the blood of an innocent substitute and by the death of another, but the Babylonians denied this and added their own works and built a tower that was to be a way to heaven and God, not by blood and death, but by the work of man's hands. That was the spirit of Babylon. It was a denial of God's way of grace. The dream of man, separated from God, is a man-made way of salvation by works, a universal federation of nations under one dictatorial leader, a universal church which denies the blood, a universal language dominated by a superstate, which will formulate the policies of both government and religion.

God Came Down

The plan, however, did not succeed for we read in Genesis 11:5-9:

> And the Lord came down to see the city and the tower, which the children of men builded. And the Lord said, Behold, the people is one, and they have all one language; and this they begin to do: and now nothing will be restrained from them, which they have imagined to do. Go to, let us go down, and there confound their language, that they may not understand one another's speech. So the Lord scattered them abroad from thence upon the face of all the earth: and they left off to build the city. Therefore is the name of it called Babel; because the Lord did there confound the language of all the earth: and from thence did the Lord scatter them abroad upon the face of all the earth (Gen. 11:5-9).

Nimrod had called Babel "the gate to God." God came down and called it "confusion" and blasted the plans for a superstate, but the spirit of Nimrod lived on in Babylonianism. Soon it asserted itself again in Egypt where Pharaoh attempted to establish his superstate. Later Nebuchadnezzar made a similar attempt followed by Medo-Persia, Alexander, the Caesars, Constantine the Great with his union of church and state, Napoleon, Kaiser Wilhelm and, more recently, Hitler. Today the dream of mankind is still a federation of nations, a superorganization—without God—that will bring the Utopia of peace of which men have dreamed since the days of Nimrod.

After the Rapture

Satan's final attempt to fulfill his dream will occur in the Tribulation *after* the Church is gone. When the true Church has been caught away, Satan will produce the personal Antichrist, the false christ of whom Nimrod was only a shadow, who will succeed in setting up a great superfederation of nations to guarantee safety

for the world, and in conjunction with the last great political head of the restored Roman Empire will seek to do
what Nimrod failed to do because he was suddenly interrupted by the coming of the Lord and scattered abroad in
confusion.

The entire story is found in these three chapters of
Revelation. The scarlet beast is the Nimrod of the end-
time, the national and international empire of revived
Babylonianism. The woman will be the apostate church,
a merging of Thyatirea, Sardis and Laodicea, *after* the
true Church has been caught away.

For a time it will seem that men have succeeded in
carrying out the dream of the devil by producing a world-
state, a universal religion of works and the denial of
grace, until suddenly it will end in confusion when the
Lord comes to destroy it by His appearing. We need
not know all the details and meanings of the horns of
the beast and the identity of all the kings that are
mentioned. The main outline is clear and the outcome
is certain.

We believe that there is today a revival of the spirit
of Babylon. Man's precarious position because of recent
developments in the science of warfare have led them
to believe that a strong federation is the world's only
hope. Not knowing or believing that the only hope for
this old world is the coming of the Prince of Peace, they
seek to bring it about by their own methods: one global
policy, one global church, one global speech. Then will
follow the catching away of the Church, and for a brief
time Satan will rapidly attempt to fulfill his plans. The
beast will appear and the woman, the false church of
the Antichrist, described as "mystery, Babylon the
Great."

The long conflict which began at the dawn of human
history will come to an end and Christ will come.

"Even so, come, Lord Jesus."

CHAPTER TWENTY-SIX

The Rise and Fall of Babylon
(continued)

And a mighty angel took up a stone like a great millstone, and cast it into the sea, saying, Thus with violence shall that great city Babylon be thrown down, and shall be found no more at all (Rev. 18:21).

And in her was found the blood of prophets, and of saints, and of all that were slain upon the earth (Rev. 18:24).

Babylon was an ancient city, the capital of the Babylonian Empire, but in Scripture, Babylon represents the program of Satan as opposed to the program of God. It began with Nimrod the rebel, of whom we read in Genesis 1, when he built the first Tower of Babel, which was destroyed by the coming of the Lord from heaven. It was a religious and political federation of all the nations of the world in opposition to God. Babylonianism has appeared in various forms, but always it has remained essentially the same. Whether in the Egyptian, Assyrian, Grecian, or Roman form, it has sought to accomplish two objectives: a world-federation which denies the right of Christ to reign and a religious system which denies the authority of Jesus Christ.

THE END IN REVELATION

Because of the important role which Babylonianism, or the spirit of the world, plays in Bible history, three entire chapters in Revelation are devoted to a discussion

of the end of this evil system. Chapters 16 to 19 record
for us the final form and destruction of the Antichristian
system of this world. Briefly stated, these chapters tell
us that after the Church has been raptured there will
arise a world-power, a dictator who will succeed in unit-
ing the nations of the world in a great federation. At the
same time the false christ, the Antichrist, the end-time
religious leader, will organize all religion into one great
world-church. Remember that at this time the true body
of Christ will have been taken out, and only professing
religion will remain. United by some common bloodless,
Christless creed, this religious global federation, in co-
operation with the world-political federation, will seek
to exterminate the ancient people of God, Israel, and set
up a kingdom in opposition to the kingdom of Christ.
This effort will be suddenly interrupted by the return
of the Lord Jesus Christ Himself.

Tne Woman in Revelation

That event, the coming of Christ to destroy this godless program of man, is described in the verses with
which we opened this chapter as the smiting of a great
stone which will destroy Babylon and all it represents.
It is the same as the stone in the vision of which we
read in Daniel 2. You will recall that in that chapter
Daniel interprets the dream of the king. He saw a
great image with head of gold, chest of silver, belly of
brass, thighs of iron, and feet and toes of iron and clay.
This was Daniel's vision of Babylonianism. The head
of gold was Babylon, the chest was Persia, the trunk
was Greece and the legs were Rome. The ten toes
represented the last form of Gentile world-power corresponding to the beast with ten horns of which Revelation
17:11 tells us. Then a great stone appeared cut out of
the mountain and struck the image in its feet and destroyed it, while the stone itself waxed greater and

greater until it filled the entire earth. The stones are the same. Both that in Daniel and the one in Revelation speak of the coming of Christ, the Rock, to destroy the wicked and put an end to man's religion and government.

WOMAN IN REVELATION

The book of Daniel is occupied almost exclusively with the political aspect of Babylonianism. John in Revelation sees, in addition to this the Antichristian, national federation of religions under the figure of the scarlet woman. It is impossible for us in the scope of these messages to discuss all the details of the vision in Revelation 16 to 18, but we shall attempt to present the general outline. There is a danger that we may become so engrossed in details that we forget the broad general plan of the book.

The beast spoken of in Revelation is the restored and revived Roman Empire, which will seek to dominate the entire earth. The woman who is seen riding the beast is the apostate church of the Antichrist, which will be established after the true church has been taken out at the Rapture. Thyatira, Sardis and Laodicea, will fuse and become religious Babylon. We have already pointed out that the last three churches mentioned in Revelation 2 and 3 will exist side by side until the Rapture. Then Philadelphia will be taken out and Thyatira, Sardis and Laodicea will remain to combine and form the great world religious hierarchy of the Tribulation Period which will seek to dominate the state and the governments of the world.

Many attempts have been made to identify a particular denomination as the scarlet woman, but Revelation tells us that she is a mother and has a brood of children, a fact which suggests that there will be a great mother church, and associated with her will be the apostate religions of the world. There are already movements which are agitating a great union and federation of all religions under one head to make one great universal world-church, but this will come only *after* the true believers have been caught away at the Translation.

History Gives Many Examples

This will not be the first time that the Church has sought to dictate the policies of the state. When Constantine the Great adopted Christianity, he paternalized and subsidized the Christian Church by gifts and grants through taxation of the citizens of the Roman Empire, but soon the situation was reversed and the state turned on the dictatorial Church and took away its temporal and political governmental powers. But the spirit of Babylon still lives, and after the Rapture the remaining false church of the Antichrist will again ride the beast and seek to dictate to the world in matters political as well as religious. However, eventually the beast will turn upon the woman and destroy her, as we read in Revelation 17:16:

> And the ten horns which thou sawest upon the beast, these shall hate the whore, and shall make her desolate and naked, and shall eat her flesh, and burn her with fire.

The ten horns are the ten kings of the final world-empire. They will destroy the false religious system and the world will remain for a time without religion of any kind.

When religious Babylon is destroyed, political Babylon must also come to an end. Soon the Lord will come and put an end to man's rule and dominion and set up His kingdom.

The spirit which will bring about the condition of which we have been speaking is already at work today. In spite of our professed belief in the separation of church and state, governments are interfering increasingly with religion and seeking to dictate its policies and restrict its liberties. The last few years have seen an alarming increase in the limitations imposed upon the free expression of our religious views and the liberties of teaching the full counsel of God. Powerful agencies are at work day and night to stop the preaching of the fundamental Gospel, and godless men who know neither Christ nor spiritual truths are posing as authorities to tell us what we can and what we cannot preach. But while this is taking place, it is true also that religion has gone beyond its bounds and has begun to interfere in politics, government and even international affairs. Great religious bodies, instead of confining themselves to preaching the Gospel, are lobbying in Washington and passing resolutions, some of which are alarmingly radical. It is the business of the Church—and the sole business of the Church—to preach Christ, and leave politics to the politicians, and it is the business of government to govern and to protect the precious liberties of the people in their belief and convictions and not to impose limitations upon the free expression of our spiritual convictions. When each stays in its own sphere, all is well, but unfortunately such is not the situation. Many politicians are attempting to tell the preachers what to do, and too many preachers are trying to tell the politicians what they should do. This condition will reach its climax when the beast suddenly destroys the woman and banishes her.

THE DOWNFALL OF BABYLON

This downfall of religious Babylon will be the signal for the end of the Tribulation and an outburst of praise from the saints of God. Listen to their exultation at the downfall of Satan's church:

And after these things I heard a great voice of much
people in heaven, saying, Alleluia; Salvation, and glory,
and honour, and power, unto the Lord our God: for true and
righteous are his judgments: for he hath judged the
great whore, which did corrupt the earth with her forni-
cation, and hath avenged the blood of his servants at her
hand. And again they said, Alleluia. And her smoke rose
up for ever and ever (Rev. 19:1-3).

The rejoicing and praise have a double motivation:
first, because Babylon the Great, the persecutor of the
saints, has been destroyed, and second, because the
time of the earth's redemption has finally come.

The Wedding of the Lamb

While this terrible tribulation was occurring upon the
earth to prepare the earth for the saints' reign, the
saints themselves were in heaven being prepared to
reign upon the earth. During the entire Tribulation
Period the Church was in heaven at the judgment seat
of Christ being made ready to come back with him to
reign upon the renewed earth. Sad to say; when Jesus
comes for His Church, all the saints will not be ready
to meet Him. There will be some who will be ashamed
at His appearing. Some will have an abundant entrance,
whereas others will be saved so as by fire. Before the
saints are ready to reign with Christ, certain difficulties
must be righted. The carnal Christian who has led a
careless life will have to give an account before the
judgment seat of Christ, and as a result of his record
he will be given his place in the kingdom reign. Some
will reign over ten cities, others over only five; some
will barely enter and receive no rewards. These rewards
will be determined at the judgment seat of Christ which
will take place in heaven while the Tribulation is taking
place upon earth. While God is preparing the earth

for the saints, He will also prepare the saints for the earth.

It is well to remember this. Too many Christians believe that because they are saved by grace they can live as they please but nevertheless go to heaven when they die or be caught up to meet the Lord when He comes. They will, however, be sadly disappointed, for when Jesus comes, all the saints shall indeed rise to meet Him, but before they can return to reign with Him they will have to give an account of their deeds and on the basis of that record the rewards will be distributed. That is why immediately preceding the account of the return of the Lord, of which we read in Revelation 19:11, is this account in Revelation 19:7-9:

> Let us be glad and rejoice, and give honour to him: for the marriage of the Lamb is come, and his wife hath made herself ready. And to her was granted that she should be arrayed in fine linen, clean and white: for the fine linen is the righteousness of saints. And he saith unto me, Write, Blessed are they which are called unto the marriage supper of the Lamb. And he saith unto me. These are the true sayings of God (Rev. 19:7-9).

Notice the statement "His wife hath made herself ready." Evidently she was not ready before. This passage in Revelation 19 speaks of events which occurred seven years after the Rapture of which we read in the fourth chapter of Revelation. In Revelation 4:1-2 we read that the Church is caught away from the earth and she does not appear again in the book of Revelation until she is seen in this passage immediately before the description of our Lord's glorious return. In chapters 6 to 19 of Revelation, God's judgments are described on the earth, while at the same time God is also judging the bride in the air. After the cleansing is complete, she reappears clean and white. The clean white robe is her righteousness. The original word translated "righteousness of saints'' means really ''the righteous acts of the saints.'' Her robe consists of the material she herself has provided here on the earth, and now, cleansed from all hay, wood and stubble, she is to be arrayed for the wedding in the robe of her own making.

What kind of robe will you wear, my friend? Is your life a life of service and righteousness, or is it a life of selfishness and fleshliness? Are you seeking your own advancement, or are you seeking the glory of God? What a disappointment it will be to stand before Him and find that we have forfeited and bartered away the opportunity for a place of highest honor in His kingdom for a few fleeting pleasures of this life. I do not know whether we will sing the songs in heaven which we sing here, but I believe that if we do, many members of the bride will sing this song with sorrow and tears:

> Oh, the years of sinning wasted,
> Could I but recall them now,
> I would bring them to my Master,
> At His feet I'd humbly bow.

Shall We Sin?

We believe that this is the truth which is needed in these last days when worldliness and carnality are so prevalent among believers. There has been much unbalanced preaching of grace, as though the very fact that it is all of grace gives the Christian the right to live as he pleases. As a result, the Church of Jesus Christ has lost her testimony and has become a reproach before the world because of her bickering, malice and selfishness.

We are saved by grace, and grace alone, without works. However, every believer will have to give an account of every deed and word committed or spoken from the day he was saved until the day on which his life here on earth ends. He will have to give an account of what he has done with his time and talents. He will have to give an account of every penny he has earned while here. If he has used his time, talents and money for selfish purposes and fleshly desires, if he has not realized that his first duty was to glorify God and spread the good news of the Gospel, then he will be judged for this and suffer loss.

How solemn this life becomes in the light of the coming of the Lord! Soon He will come and call His servants to an accounting. Every man will be called to render an account of his stewardship—he who received one talent as well as he who received ten; he who gained ten pounds as well as he who hid his pound and came before the Lord with nothing.

Oh, friend, God will require of you according to your ability! Someone has said, "God never looks at the amount on the face of your check, but He looks at the balance on the stub." Not how much you give but how much you hold back is of major importance. The greater your talent the greater your responsibility. The greater your opportunity the greater your debt.

> And that servant which knew his Lord's will, and prepared not himself, neither did according to his will, shall be beaten with many stripes. But he that knew not, and did commit things worthy of stripes, shall be beaten with few stripes. For unto whomsoever much is given, of him shall much be required: and to whom men have committed much, of him they shall ask the more (Luke 12:47-48).
>
> Let us be glad and rejoice, and give honour to him: for the marriage of the Lamb is come, and his wife hath made herself ready. And to her was granted that she should be arrayed in fine linen, clean and white: for the fine linen is the righteousness of saints (Rev. 19:7-8).

CHAPTER TWENTY-SEVEN

The Wedding of the Lamb

Let us be glad and rejoice, and give honour to him: for the marriage of the Lamb is come, and his wife hath made herself ready. And to her was granted that she should be arrayed in the fine linen, clean and white: for the fine linen is the righteousness of saints. And he saith unto me, Write, Blessed are they which are called unto the marriage supper of the Lamb. And he saith unto me, These are the true sayings of God (Rev. 19:7-10).

In our studies of the book of Revelation we have reached the end of the Tribulation Period. We have been occupied almost exclusively with the awful judgments of God upon the wicked of the earth *after* the Rapture of the Church and during the Tribulation, and have temporarily lost sight of the true Church which was caught away in Revelation 4. While she was there with her Lord, the earth was undergoing its judgments. While the Lord was judging Israel and the nations here below, He was also concerned about the Church. There was, at the same time, a judgment taking place in heaven among the believers who had been caught away at the beginning of the Tribulation. This judgment we call "the judgment seat of Christ," at which only believers will appear. At the very beginning of the Tribulation the Church will be raptured to be with the Lord, and immediately after the Tribulation she will return with her Lord to reign upon the earth.

THE BRIDE NOT READY

The sad fact is that when Christ comes for His Church, many will not be ready to enter the kingdom with Him, for they will not be prepared to meet Him and to reign with Him immediately. There must be, therefore, a period of preparation at the judgment seat of Christ where the bride will be given an opportunity to prepare herself, be cleansed of her filth, and the believers will receive rewards according to the record of their works. There are many carnal Christians who live worldly and indifferent lives who will have to pass through the fires of that judgment seat before they are ready to return with the Lord to reign upon the earth. This may not be a welcome truth, but it is the clear teaching of Scripture. Paul, in writing to the Corinthian Church, says:

> For we must all appear before the judgment seat of Christ.

In I Corinthians 3 we read:

> For other foundation can no man lay than that is laid, which is Jesus Christ. Now if any man build upon this foundation gold, silver, precious stones, wood, hay, stubble; every man's work shall be made manifest: for the day shall declare it, because it shall be revealed by fire; and the fire shall try every man's work of what sort it is. If any man's work abide which he hath built thereupon, he shall receive a reward. If any man's work shall be burned, he shall suffer loss: but he himself shall be saved; yet so by fire (I Cor. 3:11-16).

This passage indicates clearly that there will be a judgment of believers. Paul speaks of them as having built upon the foundation Jesus Christ, and they are warned to take heed how they build upon that foundation, because every man's work will be tried by fire, and the rewards in the Kingdom Age will be given on the basis of the results of that judgment of the believer's works. This has no relation to salvation, but concerns only rewards in the kingdom reign. This judgment will take place between the Rapture and the Second Coming of Christ, at the same time that God judges the wicked on earth during the Tribulation Period. That is why the wedding is mentioned in Revelation 19 before the discussion of the end of the Tribulation and the return of the Lord Jesus with His prepared and purified Church and bride.

The judgment seat which follows the Rapture will not be a pleasant experience for all. There will be suffering and rebukes, and cleansing and confessions which should have been made here. Some will be rewarded and some will suffer loss as they see the hay, wood and stubble disappear in smoke, and realize that they are "scarcely saved." Many of you who refuse to cleanse yourselves now by the washing of the Word will have to endure the purifying fires of which we have been speaking.

Finally the bride will be ready, and we read in Revelation 19:7: "His wife hath made herself ready."

THE WEDDING GARMENT

In olden times the bride made her own wedding dress. The bride of the Lord Jesus Christ, too, will have a part in making her own wedding dress. Of course, we know that every member of the bride is already clothed in the garments of the Lord's righteousness. The moment we believed on Him He imputed to us His righteousness and we were saved. There is also another robe of righteousness which will be worn on that glad day. This righteousness is the garments we make while here below and it will consist of the "good works of faith" which we have laid up, adorned with the gold, silver and precious stones of our service that will abide in that day. Let no Christian think that because he is saved his life is of no importance. There is a reckoning coming, and for Christians who believe thus it will be a sad, sad reckoning. "Be not deceived; God is not mocked: for whatsoever a man soweth, that shall he also reap."

According to Their Works

For we must all appear before the judgment seat of Christ; that every one may receive the things done in his body, according to that he hath done, whether it be good or bad (II Cor. 5:10).

Salvation depends upon grace and grace alone. By it God imputes to you His righteousness. There is another righteousness, however, which is *practical,* not *positional.* The first determines your salvation; the second determines your rewards. God makes you ready to be saved, but you must make yourself ready to reign. You can either prepare here or wait until you must do it there. I assure you it will be more pleasant, satisfactory and profitable to do it *now.*

Sanctification and Cleansing

In Ephesians 5:26 we are told that Christ will sanctify and cleanse His Church by the washing of water by the Word. The two words used, "sanctify" and "cleanse," are not the same in the Greek. The word translated "cleanse" in this verse is *katharizo,* from which our English word "cathartic" is derived. God uses two methods of making us clean. One is by "sanctifying," by washing of water by the Word. If we refuse this method, He will give us a "cathartic," but He will

have us clean. How much better to take the gentle
course now than to wait until the judgment seat of
Christ and be purged by fire!

The Wedding Gown

In Revelation 19:7 we read:

> Let us be glad and rejoice, and give honour to him: for
> the marriage of the Lamb is come, and his wife hath made
> herself ready.

Notice carefully that this event will occur *after* the
Tribulation and immediately *before* the coming of the
Lord to set up the kingdom (Rev. 19:11). Revelation
4 speaks of the Rapture of the Church and the chapters
following this, to the nineteenth, describe the seven
years of tribulation during which time the bride is
preparing for the wedding. There are many alterations
to be made, and the entire seven years will be occupied
with this task which should have been completed here
below, before the Rapture. Finally the garment is in
readiness. The spots and stains have been washed out,
the hay, wood, and stubble have been burned, and we
read:

> The marriage of the Lamb is come, and his wife hath
> made herself ready.

Note what follows:

> And to her was granted that she should be arrayed in
> fine linen, clean and white: for the fine linen is the right-
> eousness of saints.

The margin of my Bible translates the phrase "righteousness of saints" as "the *righteousnesses* of the
saints." The word is plural and means "the righteous
acts" of the saints. She will be adorned by her good
works which remained after the testing at the judgment

seat of Christ. Everything which was in the interest of self and of the flesh will have been burned, and only that which was done for the love of Christ will remain. That which remains of the precious stones will be worn as the garment for the wedding. Oh, Christian, there needs to be a burning out in our lives, and if it is not done here, it must be done there.

> Only one life, 'twill soon be past; Only what's done for Christ will last.

THE WEDDING SUPPER

The next event will be the wedding supper, which will take place after all things have been prepared, the table has been set, and the bride is ready and fit to take her place with her Lord at the table:

> And he saith unto me, Write, Blessed are they which are called unto the marriage supper of the Lamb. And he saith unto me, These are the true sayings of God (Rev. 19:9).

At this wedding supper we shall see the consummation of all our hopes and desires and all the hopes and desires of our Blessed Lord. As at any well-ordered wedding, every group will be represented. First of all, God will be the Host at the wedding. The Father will be there to smile His benediction upon the participants. There will also be the Son as the Groom who went through death to gain His precious bride. Next to Him will be the bride, who, though unworthy in herself, was made worthy by Him who gave His life for her. Finally, there will be the guests. One cannot have a wedding without guests. These are called in Scripture "the friends of the bridegroom" and consist of all the Old Testament saints who were raised at the first resurrection with the Church. They are not the bride; they are the guests, the *friends,* of the

Bridegroom. In the Song of Solomon they are called the "daughters of Jerusalem." John the Baptist was one of the Old Testament saints who died before the Cross, and he calls himself a friend of the bridegroom.

That is implied in the verse "Blessed are they which are called unto the marriage supper of the Lamb." These are not the bride, but they are guests who are invited to the marriage of the Groom and the bride. They are the Old Testament saints who will also be raised at the Rapture and be with Christ in the Kingdom Age of the Millennium. They are the ten wise virgins of which we read in Matthew 25.

When the bride is ready and the guests have assembled, the wedding of the Lamb will take place. The honeymoon of course, follows the wedding, and the record which follows immediately in Revelation 19:11 is the account of the coming again of the Lord Jesus *with* His bride to put down His enemies, to bind Satan, to destroy the Antichrist, to reassemble Israel to the land of Palestine, and then establish His kingdom on the earth and reign with His bride for a thousand blessed years. This glorious event we will study in the next chapter.

Before we close this message, however, let me make it intensely personal. I am thinking now of believers who have been saved by faith in the Lord Jesus but have never seen the truth of the judgment seat of Christ. There are many who appear to believe that because we are saved by grace we can live carelessly and "everything will be all right" when the Lord returns. Let me seriously warn you that God wants His people clean. The Lord Jesus will not tolerate a defiled bride, and you must either cleanse yourself or the Lord Himself will cleanse you at the judgment seat. Then your position in the Kingdom Age will be here and now through confession, repentance and prayer, determined on the basis of the rewards which you receive. God help us to heed the words of John when He says:

> Every man that hath this hope in him purifieth himself, even as he is pure.

I fear that when Jesus comes there will be many regrets on the part of those who refuse the cleansing of His Word *now*. The Bible speaks of those who will be ashamed at His appearing and others who will not receive a full reward. God help us to examine ourselves and make ourselves ready *now*!

CHAPTER TWENTY-EIGHT

The Second Coming of Christ

And I saw heaven opened, and behold a white horse; and he that sat upon him was called Faithful and True, and in righteousness he doth judge and make war. His eyes were as a flame of fire, and on his head were many crowns; and he had a name written, and no man knew, but he himself. And he was clothed with a vesture dipped in blood: and his name is called The Word of God. And the armies which were in heaven followed him upon white horses, clothed in fine linen, white and clean. And which out of his mouth goeth a sharp sword, that with it he should smite the nations: and he shall rule them with a rod of iron: and he treadeth the winepress of the fierceness and wrath of Almighty God. And he hath on his vesture and on his thigh a name written, king of kings, and lord of lords (Rev. 19:11-16).

In this brief but highly descriptive and clear passage we have the pointed account of the consummation of all the ages, the Second Coming of Jesus Christ in glory to set up His kingdom upon the earth. In this chapter we approach not only the climax of the entire book of Revelation, but the climax of the entire Bible as well. All the prophets looked forward to this event. When Jesus was here upon the earth, the disciples asked Him again and again concerning this event. It is the hope of Israel, the theme of all prophecy, the consummation of the ages, and the vindication of the humilation of His first coming.

The discussion of the Tribulation is concluded in

Revelation 19, the wedding of the Lamb has occurred, and the time has come for Christ to return to take the kingdoms of this world and to make them His own. This is the event for which believers have been praying for nineteen hundred years: "Thy kingdom come Thy will be done in earth, as it is in heaven." This is the event of which believers have sung throughout the centuries of the history of the Church as they lifted their voices in happy anticipation.

The great day has finally come and we read the thrilling account:

> And I saw heaven opened, and behold a white horse; and he that sat upon him was called Faithful and True, and in righteousness he doth judge and make war.

THE RAPTURE AND THE SECOND COMING

This coming of the Lord Jesus is not to be confused with His coming for the Church. Here He comes in awful judgment upon His enemies. There are two phases of the Second Coming of Christ. First He will come *for* His Church to take all believers out *before* the Tribulation. Then He will come again (about seven years later, corresponding to Daniel's seventieth week) at the end of the Tribulation with His Church to set up His kingdom upon the earth. The first event, called the Rapture is described in Revelation 4:1-3; we read in this passage, Revelation 19:11, of the second event. It is of the utmost importance that we differentiate clearly between these two events. There are two classes of passages in the Bible which concern the return of the Lord. Some speak of a secret coming as a thief in the night, whereas others speak of His coming as public, when every eye shall see Him. These two groups of passages can never be harmonized unless we distinguish between the two events, the *secret* Rapture before the

Tribulation and the *public* appearing at the close of the Tribulation.

The Old Testament prophet saw the glory of His public Second Coming only, and knew nothing about the secret coming in the Rapture. The truth concerning the Rapture is taught in the New Testament, and was unknown in the Old. The reason for this is evident when we remember that the Rapture concerns the Church, whereas the Second Coming is the time of Israel's deliverance. Hence in the Old Testament when there was no Church there was no mention of the Rapture (though it was foreshadowed in type and in figure), but when we study the New, we find many references to the blessed hope of His return *for* the Church *before* the awful day of the Lord.

The Vision of the Victorious Christ

The description in this nineteenth chapter of Revelation is one of the clearest pictures in the Bible of Christ in the majesty and glory of His Second Coming. We cannot mistake His identity. He is called Faithful and True. His eyes are as a flame of fire, revealing everything. He is clothed in a vesture dipped in blood, and His name is called "the word of God." Dreadful indeed will it be for those who have rejected Him and made light of His work on Calvary to meet Him as the all-powerful, irresistible Judge of all the earth.

It is significant that we have no picture in Scripture of the physical appearance of the Lord Jesus when He came to earth the first time to suffer and die. Though you search throughout the Bible, you will find no details concerning the appearance of Christ. Isaiah tells us that He was "marred more than any man." We are told that He was despised and rejected of men, a man of sorrows and acquainted with grief, but beyond the fact that He was a man of sorrows we know little. There is no hint in Scripture regarding the color of His hair, His stature, the color of His eyes or other details of His physical appearance. The portraits of the Lord Jesus and the pictures which appear in our Bible-story books and Bibles are merely the products of the artists' imagination and have no foundation in Scripture. The fact is that God has been pleased to keep from us all records of the appearance of Christ in His humiliation except the tragic description of the bloody sweat, the bruises and the nail-prints.

However, we are given complete details concerning His Second Coming. We have not one but many pictures of Christ in the glory of His coming again. Isaiah saw Him and describes Him as follows:

> Who is this that cometh from Edom, with dyed garments from Bozrah? this that is glorious in his apparel, travelling in the greatness of his strength? I that speak in righteousness, mighty to save. Wherefore art thou red in thine apparel, and thy garments like him that treadeth in the winefat? I have trodden the winepress alone; and of the people there was none with me: for I will tread them in mine anger, and trample them in my fury; and their blood shall be sprinkled upon my garments, and I will stain all my raiment. For the day of vengeance is in mine heart, and the year of my redeemed is come (Isa. 63:1-4).

John, in the first chapter of Revelation, pictures Him in this graphic manner:

> And in the midst of the seven candlesticks one like unto the Son of man, clothed with a garment down to the foot, and girt about the paps with a golden girdle. His head and his hairs were white like wool, as white as snow; and his eyes were as a flame of fire; and his feet like unto fine brass, as if they burned in a furnace; and his voice as the sound of many waters. And he had in his right hand seven stars: and out of his mouth went a sharp twoedged sword:

and his countenance was as the sun shineth in his strength
(Rev. 1:13-16).

THE INESCAPABLE BLOOD

Perhaps the most striking statement in this description of Christ in the glory of His Second Coming is
this: "He was clothed with a vesture dipped in blood."
His garments are bloody as He comes from heaven.
Men in all ages have tried to escape the blood of Christ
but a Christ without blood can be no Saviour. When He
came the first time He died in blood and agony. In the
garden His sweat was as it were great drops of blood
falling upon the earth. In the judgment hall the blood
flowed as the cruel scourger lashed His innocent back
with the cruel flail. When wicked men pushed the crown
of thorns upon His head the blood flowed down, and
when they pierced His hands and His feet his blood
flowed freely. Last of all, when after His death the
soldier plunged the spear into His side, there came
forth blood and water. That blood which flowed is the
cleansing blood in which He died but by which we live.
The poet expresses this thought effectively:

> His dying crimson like a robe
> Spreads o'er His body on the tree;
> Then I am dead to all the globe,
> And all the globe is dead to me.

That blood cannot be evaded. You may reject it,
ridicule it, tread it under foot and despise it, but that
blood remains the witness of God either for or against
you. If you by faith receive Him, that blood will cleanse
you from all sin and save you forever. If you reject that
blood now, you will have to face it later, for note well
the fact that when He comes again He will come clothed
in a vesture dipped in blood. Either you must accept
the blood of Christ or He will require your blood.

Isaiah tells us that when He comes again He will stain His raiment with the blood of His enemies. This may shock you, but it is the clear teaching of the Word of God. Jesus Christ is not a weakling. He is not only a tender and compassionate Saviour to all who believe on Him; He is also the righteous and eternal Judge of all those who reject. There is a teaching abroad in the world which robs Christ of one of His principle attributes: His justice. To be sure, He is love, but He is also justice, and while He deals in infinite mercy with those who believe on Him, He deals also in infinite justice and righteousness with those who turn their backs upon Him. For this reason Isaiah tells us in that chapter which speaks of His glorious Second Coming that He will wreak vengeance upon the wicked. Here is the record:

> Wherefore art thou red in thine apparel, and thy garments like him that treadeth in the winefat? I have trodden the winepress alone; and of the people there was none with me (a reference to His death on the Cross).

The tense changes from the past to the future and we read:

> For I will tread them in mine anger, and trample them in my fury; and their blood shall be sprinkled upon my garments, and I will stain all my raiment (Isa. 63:2-3).

The next verse tells us when He will do this:

> For the day of vengeance is in mine heart, and the year of my redeemed is come.

THE ARMIES OF HEAVEN

When the King comes at the end of the Tribulation Period He will not come alone: He will be attended by the redeemed company of resurrected and redeemed saints as well as the hosts of angels who constantly attend Him. John declares:

> And the armies which were in heaven followed him upon white horses, clothed in fine linen, white and clean (Rev. 19:14).

We know that these armies are the members of the bride of Christ, the purified Church which was caught up in the Rapture. They are said to be clothed in fine linen, white and clean, and we have already seen that this is the wedding garment of the Lamb's wife, the glorified purified Church (Rev. 19:8).

ARMAGEDDON

The next event will be Armageddon, the last great battle of the ages. The kings of the earth are gathered about the city of Jerusalem, ready to make the last great effort to destroy God's earthly people, and it seems as though their end has come when suddenly the heavens open and the King comes forth. So great is the slaughter of the enemies of the Lord that it is described in the following graphic account:

> And I saw an angel standing in the sun; and he cried with a loud voice, saying to all the fowls that fly in the midst of heaven, Come and gather yourselves together unto the supper of the great God; that ye may eat the flesh of kings, and the flesh of captains, and the flesh of mighty men, and the flesh of horses, and of them that sit on them, and the flesh of all men, both free and bond, both small and great. And I saw the beast, and the kings of the earth, and their armies, gathered together to make war against him that sat on the horse, and against his army (Rev. 19:17-19).

So great will be the slaughter of that day that the Bible tells us seven months will be required to clear the battlefield and bury the dead. Yes, my friend, awful days are coming. There is no need to dodge the facts. Not only does the Word of God clearly predict these events, but history and current events unite in their testimony that we are rapidly approaching the end of the age, the judgment of God and the day of final reckoning.

AN ALARMIST

I hear someone say, "That preacher is an alarmist; I won't listen to him." I plead guilty to the charge of being an alarmist. That is precisely what I am trying to do: I am attempting to "sound an alarm." I would be the most despicable man in the world if I did not sound an alarm. God has ordered me to do it and said, "When I say unto the wicked, O wicked man, shalt surely die; if thou dost not speak to warn the wicked . . . that wicked man shall die in his iniquity; but his blood will I require at thine hand."

The recent war should teach us lessons. If a watchman on guard saw a squadron of enemy bombers, would you call him an alarmist if he sounded the sirens? What would you think of him if he said, "All the people are peacefully sleeping. I won't awaken them. They might be alarmed." Suppose that I walked past your house while you were asleep and I saw a fire in your basement, would you call me an alarmist if I ran with all my might to rap at your door and batter it down to warn you of your danger? If I saw a car heading down the road toward a precipice while I rocked on my front porch, what would you think of me if, fully aware of the danger, I did not try to stop it? What would you think of me as a preacher who believes the Bible's emphatic declaration that you are a sinner plunging into a hopeless eternity, if I did not lift up my voice and cry, "Flee from the wrath to come!" I believe

God's Book. I believe that men are lost and on the way to an eternal hell without Christ. I believe that only faith in Jesus Christ can save these men and women. And I believe that God commissioned me as a spiritual air-raid warden to sound the alarm. Yes, I am an alarmist. If there had been more alarmists in Europe, conditions would perhaps be different today. If we here in our beloved land had given more heed to the alarms sounded by our leaders months before the war and even after the war, perhaps the deadly complacency of the American people would have been shaken and the unpreparedness and subsequent loss of thousands of lives prevented. If the alarm had been sounded before Pearl Harbor, catastrophe would perhaps have been averted.

WE PREACH BECAUSE WE MUST

Christian, have you caught the vision? Do you believe that there is a judgment coming? Do you believe that the men and women around you are lost in sin and that they cannot be saved without the Gospel? Do you believe that? If so, what are you doing about it? Are *you* sounding the alarm? Are *you* helping those who are sounding the alarm? The guardians of our country and those who are entrusted with the responsibility of looking out for the enemy and to warn of impending danger must be given the equipment and support they need. Are you, as a Christian, supporting those who seek to warn sinners of their doom? Do you pray for them? How long could we sound the alarm if everyone was as interested as you are and did what you are doing to guarantee that the alarm will not be silenced? God help you to awaken to the danger and get busy for Him!

CHAPTER TWENTY-NINE

The Binding of Satan

And I saw the beast, and the kings of the earth, and their armies, gathered together to make war against him that sat on the horse, and against his army. And the beast was taken, and with him the false prophet that wrought miracles before him, with which he deceived them that had received the mark of the beast, and them that worshipped his image. These both were cast alive into a lake of fire burning with brimstone. And the remnant were slain with the sword of him that sat upon the horse, which sword proceeded out of his mouth: and all the fowls were filled with their flesh. And I saw an angel come down from heaven, having the key of the bottomless pit and a great chain in his hand. And he laid hold on the dragon, that old serpent, which is the Devil, and Satan, and bound him a thousand years, and cast him into the bottomless pit, and shut him up, and set a seal upon him, that he should deceive the nations no more, till the thousand years should be fulfilled: and after that he must be loosed a little season (Rev. 19:19— Rev. 20:3).

Scripture says that Satan is the "god of this age" and the prince of the power of the air, but there is a time coming when Satan shall be cast into the bottomless pit for a thousand years, and then, after being loosed for a little season, he will be cast forever into the lake of fire with his followers. In our studies in Revelation we have considered the general outline of the course of events. At the close of this age the true Church will be caught out of the earth. Then will

follow a period of seven years during which Satan will
be permitted to hurl all his fury against God and His
people. This will end in Armageddon and the return
of the Lord in glory. The first act of judgment at the
return of the Lord Jesus will be against the two beasts
of Revelation, the beast out of the sea and the beast
out of the land.

The First Occupants of Hell

In Revelation 19 we read of the establishment of
Christ's millennial reign upon the earth, but it is necessary first of all that He take care of His enemies who
have opposed His program up to this time. You will
recall that Satan has two chief representatives during
the Tribulation Period, described in detail in Revelation
13. These are called the beast out of the sea and the
beast out of the earth. The first is the political dictator
of the end-time, the despot who will manage to gather
all nations into one mighty international bloc to destroy
God's people, Israel, and establish a mock millennium
and a false kingdom. Associated with him is the false
prophet, the Antichrist, the head of the religious federation of that day. When Christ returns, these two
men—for they are men—will be cast into the lake of
fire and brimstone. This is the Biblical description
of hell. Until the events spoken of in the nineteenth
chapter of Revelation, hell will be empty; it will have
not even one occupant. These two, "the beast and the
false prophet," therefore, are the first two individuals
to be cast into this horrible place.

Hell and Hades

It is unfortunate that in our King James Version the
words "hell" and "hades" have been confused. The
word "hell" never occurs in the original of the Old

Testament. The word translated thus is *sheol* in the Hebrew. It is the equivalent of *hades* in the Greek. This place, hades, was the abode of the souls of all men and women who died before the Cross. When Old Testament men died, their bodies, of course, returned to the earth, but their souls went into hades in the lower parts of the earth. This place is clearly and graphically described by Jesus in the historical narrative of the rich man and Lazarus. When Jesus died upon the Cross, He descended into hades and brought forth all the spirits of the saved and took them to heaven, while the souls of all the lost were left in hades until the last judgment of the Great White Throne, which we will discuss in one of our messages when we study the twentieth chapter of Revelation. At this judgment the wicked, who have been kept in hades, will be cast finally into the lake of fire.

The lake of fire, also called ''hell,''is quite different from hades. We do not know when it was created. It is not mentioned in the account of the creation of the heavens and the earth, of which we read in Genesis 1, but we are distinctly told that it was specially prepared for the devil and his angels Remember these facts. There is a place called ''sheol'' or ''hades,'' usually translated —or, rather, mistranslated—''hell,'' where the souls of the wicked are today. It is described in Ephesians 4 as being in the lower parts of the earth (Eph. 4:9). (For a full discussion of hell and hades see the author's booklet entitled *The Gates of Hades*.) We shall deal with this subject more fully when we reach the discussion of the judgment of the Great White Throne.

THE LAKE OF FIRE

The lake of fire, as we said, was a place prepared for the devil and his angels. It is empty now, and is without occupants, but at the close of the Tribulation, just before

252 Studies in Revelation

the Millennium, two persons will be cast alive into this place: the last great world-dictator and the Antichrist. This place is not, as many would teach, a place of annihilation, but a place of eternal torment. The words of Scripture are unmistakable. Read them carefully:

> And the beast was taken, and with him the false prophet that wrought miracles before him, with which he deceived them that had received the mark of the beast, and them that worshipped his image. These both were cast alive into a lake of fire burning with brimstone.

In the next chapter we are told that after a thousand years these two men are still alive in the lake of fire. After a thousand years they have not yet been annihilated, for when the devil is cast into the same place with them at the end of the Millennium we read:

> And the devil that deceived them was cast into the lake of fire and brimstone, where the beast and the false prophet are, and shall be tormented day and night for ever and ever (Rev. 20:10).

THE FATE OF THE WICKED

Immediately after the beast and the false prophet have been cast into the lake of fire their wicked followers are slain and cast into hades. These will, together with the remainder of the wicked, be cast into the lake of fire *after* the millennial reign of Christ. The same is true of Satan, who will not be cast into the lake of fire until *after* the Millennium. During the Millennium he will be kept in the bottomless pit.

The twentieth chapter of Revelation opens with the account of the binding of Satan at the beginning of the kingdom reign. John sees an angel come down from heaven with the key of the bottomless pit and a great chain in his hand. In this connection another place is mentioned: the bottomless pit, the temporary abode of Satan while he is bound for a thousand years. Whether this bottomless pit and hades are the same is not clear, but it is the prison house of Satan during the reign of Christ upon the earth. Scoffers have ridiculed the idea that a spirit could be chained with a great iron chain, but the Bible does not say that it was an *iron* chain. There are other chains besides those of iron. Jude tells us that the angels which kept not their first estate are kept in *chains* of everlasting darkness.

The idea is that Satan is restrained, isolated and prevented from deceiving the nations. The devil's business today is to deceive the nations. He would have them believe that man can make the world better without Christ. Satan deceives the nations into believing that the world's problems can be solved by war, and when that has failed, he cleverly convinces them that the world can be saved by education, reformation, religion and conferences. However, when Christ comes, Satan will be cast into the bottomless pit where he can practice his deception no longer.

After a thousand years he will be loosed for a short time. He will immediately gather all the wicked of the earth and once more attempt to defeat God and Christ; but he will be taken with his wicked followers and cast finally and permanently into the lake of fire. The record is plain in Revelation 20:7-10:

> And when the thousand years are expired, Satan shall be loosed out of his prison, and shall go out to deceive the nations which are in the four quarters of the earth, Gog and Magog, to gather them together to battle: the number of whom is as the sand of the sea. And they went up on the breadth of the earth and compassed the camp of the saints about, and the beloved city: and fire came down from God out of heaven, and devoured them. And the devil

that deceived them was cast into the lake of fire and brimstone, where the beast and the false prophet are, and shall
be tormented day and night for ever and ever.

THE MILLENNIUM

You have probably noticed in this chapter the oft-
recurring expression "a thousand years." Six times
it is used to describe the reign of Christ on the earth
after the Tribulation. We are told that Satan was
bound for a thousand years, that he would not deceive
the nations until the thousand years were past and we
are told also that the saints of God lived and reigned
with Christ a thousand years. We are informed, furthermore, that the rest of the dead lived not again till the
thousand years were finished, that the saints lived and
reigned with Christ a thousand years, and then, finally,
we learn that Satan will be loosed again after a thousand
years.

It seems strange that there could be a person with
an open Bible who would deny the teaching of the
Millennium. It is a result of that cancerous curse of
Bible teaching which we call "spiritualizing Scriptures."
No less than six times in one chapter the Lord tells
us of the coming Millennium, and yet men deny the
truth and say that a thousand years does not mean a
thousand years.

Some argue that the word "millennium" never occurs
in the Bible. To this assertion we reply that it occurs
six times in Revelation 20 alone. The word "millennium"
is the Latin term meaning "a thousand years." It is
derived from two words: *mille,* meaning "thousand,"
and *annum,* meaning "year." It is, therefore, simply
the Latin word meaning "a thousand years."

WHY MUST SATAN BE LOOSED AGAIN

A question which arises naturally in this connection is: Why must Satan be loosed for a little season after the Millennium? We believe that there are two reasons: to prove the incorrigibility of Satan himself and, second, to show the absolute justice of God in casting the wicked into the lake of fire forever. For a thousand years the devil will be bound, and therefore during that time men will be free from his wicked influence. Moreover, during those thousand years Christ will reign in person on the earth. However, at the end of that thousand years there will be a great multitude of men who have given only lip service to the King, whose hearts had never been changed, and, who as a result, are ready to follow Satan the moment he is loosed. Remember that during the Millennium the population of the world will increase tremendously. Death and sickness will be uncommon. People will live a thousand years. Countless children will be born during this time when men will have to obey the command of God, "Be fruitful, and multiply, and replenish the earth." But all these children will have to be born again just as they do today.

Everyone who lives during the Millennium will have to do homage to the King, Christ Jesus, even those who are not saved. Failure to do so will result in sudden death. Open rebellion will be summarily punished by death. In that age truly every knee shall bow to Him, but all will not be saved. This becomes immediately apparent from the fact that when Satan is loosed out of his prison, he will instantly find a tremendous host ready to follow him and forsake the Christ. Consider carefully the brief record as John gives it:

And when the thousand years are expired, Satan shall be
loosed out of his prison. And shall go out to deceive the
nations which are in the four quarters of the earth, Gog
and Magog, to gather them together to battle: the number
of whom is as the sand of the sea. And they went up on
the breadth of the earth, and compassed the camp of the
saints about, and the beloved city: and fire came down
from God out of heaven, and devoured them (Rev. 20:7-9).

God is going to prove that the human heart is corrupt
beyond help and only through personal faith in Jesus
Christ can men be saved. He is going to let man prove
that "the heart is deceitful above all things, and desperately wicked." That is why God gives us the revelation
that the unregenerate heart has not improved even after
a thousand years of blessing and prosperity.

What Is the Lesson

Jesus said, "Except a man be born again, he cannot
see the kingdom of God." The devil tries to tell us that
we need merely better our environment, improve the
physical quality of the race by eliminating the weak
and mentally unfit, and promote education, reformation
and better social understanding, and consequently man
will become better and better until we have a world of
perfect peace and perfect people. God is going to prove
twice that this is the devil's lie. He proved it once in
the Garden of Eden. He placed two people in a beautiful garden with perfect heredity and environment.
By heredity they had been created in the image of God.
They were pure. They had no inherited taint of sin.
Their hearts were not corrupt. God placed them in a
perfect environment. There were no evil associates to
influence them; they were not beset by the corruptions
and evils which menace us today. Yet these two, although their environment and heredity were perfect,

fell. They sinned, broke with God and rebelled against Him.

At the end of human history God will once more prove man's need of Him, for after one thousand years of ideal environment, in which he basked in the indescribable blessing of the beneficient King of kings, the unregenerate man will remain the same, and when the opportunity comes, he will be ready to rise up against God and defy his Benefactor and Creator.

This will prove the need of the injunction "Ye must be born again" and also vindicate God in His rightousness when He condemns those who have spurned His love and salvation. Look away from self and man! "believe on the Lord Jesus Christ, and thou shalt be saved!"

CHAPTER THIRTY

The Two Resurrections

Marvel not at this: for the hour is coming, in the which all that are in the graves shall hear his voice, and shall come forth; they that have done good, unto the resurrection of life; and they that have done evil, unto the resurrection of damnation (John 5:28-29).

While He was here on earth the Lord Jesus taught that all men who die will be raised again at some future time. His words are unmistakably clear: "*All* that are in the graves . . . shall come forth." Belief in the resurrection and life after death has characterized all men from the earliest dawn of history and is taught consistently from Genesis to Revelation. All Christians believe, therefore, in a bodily resurrection, not only of the Lord Jesus Christ, "the firstfruits" of the resurrection, but also of all those who have died from the time of the first man, Adam, until the present. But all Christians do not believe alike concerning the nature and the order of this resurrection. Tradition, false doctrine and failure to study the Scriptures carefully have resulted not only in untold confusion on the subject of life after death but have led also to serious error and resultant loss of joy and victory.

THE COMMON BELIEF

Most Christians have been taught to believe in a "general" resurrection, a resurrection of all men at the

258

end of the world. They believe that at the end of the world Christ will return to sit on the throne of judgment, and all the dead will arise. The saved will go into glory at that time and the wicked will be turned into hell. Such people believe that at that time all our works will be brought forth, the books will be opened, and amid the rending of rocks and the thunders of God's wrath, all men, saved and lost, will stand before God and hear the final verdict which will determine their eternal destiny and abode. Is it strange, then, that people who believe this wholly erroneous doctrine, without a shred of support in Scriptures, should be afraid of the coming again of Jesus Christ? Is it strange that the blessed hope means nothing to them?

THE PREMILLENNIAL VIEW

However, the Bible and the Lord Jesus teach a view entirely different from this. According to Jesus and all New Testament apostles, there will be two distinct resurrections separated by at least a thousand years during which Jesus will reign upon the earth and set up His millennial kingdom. The saved of both the Old and the New Testament, before and after the Cross, will be raised from the dead *before* this blessed Kingdom Age, whereas the lost of all ages will not be resurrected until after "the thousand years are ended." The resurrection of the saved at Jesus' coming *before* the Millennium is called "the first resurrection." The raising of the lost at the close of the Millennium is called "the second death." In the following messages we shall study the Scripture passages which give the details of these two sharply-differentiated events, the first and the second resurrections. In the passages quoted at the beginning of this message Jesus mentions these two groups:

> All that are in the graves shall hear his voice, and shall
> come forth; they that have done good, unto the resurrection
> of life; and they that have done evil, unto the resurrection
> of damnation (John 5:28-29).

Here Jesus distinguishes between the two resurrections and calls the first a "resurrection of life" and the
second a "resurrection of damnation." If there were
but a single event when all the dead would be raised
at one and the same time, there would have been no
reason to mention two separate resurrections. Jesus
was never ambiguous in His teaching, and here He
merely mentions the fact that there are two resurrections, without mentioning the time which elapses between
them.

In Luke 14:14 our Lord makes mention of the *first*
resurrection without referring to the second when He
says concerning the faithful ones:

> And thou shalt be blessed; for they cannot recompense
> thee: for thou shalt be recompensed at the resurrection of
> the just.

Paul's Testimony

In perfect harmony with the teaching of the Lord
Jesus is the teaching of the Apostle Paul. In First
Thessalonians 4:16 He declares:

> For the Lord himself shall descend from heaven with a
> shout, with the voice of the archangel, and with the trump
> of God: and the dead in Christ shall rise first.

The dead in Christ shall rise first, which of course,
implies that the dead out of Christ will be raised last,
for the term "first" implies a "last." Again in this
passage there is no hint given regarding the length of
time which will elapse between the "first" and "last,"
but we are given a mere statement of the fact that there

is a difference in time between the two. This first resurrection is called in the Bible a resurrection "out from among," implying that there are some which will not come forth, but only some are raised "out from among the others."

Unfortunately, the translators of the King James Version of the Scriptures have not transferred this translation correctly from the Greek. The Greek word for resurrection is "anastasis." Whenever reference is made to the resurrection of Jesus or the resurrection of the saved, the expression *ek ton nekron* is usually employed. *Anastasis* means "resurrection." *Ek* means "out from," and *nekron* means "dead." Thus, whenever this expression is used (and it is never used with reference to the wicked dead), it should have been translated "out from among the dead," meaning that some remained dead and were not raised.

THE TIME OF THE FIRST RESURRECTION

The first resurrection will occur at the coming again of the Lord Jesus Christ when He descends upon the clouds of heaven, and all the saints' bodies which have been sleeping in the grave will be raised and joined to their redeemed souls, which have been in the presence of the Lord, conscious and happy and awaiting the time of the resurrection of the body. This is taught in First Thessalonians:

> For this we say unto you by the word of the Lord, that we which are alive and remain unto the coming of the Lord, shall not prevent them which are asleep. For the Lord himself shall descend from heaven with a shout, with the voice of the archangel, and with the trump of God: and the dead in Christ shall rise first: then we which are alive and remain shall be caught up together with them in the clouds, to meet the Lord in the air: and so shall we ever be with the Lord (I Thess. 4:15-17).

BEFORE THE MILLENNIUM

This resurrection of the saints will occur *before* the Millennium. The remainder of the dead will remain in their graves for another thousand years. At the close of the Bible, in Revelation 20, this truth is clearly and indisputably taught:

> And I saw thrones, and they sat upon them, and judgment was given unto them: and I saw the souls of them that were beheaded for the witness of Jesus, and for the word of God, and which had not worshipped the beast, neither his image, neither had received his mark upon their foreheads, or in their hands; and they lived and reigned with Christ a thousand years. But the rest of the dead lived not again until the thousand years were finished. This is the first resurrection.
>
> Blessed and holy is he that hath part in the first resurrection, on such the second death hath no power (Rev. 20:4-6).

This *first* resurrection at the return of the Lord Jesus Christ before the Tribulation is called in the word "that blessed hope." Our hope is not the setting up of a kingdom of peace by man's efforts, and our comfort when we bid our loved ones farewell is not that they are now in heaven while their bodies crumble in the dust. We are not comforted by the fact that our loved ones are "absent from the body, and . . . present with the Lord." Our comfort is not this, that while their bodies are decaying in the dust they are disembodied spirits, but this is our blessed hope: Jesus Christ is coming again to raise those bodies of our loved ones and unite them with their redeemed spirits. We shall meet them again, not as ghosts and spirits, but as human beings with bodies redeemed and glorified. We will meet never to part again, but to enjoy forever and forever the fellowship of our Lord and the fellowship of those who were so dear to us here below.

This is the hope of all who have a part in the first resurrection.

A TIME OF REUNION

This glorious and imminent event will be the greatest reunion the world has seen or known. Not only will we meet Him, the One who died for us, but we will be reunited, never to part again, with our loved ones who have died in the faith. The question is often asked: "Will we know our loved ones in heaven?" When we consider the clear statements in Scripture, we wonder how people can ask the question. The Bible tells us plainly that our bodies will be conformed to the body of the Lord Jesus. After His resurrection He was recognized by His disciples. Although at first they did not recognize Him, we are plainly told the reason: their eyes were "holden." The three disciples, Peter, James and John, immediately recognized Moses and Elijah on the Mount of Transfiguration, although they had never seen the Old Testament prophets. They recognized them by their individual characteristics. Recall the experience of Abraham in hades as recorded in the Gospel of Luke. The rich man in torment pleaded that Abraham send someone from the dead to warn his five brothers lest they, too, should come into the place of torment. What was Abraham's answer?

> They have Moses and the prophets; let them hear them (Luke 16:29).

How did Abraham know about Moses and the prophets? Abraham died hundreds of years before Moses. He had probably met him. Yes, my friend, there is con-

sciousness after death. The soul does not slumber; only
the body sleeps.

ABRAHAM, ISAAC AND JACOB

Our Lord Jesus, on the occasion of the healing of the
centurion's servant, described in Matthew 8, spoke these
words:

> Many shall come from the east and west, and shall sit
> down with Abraham, and Isaac, and Jacob, in the kingdom
> of heaven (Matt. 8:11).

This promise would be valueless if the inhabitants of
heaven were not recognizable. At the first resurrection,
therefore, there will first of all be a great and glorious
meeting and reunion of all God's people. Even before
we rise to meet the Lord in the air we will be given time
to meet and to greet our loved ones who have gone on
before. Our Lord does not forget that we are human,
and we will still be human when we get to heaven. He
knows the human ties which bound us here and sympa-
thizes with us when those tender ties are broken. Consequently, when He comes, He will heal the wounds
that were caused by the separation of death, and will
permit us to greet our loved ones first of all. There can
be no mistaking this teaching of the Word. Referring
again to First Thessalonians 4, we read:

> The dead in Christ shall rise first: then we which are
> alive and remain shall be caught up together with them
> in the clouds, to meet the Lord in the air (I Thess. 4:16-17).

Notice carefully these words: "Then we which are
alive and remain shall be *caught up together with them,*"
that is, with the dead who were raised first. We will be
caught up *together*. In other words, we will be reunited,

brought together, before we rise to meet Him in the air. That is why we speak of our anticipation as "the blessed hope." We will experience the thrill of thrills when we together meet Him—meet our Lord, our Beloved, our Saviour, the man who died on the Cross for us. The first glimpse of Him will repay us for all the suffering which came to us during our lives.

THIS COMING IS IMMINENT

We believe that this event, the coming of the Lord, the first resurrection and the Rapture of the Church, is imminent. By "imminent" we mean that it *may* occur at any time. We do not prophesy the day or the hour. We do not set dates but look for our Saviour every day. One of these days He is coming back again. He said He would, and we are already nineteen hundred years nearer that day than when He promised that He would return. Yes, one of these days the heavens will open, the Lord will descend, the dead in Christ will be raised, the living believers will be changed in a moment, and we will leave this old world of sin, turmoil and suffering in redeemed, immortal, incorruptible, sinless bodies to meet Him. I shall see my mother again, and know her. I shall greet my godly father, my brother and my sister, all of whom are now with the Lord anxiously waiting for that great day when our family will again be reunited.

GLORY FOR HIM

Not only will it be a glad day for us, but what a day it will be for Him who made this possible! What joy it will bring to the heart of the One who hung on the Cross and bled and died to make this glad day the culmination of the joy for which He came into the world.

My friend, are *you* ready? He who said He would come will come. Men may scoff and mock at the coming of the Lord, but He will come, and then there will be joy unspeakable for the believer, but only judgment and damnation for those who have rejected the glad offer of salvation. Will *you* receive Him today?

CHAPTER THIRTY-ONE

The Two Resurrections

For as in Adam all die, so in Christ shall all be made alive. But every man in his own order: Christ the firstfruits; afterward they that are Christ's at his coming. Then cometh the end, when he shall have delivered up the kingdom to God, even the Father; when he shall have put down all rule and all authority and power. For he must reign, til he hath put all enemies under his feet (I Cor. 15:22-25).

The Bible teaches that there will be two resurrections of the bodies of those who have died, and whose bodies now sleep in the graves while they await the time of their resurrection. The first resurrection includes all believers of both the Old and the New Testaments who have died in the faith. The last resurrection will not occur until a thousand years afterward at the end of time and at the beginning of eternity. This last resurrection will include all the lost—and only the lost—who have died without Christ. The destiny of those who have part in the first resurrection will be to reign with Christ in His kingdom for one thousand years and after that to spend eternity with Him in the new heavens and the new earth. The destiny of the lost who are to be raised *after* the Kingdom Age is the lake of fire and separation from the presence of God forever. In our previous message we merely pointed out the Scripture teaching concerning these two resurrections, and in this message we will study only the *first* resurrection and the saints of God at the coming again of the Lord Jesus Christ.

The Time

The first resurrection will occur at the return of the Lord Jesus according to His promise at the close of this dispensation and before the day of the Lord, the Tribulation. The Bible says concerning this:

> Blessed and holy is he that hath part in the first resurrection: on such the second death hath no power (Rev. 20:6).

The first resurrection of believers consists of at least three distinct companies as concerning the time of their resurrection. The first stage of the first resurrection, having occurred nineteen hundred years ago is history. The second stage of this blessed event lies in the near future and the last stage will occur approximately seven years after the second.

Israel's Feast of Firstfruits

In the ritual of Israel there were at least seven annual feasts which were prophetic of the work of the coming Redeemer. These feasts were in this order:

1. The Passover (the death of Christ)
2. The Feast of Unleavened Bread (the burial of Christ)
3. Feast of Firstfruits (the resurrection of Christ) Christ)
4. Pentecost (the coming of the Spirit)
5. The Feast of Trumpets (the second coming of Christ)
6. The Atonement (the Tribulation Period)
7. The Feast of Tabernacles (the Millennial Age)

These seven feasts are a prophetic picture of the entire plan of God from the first coming of Christ as the Passover Lamb until His second coming again as the full Redeemer and Rest-Giver of His people. The Feast of Firstfruits was the third in order of these yearly feasts and was a day of solemn consecration. This feast, which occurred at the beginning of the harvest season, had three parts: the firstfruits, the harvest proper, and the gleaning. These three constituted the full harvest. When the first ears of corn were ripe, the Israelite gathered a handful of ears from this coming crop and took it to the priest, who presented it before the Lord, and waved it before Jehovah in the Tabernacle as a promise that the entire harvest would be dedicated to the Lord. The firstfruits were an earnest of the coming harvest and a promise that all would be dedicated to God.

A Handful of Ears

Note carefully that not the word "firstfruit" (singular) but "firstfruits" (plural) is used. The firstfruits consisted not of one ear but a handful of several ears. These were presented to the Lord and then followed the full harvest when the reapers gathered the wheat into sheaves, the fulfillment of the promise of the firstfruits. However, there still remained the gleanings to be gathered, and so the gleaners followed the reapers and gathered the ears which had been left and trodden under the feet of men, and when these gleanings had been gathered with the harvest, the reaping time was done. With the firstfruits and the main harvest they constituted and completed the full harvest.

So Also Christ

In the first resurrection, which was a fulfillment of the type of the Feast of Firstfruits, we find these three stages or parts of the resurrection. The first resurrection covers a period of centuries and has these three divisions. To this Paul refers in the following Scripture passage:

> For as in Adam all die, even so in Christ shall all be made alive (I Cor. 15:22).

The apostle is speaking of the *first* resurrection and is *not* referring to the lost. The entire fifteenth chapter of First Corinthians concerns the resurrection of believers, and there is no reference in this chapter to the resurrection of the lost. Everything which Paul discusses has reference to the raising of believers at Christ's coming. He is, therefore, telling us that all who are *in* Christ shall be made alive. Then he gives the order or arrangement in time of this event and declares:

> But every man in his own order.

The word translated order is *tagma* and the Greek dictionary tells us that it means literally a "troop" or a "company," so that the verse can be rendered "each in his own company." He tells us also that there will be three of these "troops" or companies in the resurrection of the saints. He is definite in his description of these three orders:

> Christ the firstfruits.

The first troop is the troop of the firstfruits, and Christ is called "the firstfruits." As we have observed, the word "firstfruits" is plural reminding us that a handful of ears, not merely one ear, was presented. Similarly, when Jesus arose He did not arise alone, but with Him came forth from the graves a handful, a company, a troop of others who had been sleeping in the graves. When Jesus ascended into heaven to present the blood upon the mercy seat after His resurrection, He led with Him a troop of resurrected believers of the Old Testament who are in heaven today in resurrection bodies as the promise and earnest, the guarantee and the assurance that the remainder of the saints of God will also be raised when the harvest at Jesus' coming occurs.

MATTHEW 27

We have a clear description of this "troop" of the firstfruits given us in Matthew 27, beginning at verse 50. Here we read:

> Jesus, when he had cried again with a loud voice, yielded up the ghost. And, behold, the veil of the temple was rent in twain from the top to the bottom; and the earth did quake, and the rocks rent; and the graves were opened; and many bodies of the saints which slept arose, and came out of their graves after his resurrection, and went into the holy city, and appeared unto many (Matt. 27:50-53).

First the veil was rent, signifying that the blood had been shed for the last and final time, and now the veil which forbade the sinner to approach God was taken away and there was nothing to prevent man from coming directly, by way of the altar, into the very presence of God. The price had been paid and nothing remained to separate man from God. Before Jesus' body, which is the veil, was broken, there could be no approach to God, for the veil of the temple was only a shadow and a type of the body of Christ. For this reason no one could go into the presence of God *until* Christ's blood had been shed. But when that was accomplished, the way was opened. Then there was an earthquake and as a result the rocks rent, the graves split open and the bodies of many saints arose after His resurrection. Christ, and

these were the firstfruits. Until Christ arose this could
not happen, for He is the "firstborn from the dead"
(Col. 1:18).

That occurred nineteen hundred years ago. The first
troop is already in heaven as the promise of the coming
harvest when all the saints shall be raised.

THE SECOND TROOP

The second group of the first resurrection will follow,
according to Scripture, at Jesus' coming, and so Paul
says, "Christ the firstfruits; *afterward* they that are
Christ's at his coming." This event will occur just before
the Rapture of the Church. One of these days the One
who said, "I will come again, and receive you unto
myself," will shout from the air and the dead in Christ
shall arise. This is the unfailing testimony of the Word.
Paul says in this same chapter (I Cor. 15:51-52):

> Behold, I shew you a mystery; We shall not all sleep, but
> we shall all be changed, in a moment, in the twinkling of
> an eye, at the last trump: for the trumpet shall sound, and
> the dead shall be raised incorruptible, and we shall be
> changed.

In I Thessalonians 4:16 we read:

> For the Lord himself shall descend from heaven with a
> shout, with the voice of the archangel, and with the trump
> of God: and the dead in Christ shall rise first.

Philippians tells us:

> For our conversation is in heaven; from whence also we
> look for the Saviour, the Lord Jesus Christ: who shall change
> our vile body, that it may be fashioned like unto his glorious
> body, according to the working whereby he is able even to
> subdue all things unto himself (Phil. 3:20-21).

THEN THE END

At this point the firstfruit troop are joined by the harvest group at Jesus' coming, but before the first resurrection is complete the gleaning must be brought in. The Rapture of the Church will precede the Tribulation Period. During this period 144,000 of the twelve tribes of Israel will be saved and become Christ's missionaries, and as a result of their preaching, a great multitude of every tribe, tongue and nation will believe and be saved, but be martyred for their faith because they would not receive the mark of the beast in their foreheads and hands. These saved ones of the Tribulation Period will be raised at the end of the Tribulation and just before the coming again of the Lord to the earth to set up His millennial kingdom. They are the gleanings *after* the harvest. First Christ will come for His Church. Then the Tribulation will occur, followed by His second coming to the earth, but before He comes, the martyred Tribulation saints, the gleanings, must first be added to the harvest.

REVELATION 20

Again Scripture leaves no room for doubt. In Revelation 20 we read:

> And I saw thrones, and they sat upon them, and judgment was given unto them: and I saw the souls of them that were beheaded for the witness of Jesus, and for the word of God, and which had not worshipped the beast, neither his image, neither had received his mark upon their foreheads, or in their hands; and they lived and reigned with Christ a thousand years. But the rest of the dead lived not again until the thousand years were finished. This is the first resurrection (Rev. 20:4-5).

In this reference the expression "first resurrection" occurs in the Bible for the first time. It is not mentioned

before because the first resurrection is not complete
until these gleanings, these Tribulation martyrs, have
also been raised and added to the firstfruits to complete
the harvest, the first resurrection. John speaks thus of
this completed harvest: "This is the *first resurrection*."

> Blessed and holy is he that hath part in the first resurrec-
> tion: on such the second death hath no power, but they shall
> be priests of God and of Christ, and shall reign with him
> a thousand years (Rev. 20:6).

Are you blessed and holy, and will you have a part
in that glorious resurrection of the just? Or will you
have to wait until the judgment of the Great White
Throne and then be cast into outer darkness forever?
Jesus Christ is coming again, and when He comes, all
the saints shall be caught away in the clouds and then
there will break forth upon the earth a time of war,
suffering and death such as history has never known.
God says that it will be a time such as never was nor
ever shall be again, but when that time comes, all believers will be safe with the Lord Jesus Christ. Receive
Him today, before it is too late!

CHAPTER THIRTY-TWO

The Great White Throne Judgement

In previous messages we have spent considerable time discussing the two resurrections. We have given special attention to this subject because of the prevailing ignorance and misunderstanding concerning this important and clearly-taught doctrine of Scripture. In spite of the clearness of the revelation of the Bible it is strange indeed that the great mass of Christendom still believes in the totally unscriptural doctrine of a general resurrection at the end of time, when the saved and the unsaved will appear before the Great White Throne, and then, finally, discover their eternal destiny.

No wonder that the coming of the Lord is viewed as a terrifying and unwelcome event! However, once the believer sees the biblical picture of a resurrection of the saved at the Rapture, and the resurrection of the lost one thousand years later, all his fear disappears. John declares in Revelation 20 that the saved are raised before the thousand-year reign of Christ for--

> they lived and reigned with Christ a thousand years. But the rest of the dead lived not again until the thousand years were finished.

Surely, the Lord could not have stated this truth more plainly. It is presented so clearly that even a child can understand it, and yet so subtly has Satan blinded men's eyes that they cannot see it.

The Second Death

Someone has said, "They that are born but once will have to die twice, and they who have been born twice will die but once." This statement is entirely true, if we "except" those believers who will be alive at the coming of the Lord Jesus. These believers, of course, will never die, for the Lord Jesus Himself said:

> I am the resurrection and the life: he that believeth in me, though he were dead, yet shall he live: and whosoever liveth and believeth in me shall never die (John 11:25-26).

With this exception it is true that all who have been born of Adam's seed will die twice: once in physical death, and the second time, in the lake of fire. If, however, you have been born twice, once naturally and again spiritually, there will be no eternal death for you.

The Thousand Years

There are two resurrections distinguished in Scripture: these are called "the first resurrection" and "the second death." Jesus spoke of these two as a "resurrection unto life" and a "resurrection unto damnation." These two resurrections are separated in time by a period of a thousand years:

> And I saw thrones, and they sat upon them, and judgment was given unto them: and I saw the souls of them that were beheaded for the witness of Jesus, and for the word of God, and which had not worshipped the beast, neither his image, neither had received his mark upon their foreheads, or in their hands; and they lived and reigned with Christ a thousand years (Rev. 20:4).
> But the rest of the dead lived not again until the thousand years were finished. This is the first resurrection (Rev. 20:5).

> Blessed and holy is he that hath part in the first resurrection: on such the second death hath no power, but they shall be priests of God and of Christ, and shall reign with him a thousand years (Rev. 20:6).

How clear this becomes if we are willing to believe the record as God has set it forth. How tragic that man, with his preconceived ideas and traditions, has so twisted and perverted Scripture that it loses its meaning. At the coming of Christ every believer will be raised. When the Tribulation saints have joined them, they will all reign with Christ a thousand years. After this period of millennial reign, Satan will be loosed for a little season, only to be finally destroyed with all his followers and cast into the lake of fire. The end will be the last resurrection of the lost. We have the record in Revelation 20:11-15:

> And I saw a great white throne, and him that sat on it, from whose face the earth and the heaven fled away; and there was found no place for them. And I saw the dead, small and great, stand before God; and the books were opened: and another book was opened, which is the book of life: and the dead were judged out of those things which were written in the books, according to their works. And the sea gave up the dead which were in it; and death and hell delivered up the dead which were in them: and they were judged every man according to their works. And death and hell were cast into the lake of fire. This is the second death. And whosoever was not found written in the book was cast into the lake of fire.

Although this passage is not pleasant to hear, it is as much the Word of God as any other portion, and woe to the preacher who fails to proclaim the full counsel of God! Let us consider these verses.

John saw the "dead, small and great" stand before God. All these whom John saw were the lost dead, from wicked Cain to the last one who with Satan rebelled at the end of the Millennium. Every man and woman who has rejected Christ is there: those who were drowned in the sea; those who were eaten by animals; those whose ashes were scattered to the winds of heaven. God who made the elements of which those ashes are composed knows where to find every molecule and atom when the time for bodily resurrection comes. He calls them forth, says John, from "death and hell." The bodies are in the graves; they are dead. Their souls are in hades; they are conscious. The graves give up the bodies and hades gives up the souls of the lost, and they come together in this last resurrection to stand before God, there to receive the final word of destiny.

This judgment is not arbitrary, but is based on absolute justice. The record books are opened and every thought, word and deed of these lost ones is brought forth as evidence of the justice and righteousness which He (God) is about to mete out to those who have rejected Him. "Why is the Book of Life brought out here?" you may ask. God had said, "Blessed and holy is he that hath part in the first resurrection." They all have their names in the Book of Life. If all these at the Great White Throne are lost, why is this Book of Life here? The answer is plain. Read verse 15 of Revelation 20. It is God's "double check" on the lost. First they are judged because of what is written in the book of their deeds, and then they are judged as a double proof of the righteousness of God by the fact that their names are missing from those in the Book of Life.

And whosoever was not found written in the book of life was cast into the lake of fire (Rev. 20.15).

This is God's "double check." "Let God be true, but every man a liar."

DEGREES OF PUNISHMENT

This judgment at the Great White Throne concerns the degree of the eternal punishment of the lost and not the fact of their punishment. The place of punishment was determined when they died. The moment these lost ones died, their eternal abode was forever settled. Now, however, before they are cast into that place of eternal separation, God declares the degree of punishment that each will receive on the basis of His record. There will be many degrees of punishment in hell. Not all the lost will receive the same punishment. The degree of punishment, determined here at the judgment of the Great White Throne, will depend upon many factors. God is just and righteous in all His dealings, even with the lost. He will take into account the opportunities each has had to accept Christ, the amount of light he has enjoyed, the environment in which he has lived and the degree and amount of his sin. Jesus said in Matthew:

> Woe unto thee, Chorazin! woe unto thee, Bethsaida! for if the mighty works, which were done in you, had been done in Tyre and Sidon, they would have repented long ago in sackcloth and ashes. But I say unto you, It shall be more tolerable for Tyre and Sidon at the day of judgment, than for you. And thou, Capernaum, which art exalted unto heaven, shalt be brought down to hell: for if the mighty works, which have been done in thee, had been done in Sodom, it would have remained until this day. But I say unto you, that it shall be more tolerable for the land of Sodom in the day of judgment, than for thee (Matt. 11: 21-24).

Sodom never had the opportunity which Capernaum enjoyed, and Tyre and Sidon did not have the advantages of Bethsaida and Chorazin. This fact will be considered, and they will be dealt with in mercy and justice even at the judgment. I fear the teaching that

there is a general hell where all sinners, regardless of
their light, opportunity and conduct, will be eternally
tortured to the same degree without regard to the cir-
cumstances has caused many people to reject this truth
so plainly set forth, namely, that the lost will perish
forever in outer darkness. The ignorant savages in
the jungle certainly will not be held responsible to the
extent that you who read this will, if you still reject the
message of salvation.

Again and again people who have more argument
than conviction in their hearts come to me and ask,
"What about the heathen who have never heard the
Gospel? Will they be lost?" I have learned to answer
that question, for I have found that nine times out of
ten, people who ask this question are not saved themselves and make the query to justify themselves and
accuse God of being unfair. Therefore I always respond
to that question with this one: "My friend, are *you*
saved?" Usually, after considerable hesitation, such
people finally say, "No." "If you are not saved, why
should you worry about the heathen?" I ask. My
friend, if you have not accepted Christ as your Saviour, your plight is ten thousand times worse than
theirs, for you have heard the Gospel, have had the light,
and have rejected it. Let me tell you earnestly that
hell for the pagan Hottentot who has never heard the
Word is going to be heaven compared with what it will
be for you who have heard the pleading of the Gospel
and have rejected it.

What the punishment of the unenlightened heathen
will be we may not know, but be assured that God always
deals in justice and righteousness. You may rest assured
that God will do everything right. But you who know
the way and then reject it—you will have no excuse

to offer and can expect no mercy. They who have had the maximum of light and opportunity will receive the maximum of just and righteous punishment.

As we approach the end of the book of Revelation, the need for a personal application of its truths and warnings becomes more and more apparent. If there is one fact which is clear in the Scriptures, it is this: God will hold every man responsible according to the degree of light and the opportunity which he or she has had. It were a thousand times better not to have known the way than to have known it and not to have walked in it. This is true of both the believer and the unbeliever.

Every child of God must appear before the judgment seat of Christ to give an account of the things he did after he was saved. Do not confuse the judgment seat of Christ with the judgment of the Great White Throne of which we read in Revelation 20. The judgment seat of Christ will occur *before* the Millennium, and there will be only *believers* there. There will be no unsaved at the judgment seat of Christ. Believers will be judged *not* according to their salvation, for that is done by *grace,* but according to what they have *done* with the light and the opportunities God has given them. They will be saved, but their rewards will depend upon the record of their works. The judgment of the Great White Throne, on the other hand, will occur at the *close* of the Millennial Kingdom Age, and there will be *no believers* there. This is the judgment of the lost.

We believe that soon the Lord will come and we shall have to give an account to *him.* No one can escape meeting Him. If you are saved, you will meet him at the Rapture and be taken out before the great and terrible day of the Lord comes. Christian, to you, indeed, the coming of the Lord is *that blessed hope,* but, sinner, unsaved, what a terrible day, yea, what a terrible eternity, lies ahead of you. Perhaps you are hearing the last call even now. Will you receive Him *now,* accept His kind invitation and be saved?

> Come unto me, all ye that labour and are heavy laden, and I will give you rest.

CHAPTER THIRTY-THREE

The New Heavens and the New Earth

And I saw a new heaven and a new earth: for the first heaven and the first earth were passed away; and there was no more sea (Rev. 21:1).

In our studies of the book of Revelation we have reached the end of time and the beginning of eternity. We have traced the course of the history of the Church, the nations and the nation of Israel through this present age and also through the Tribulation Period. The Millennium is over, Satan has been judged, the wicked have all been raised and cast into the lake of fire, and only eternity remains. Every trace and vestige of sin and its curse is now to be removed, and everything will be made new. Seven new things are mentioned in the last two chapters of Revelation. Seven is the number of perfection and reminds us that when God says, "Behold, I make all things new," He refers to absolute perfection. The seven new things are as follows:

1. A new heaven
2. A new earth
3. New inhabitants
4. The New Jerusalem
5. A new temple
6. A new light
7. A new paradise

283

The first of these new things mentioned is the new heavens and the new earth. The word "heavens" in this connection refers, of course, to the atmospheric heaven. In Scripture there are three heavens mentioned. First, the atmospheric heavens of gas around the earth; second, the planetary heaven of the stars and sun and moon; third, the heaven of heavens, the dwelling place of God Himself. It is to the atmospheric heavens that John refers here. This is evident from the other passages which mention the new heaven. In Isaiah 65:17 we read:

> For, behold, I create new heavens and a new earth: and the former shall not be remembered, nor come into mind.

Everything which has been defiled by sin and Satan will be purified by fire and made new. Since the earth was defiled by sin, it will be destroyed, and since the atmosphere, the air, is the present domain of the "prince of the power of the air," this also will be purified by fire.

The Method of Purification

The Apostle Peter in his second epistle gives us what probably is the most thorough description of how the Lord is going to create the new heavens and the new earth. Here we have one of the most advanced and scientific statements of the composition of the earth and its final destruction found anywhere in Scripture. He says:

> But the heavens and the earth, which are now, by the same word are kept in store, reserved unto fire against the day of judgment and perdition of ungodly men (II Peter 3:7).

The free literal rendering of this verse is as follows:

But the present heavens and earth are held in check by
the same word of God, stored with fire, and reserved unto
the day of judgment and perdition of the ungodly.

STORED WITH FIRE

Peter says that the earth is *stored with fire*. We know
this to be scientifically true, but Peter knew all this
nineteen hundred years ago, Isaiah knew it twenty-five
hundred years ago, and God always knew it, for He
is the One who made the earth.

THE EARTH A GIANT BOMB

The earth on which we live is approximately twenty-
five thousand miles in circumference and eight thousand
miles in diameter. It is formed like a hollow ball with
an outer crust and a core which is liquid, consisting of
molten elements, seething and boiling in the heart of
the earth. The thickness of this crust or shell is
variously estimated, and varies in different parts of
the earth, but science tells us that the crust compares
in thickness or depth with its superheated liquid content
as the shell of an egg compares with its viscous interior.
On this outer solid crust man lives, builds homes, con-
ducts warfare and shakes his fist in the face of the
Creator while he walks on a boiling, seething firepot
which God Himself has made.

We are told that the temperature in the core of the
earth becomes unbelievably hot. In some places of the
earth's crust the molten, superheated elements are
near the surface and the pressure becomes so great that
suddenly a piece of the crust blows away, usually at
some mountain whose roots reach into the caldron of
fire, and millions of tons of rock and earth are blown

away, shooting flames hundreds of feet into the air, and
emitting a stream of glowing, burning lava down the
mountain side, inundating whole cities and causing tens
of thousands to perish in the river of fire. All this is
history. Suddenly a great part of the earth reels with
the internal explosion, the earth trembles and cracks
open, rocks are hurled into the air, and the ash from the
spewing volcano drifts for a thousand miles to be de-
posited upon some ship in the middle of the ocean, while
the tidal wave caused by the upheaval on the ocean floor
hurls waves twenty feet high on shore a thousand miles
from the explosion.

Is It Possible?

Do you continue to doubt God's Word when He
says that someday this old world will be destroyed by
fire? Astronomers tell us that during the past few
hundred years dozens of worlds have burned out before
the very eyes of scientists. Worlds that once traveled
their majestic way through the heavens suddenly exploded and disappeared, and all over this old earth are
these volcanos, hot springs, rivers, and spouting geysers
of steam to remind us that inside the old earth is a sea of
fire and that Peter knew whereof he spoke when he
declared by the inspiration of the Holy Ghost:

> But the heavens and the earth, which are now, by the same
> word are reserved, (stored with fire), against the day of
> judgment and perdition of ungodly men.

One wonders, therefore, why this old world has not
blown up before. When one considers these facts both
from the Scriptures and from science, he shudders to
think of the precarious place in which he lives. Yet
there is no fear for those who believe on the Lord Jesus

Christ, the Word, who created these elements, for He has promised that this disaster will never occur while we, His people, are here on the earth. When that happens, only the wicked will be here. By that time we will have been with the Lord Jesus for a millennium, and after the world has been destroyed by fire, He will make a new heaven and new earth which will be the abode of His people forever and forever. You may ask, "What is keeping this bombshell, eight thousand miles in diameter, from blowing up?" Again the Word of the Lord gives the answer in II Peter 3:9:

> The Lord is not slack concerning his promise, as some men count slackness; but is longsuffering to us-ward, not willing that any should perish, but that all should come to repentance.

THE LONG-SUFFERING OF GOD

God is long-suffering. I wonder whether we have yet grasped the meaning of that truth. The world crucified His son. Raining death and destruction upon women and children, mowing men down like hay, despots have torn Christ from His throne and set themselves up as God. They have scrapped the Bible and substituted pagan tradition and mythologies. The entire world has been drenched in blood; nations have defied God and shaken their puny fists in His face. Yes, they have defied the God who said that all nations are before Him as the small dust of the scales and as a drop in the bucket. Men curse Him, revile Him, challenge Him, and yet God does not plunge them into perdition.

I have wondered in view of the events of recent years, with the increase of violence and the hell-bent programs of the world-dictators, why God has not yet rent the heavens and poured out His judgments upon the wicked. There is but one answer: God is indeed long-suffering.

In spite of the delay and the long-suffering of God, there is a day coming when this world will be destroyed. Consider the words of Peter:

> But the day of the Lord will come as a thief in the night; in the which the heavens shall pass away with a great noise, and the elements shall melt with fervent heat, the earth also and the works that are therein shall be burned up (II Peter 3:10).

THREE REALMS

This coming cataclysm will be confined, according to Peter, to three realms, all part of this earth, but its effects will be felt even in the sun, ninety-three million miles away, and the stars, some of them countless billions of miles distant. The heavens will explode. The elements will burn and the earth will melt. The heavens here referred to are the atmospheric heavens, the capsule of air surrounding the earth.

Three heavens are mentioned in Scripture. There is no "seventh heaven." That is merely a figment of man's imagination. There is, however, first of all the atmosphere or air around the earth, which we call the atmospheric heaven. Beyond that is the planetary or starry heaven, and beyond the heaven of stars is the third heaven, the heaven of Heavens, where God dwells. The heaven to which Peter refers is evidently the air about the earth. This heaven, says Peter, will at the end of time explode with a great noise or detonation.

If this seems fanciful to you, let us hear the evidence about the world reveals that it is composed of several gaseous elements, but the two predominating substances are nitrogen and oxygen. These two, nitrogen and

oxygen, are two of the most combustible gases in existence. Oxygen a basic necessity for all combustion. In
fact, burning is merely the oxidation of matter. Without oxygen there can be no combustion. Whether in the
slow combustion of metabolism in our bodies or the im-
mediate violent combustion of gas in a motor's cylinder
or in a bomb, oxidation is essential. When you want
more heat, you open the draft in a stove, admit more
oxygen and thus speed combustion. When you want
less heat you close the draft and shut off the supply of
oxygen. The air about us is composed largely of this
combustible gas. The other element in air is nitrogen,
the basic element in most of our high explosives such
as dynamite and T.N.T. The word "nitroglycerin"
tells its own story.

OXYGEN AND HYDROGEN

Besides these two highly inflammable and combustible
gases there is present in the atmosphere a large amount
of water, and water consists of oxygen and hydrogen.
Hydrogen is the highly explosive gas once used for in-
flating dirigibles, but because of its combustibility it
has been replaced by less combustible gases. Think of
the air you breathe as consisting of these various gases,
every one of them a combustible element if the proper
combinations and conditions are present.

When Peter tells us that the heavens shall pass away
with a great noise, is he fanatical and fanciful? To
the contrary, he is thoroughly scientific. The atmospheric heaven about us is a veritable storehouse of fire,
ready to explode when God gives the signal. Then indeed
we can understand the expression "with a great noise."
What a noise a firecracker makes! We are told that the
fire of one twelve-inch shell can be heard for fifty miles.

Imagine the deafening roar when the air, containing countless billions of square miles of nitrogen, oxygen and hydrogen, suddenly explodes, as we read in Scripture. Yes, it will be "a great noise." So tremendous will be the explosion that stars millions of miles from the earth will be jarred out of their courses and fall from the heavens. No wonder, then, that Isaiah describes the effect of that explosion in these words in Isaiah 13:

> Therefore I will shake the heavens, and the earth shall remove out of her place, in the wrath of the Lord of hosts, and in the day of his fierce anger. And it (the earth) shall be as the chased roe, and as a sheep that no man taketh up (Isa. 13:13-14).

A few years ago men scoffed at Peter's words as the apostle predicted they would:

> Knowing this first, that there shall come in the last days scoffers, walking after their own lusts, and saying, Where is the promise of his coming? for since the fathers fell asleep, all things continue as they were from the beginning of the creation (II Peter 3:3-4).

Yes, men scoffed at the idea that the world would be destroyed, and then suddenly these scoffers were silenced by the atomic bomb. If they had doubted the possibility of Peter's prediction, all doubt was dispelled by the discovery of this instrument of destruction, the atomic bomb.

Eclipsing every other event in the late eventful war was the loosing of this comparatively "little" bomb, weighing about six hundred pounds, which when it exploded fifteen hundred feet above the city of Hiroshima virtually destroyed that entire community and left in its wake more than a hundred thousand dead and dying. Probably the greatest surprise of all human history in the annals of man's scientific development was this creation of science in the perfection of this latest and most horrible instrument of destruction. How thankful we ought to be that it was not discovered first by our enemies! But it is here, and no one knows how it will effect the future of our world.

The creators of this bomb, we are told, are desperately afraid of this, their own brain child. They tell us that the atomic bomb contains all the potentialities and possibilities of destroying this entire earth in one mighty blast. Some believe that it will cause the destruction of the globe on which we live, but we Christians know that this will never happen. God will never permit man to accomplish this. The Bible does tell us, however, that unless the Lord intervened, this would be the result, but God is going to shorten man's day before he utterly annihilates himself. We read plainly and assuringly "that except those days be shortened, there should no flesh be saved." God will cut short man's destructive program, and at the end of the age this world will be destroyed by fire, to prepare for a new heaven and a new earth wherein dwelleth righteousness.

In view of these facts it is not difficult to believe that the Lord will destroy this earth by fire and then make the new heavens and the new earth. This destruction of the earth and the atmosphere does not mean its annihilation but, rather, its purification by fire and the recasting of these purified elements into a new, more beautiful, sinless and perfect earth to be the dwelling place of a sinless and purified people forever and ever. Immediately after John makes the statement concerning the new heavens and the new earth, he mentions a new city, the New Jerusalem, coming down from God out of heaven. This we will study in detail in our next chapter, but let us consider John's statement regarding it:

And I John saw the holy city, new Jerusalem, coming
down from God out of heaven, prepared as a bride adorned
for her husband (Rev. 21:2).

The heavens and earth have been cleansed and made
a fit dwelling place for the bride of the Lamb. She
descends from heaven and at the same time her new
home descends with her. The city and the bride are
so closely identified that they are here spoken of as
one. There is a literal city, and it is called the bride.
The terms "Holy City" and "New Jerusalem" are
used to describe both the glorified Church and her home.
We shall consider this more fully in our next chapter.

Before we close this chapter, however, I ask you to
face this important question? *Do you belong to the
bride?* Are you one of those who, when the earth passes
away with a great noise and when the elements explode,
will be safe with the Lord in heaven, to return and inherit the earth after it has been prepared for the dwelling place of the saints forever? If you are not ready,
I plead with you once again:

Believe on the Lord Jesus Christ, and thou shalt be saved.

CHAPTER THIRTY-FOUR

The New Jerusalem

And there came unto me one of the seven angels which had the seven vials full of the seven last plagues, and talked with me, saying, Come hither, I will shew thee the bride, the Lamb's wife. And he carried me away in the spirit to a great and high mountain, and shewed me that great city, the holy Jerusalem, descending out of heaven from God. Having the glory of God: and her light was like unto a stone most precious, even like a jasper stone, clear as crystal; and had a wall great and high, and had twelve gates, and at the gates twelve angels, and names written thereon, which are the names of the twelve tribes of the children of Israel: on the east three gates; on the north three gates; on the south three gates; and on the west three gates. And the wall of the city had twelve foundations, and in them the names of the twelve apostles of the Lamb. And he that talked with me had a golden reed to measure the city, and the gates thereof, and the wall thereof. And the city lieth foursquare, and the length is as large as the breadth: and he measured the city with the reed, twelve thousand furlongs. The length and the breadth and the height of it are equal. And he measured the wall thereof, an hundred and forty and four cubits, according to the measure of a man, that is, of the angel. And the building of the wall of it was of jasper: and the city was pure gold, like unto clear glass. And the foundations of the wall of the city were garnished with all manner of precious stones. The first foundation was jasper; the second, sapphire; the third, a chalcedony; the fourth, an emerald; the fifth, sardonyz; the sixth, sardius; the seventh, chrysolyte; the eighth, beryl; the ninth, a topaz; the tenth, a chrysoprasus; the eleventh, a jacinth; the

> twelfth, an amethyst. And the twelve gates were twelve
> pearls; every several gate was of one pearl: and the street
> of the city was pure gold, as it were transparent glass
> (Rev. 21:9-21).

In our previous message we studied the New heavens
and the new earth which God will prepare for the redeemed after the Millennium and after He has destroyed
and purified the old earth and heavens by fire. Let us
now consider the description of the Holy City, the New
Jerusalem, the Lamb's wife. Theologians have been
confused by this expression "the holy Jerusalem, the
Lamb's wife." How can the New Jerusalem be a city
and at the same time be the wife of the Lamb, the bride
of Christ? If we study the passage carefully, there
need be no difficulty. The city and its occupants are
one. This chapter of Revelation concerns a literal city
of inexpressible beauty. It is the New Jerusalem. The
redeemed Church of Christ, the bride of the Lamb, is to
dwell in that New Jerusalem. The city and its inhabitants are one.

Today we speak in the same manner concerning
cities. When I mention a certain city, for example,
Grand Rapids, Michigan, I may mean either or both
the material city and its buildings or the inhabitants
of Grand Rapids. From one point of view Grand Rapids
is a city. However, Grand Rapids is also a company of
people who, like myself, live here. For instance, if I say
that Grand Rapids is a beautiful city, you know that I
refer to its beautiful location and its fine buildings and
streets. But if I say that Grand Rapids is a wicked
city, you know immediately that I am referring to the
people of Grand Rapids and not to its buildings, streets
and trees. The term "Grand Rapids" may refer either
to the city itself or to the people who live there. In the
same way God speaks of the New Jerusalem. The

term indicates both a literal city and also the occupants of that city; it is both the city and the bride, the building and its occupant. That is why God calls it both "the holy city" and "the wife of the Lamb."

A Literal City

Remember first of all that this description of the New Jerusalem is of an actual material literal city in which the Church of Jesus Christ will dwell and reign over the earth, the new earth, forever and ever. In this chapter we shall attempt to speak of its beauty and purpose.

Its Derivation

Notice first of all that this literal city is specially prepared by God and comes down from heaven. So huge is this city that John was carried away to a very high mountain in order that he might catch a glimpse of its transcendent beauty. The city itself was a cube equal in length, breadth and height. The dimensions of the city, as given to John, were as follows: it was fifteen hundred miles long, fifteen hundred miles wide and fifteen hundred miles high. It is a city, a literal city, containing one billion eight hundred and seventy-five million cubic miles, and is prepared to be the habitation of the redeemed of the Lord of all ages. The implication, of course, is that there are streets running like blocks in all directions, and the streets are superimposed one above the other, while through the middle of the streets runs the river of life, bordered on either bank by the tree of life, originally placed in the Garden of Eden, but from which man was barred after he had sinned.

The Materials

The city was surrounded by a great and magnificent wall with twelve great gates which were never shut, and

on the gates were the names of the twelve tribes of
Israel. The wall itself rested upon twelve foundations
and on the foundations were written the names of the
twelve apostles of the Lamb. The entire city, therefore, is connected with and rests upon the twelve tribes
of Israel and the twelve apostles of the Lamb. This is
the teaching of Paul as well in Ephesians, where he
tells us that the Church, the body of Christ, is—

> built upon the foundation of the apostles and prophets,
> Jesus Christ himself being the chief corner stone.

This great city, which comes down from heaven, was
so huge that if you can imagine a city stretching from
Boston to Miami and from New York to Denver, Colo-
rado, and towering fifteen hundred miles into the air, you
can visualize the dimensions of that place of many
mansions which is being prepared for our eternal abode.
The wall of the city is made of jasper, and the city
itself was made of pure transparent gold, as clear as
glass.

I hear one of you ask, "But surely you do not interpret
that literally, do you? Surely these are figures of speech
and cannot refer to an actual city!" Why not? If man
can make cities, cannot God do so? If man can build
great cities, cannot God build greater? He who created
the jewels and the precious stones, the gold and the
silver, yea, the universe, by the word of His mouth—is
He not able to do with it what He will? I interpret this
passage in Revelation literally, and in so doing I have
absolutely no difficulty. Any child can read this chapter
and understand it, but when we begin to spiritualize
this passage and change its meaning, confusion results.
That is why there are a legion of interpretations and
explanations which serve only to confuse Bible students
and frighten them from this blessed book of Revelation.

Read this chapter and believe it literally as God expects you to do, for it is a description of your literal future home—if you are saved.

THE FOUNDATIONS

The foundations of the city are garnished with all manner of precious stones. The twelve gates of the city are twelve huge pearls, and the streets are paved with pure gold, a special kind of gold, transparent and clear as glass. John says he saw no temple therein, for the Lord God Almighty and the Lamb are the temple of it. The Tabernacle and the Temple in the Old Testament were the rallying points for the worship and adoration of the children of Israel. Every part of the Tabernacle and Temple pointed to the Lord Jesus Christ. The gate pointed to Him as the Door. The altar pointed to the Cross, the laver, to His cleansing Word. The table of shewbread spoke of Him as the Bread of Life; the candlestick pointed to the Light of the World; the altar of incense spoke of Him as the interceding High Priest. The ark of the covenant was a picture of Christ who by His blood redeemed us from the curse of the law. The linen in the Tabernacle spoke of His righteousness, the brass, of the judgment He bore; the gold, of His deity; the silver, of His blood; the wood, of His humanity. Every part of the building revealed a special aspect of His glorious relationship to His people.

When we reach the New Jerusalem, we will not need all these, for there we will have Him. He will be with us forever. We shall follow the Lamb withersoever He goeth. Yes, we shall have Him, and we shall be like Him.

THE CITY'S ILLUMINATION

We are told that the lighting of this city will also be new. John says:

> And the city had no need of the sun, neither of the moon, to shine in it: for the glory of God did lighten it, and the Lamb is the light thereof. And the nations of them which are saved shall walk in the light of it: and the kings of the earth do bring their glory and honour into it. And the gates of it shall not shut at all by day: for there shall be no night there (Rev. 21:23-25).

Can you imagine what this glorious sight will be? Picture a new earth on which dwells the restored and redeemed nation of Israel, and around them are literal nations of redeemed people, consisting of the saved of the nations before the Cross and the nations which came through the Millennium. All dwell on the new earth. Hanging over that new earth, suspended in the sky, is this gigantic city, the New Jerusalem, the habitation of the bride of Christ.

Christ is the light of it, and this light streams forth over all the earth, dispelling all darkness forever. Remember that the city is made of transparent gold, so that the light from the Person of Christ dwelling with His bride in the New Jerusalem streams forth from this lamp, fifteen hundred miles cube, lighting the entire earth.

When the Lord makes the new earth, He, of course, makes it to be inhabited. There will be people living here in a perfect and sinless world. Israel will be in the land of Palestine under their own King David of old. The saved nations will inhabit the earth, while the church dwells with Christ and reigns over this new earth from her glorious place in the New Jerusalem.

And there shall be no night there; and they need no candle,
neither light of the sun; for the Lord God giveth them light:
and they shall reign for ever and ever.

We shall reign forever and ever. That is the heritage
of the saints of God. Those of us who believe the Old
Book and the old way are ridiculed, but listen, friend,
someday, when Jesus comes, we despised believers will
judge the angels. In the Millennium we shall rule the
nations with a rod of iron and throughout all eternity
we shall dwell with Him in the New Jerusalem and
reign over the earth and the nations forever and ever.
Let the foes of Christ despise us now and even persecute us; we can wait for that glad and glorious day
when we shall reign with Him, not for a few brief
years, but forever and ever.

One more interesting fact is mentioned concerning
this wonderful city:

And he shewed me a pure river of water of life, clear as
crystal, proceeding out of the throne of God, and of the
Lamb. In the midst of the street of it, and on either side
of the river was there the tree of life, which bare twelve
manner of fruits, and yielded her fruit every month: and the
leaves of the tree were for the healing of the nations (Rev.
22:1-2).

In the midst of the city will be the throne of God and
of the Lamb. Out of the throne flows a river of life and
beside the river, on either side, is the tree of life. Since
Adam was driven out of Eden we had lost sight of
that tree. You will recall that there were many trees
in the garden, but two are mentioned in particular:
the tree of knowledge of good and evil and the tree of
life. After Adam sinned by eating of the first, God
drove him out lest he eat also of the tree of life and
live forever in his sinful lost estate. When sin is gone
and the redeemed are all at home, the tree of life will

again appear—the tree which will stay alive forever.
Actual literal fruit grows on these trees—twelve kinds
and at one time. There will be twelve crops yearly, so
that there will be plenty for all. Remember again that
these are literal trees. As we believe the tree of life in the
Garden of Eden to be literal, so, too, we believe that
this is a literal tree.

The leaves are for the healing of the nations. As the
eating of the fruit gives eternal life to the saints in
the city, so the leaves are used to give undying bliss
and joy to the nations dwelling upon the new earth.
In the beginning God created the earth for man to dwell
in and enjoy. Sin entered, but God will not abandon His
original purpose. He will not allow Satan to thwart
His plan to have an earth full of people worshipping
Him. Through all eternity, therefore, there will be
people dwelling upon the earth while we reign with
Christ over the earth.

Before we close this chapter we must call your attention to a sad warning in this passage:

> And there shall in no wise enter into it any thing that
> defileth, neither whatsoever worketh abomination, or maketh
> a lie: but they which are written in the Lamb's book of life.

If you are not saved, my friend, you will never see
that glorious city. Instead, you will dwell in outer
darkness, separated from God in the place of eternal
remorse. I ask you, is your name written in the Lamb's
Book of Life? Is your name on the social register of
the New Jerusalem? If not, again I plead with you to
receive Christ by faith and be saved. Then you can
join that happy throng of whom John says:

> Blessed are they that do his commandments, that they
> may have right to the tree of life, and may enter in through
> the gates into the city (Rev. 22:14).

CHAPTER THIRTY-FIVE

"Even So, Come, Lord Jesus"

And he shewed me a pure river of water of life, clear as crystal, proceeding out of the throne of God and of the Lamb. In the midst of the street of it, and on either side of the river was there the tree of life, which bare twelve manner of fruits, and yielded her fruit every month: and the leaves of the tree were for the healing of the nations. And there shall be no more curse: but the throne of God and of the Lamb shall be in it; and his servants shall serve him: and they shall see his face and his name shall be in their foreheads. And there shall be no night there and they need no candle, neither light of the sun; for the Lord God giveth them light: and they shall reign for ever and ever. And he said unto me, These sayings are faithful and true: and the Lord God of the holy prophets sent his angel to shew unto his servants the things which must shortly be done (Rev. 22:1-6).

The twenty-second chapter of Revelation is a continuation of the preceding chapter, which speaks of the New Jerusalem, the eternal home of the saved. It is the final description in the Bible and concludes God's revelation. The first five verses present five facts concerning this New Jerusalem, the abode of the saints. We are told of a river, the tree of life, the government of the city, the illumination of the city and its eternal duration.

THE RIVER OF LIFE

Mentioned first in the chapter is the river. It is described as pure, clear as crystal, and is said to proceed

out of the throne of God. The water supply of a city
is of utmost importance. Throughout human history
man has been concerned about and influenced by the
source of water. Ancient cities were built where there
was a sure and pure supply of water. Man can live
longer without food than without drink, and water is
indispensable both for refreshment and the life of men.
In the New Jerusalem the source of refreshment is
the throne of God. He is the source of life, and therefore the river is called the river of the water of life. It
is pure water because of its source. It is clear as
crystal because it is free from all impurities and con-
tamination. There are those who would make this
water spoken of in Revelation 22 symbolic of something
else, but there is no reason for doing so. This passage
undoubtedly refers to literal water to be enjoyed by
literal human beings in a literal New Jerusalem.

Not Angels

The same is true of the second thing mentioned in the
chapter: the tree of life. We believe that the tree of
life mentioned in the first book of the Bible, Genesis,
was a literal tree, in a literal Paradise, for literal human
beings, Adam and Eve. Why, then, should we view
the tree differently when it is referred to again in the
last book of the Bible? You have already noticed, I am
sure, that the description of this New Jerusalem follows
closely the description of the first abode of mankind in
the Garden of Eden. There, too, was the literal river
with its three heads, and there, too, were trees, and
in the midst, the tree of life. On this tree grew literal
fruit and literal leaves.

The tendency to spiritualize is the result of a wrong
conception of the life hereafter, of heaven and the New
Jerusalem. We are liable to think of heaven as a place

with golden streets, where angels and the saints play golden harps all day long. This is, however, wholly erroneous. When we get to glory, after the resurrection, we will still be human beings. Our resurrection bodies will be literal human bodies and we shall eat and drink and act like human beings. Scripture seems to indicate that we will not have to eat, but we will be able to eat. After His resurrection, Jesus ate literal food, and here we can believe that the tree of life is for our pleasure and enjoyment. We will be higher than the angels. They will be our ministering servants, appointed of God to wait upon us as our servants, ministering to us, the heirs of salvation.

LEAVES FOR HEALING

How glorious it will be to see that river flowing through the city lined with these beautiful trees—trees bowed down with twelve kinds of fruits for our pleasure and enjoyment. Furthermore, Scripture tells us that the leaves will also have a ministry: they are for the healing of the nations. Evidently there will be nations of people on the earth throughout eternity. This may be a rude shock to many who have conceived of eternity as a time when all men will be the same and dwell together in heaven as spirits or, at least, angels, but such is not true. The Church will be the bride of Christ forever. Believers will be literal human beings in perfect resurrection bodies, but there will be other peoples also. There must be, for it is said of us, the saints of God, that we shall reign with Him forever and ever.

Note the words "reign with Him." If we are to reign, there must be subjects over which we are to reign. You cannot reign over nothing. A king implies a kingdom. All the details are not clear, but the teaching of Scripture seems clearly to indicate that there will always

be nations upon the earth, even the new earth, and we
shall reign over them. We are told that while the
bride of Christ feasts upon the fruit of the tree of life,
the nations will partake of the leaves of the tree of life.
They, too, will live forever, and the leaves will be for
their eternal sustenance. How the leaves will be applied
I do not know, but I believe what the text says: "and
the leaves of the tree were for the healing of the nations."

Its Government

This passage describes also the government of this
eternal city, for John sees the throne of God in the
midst. Out of it proceeds the river, and the river
supplies the trees, and the trees supply the saints and
the nations. The throne of God is the source of all.
There will be only one ruler, one governor—the Lord
Jesus Christ—and only one throne, the throne of God. So
perfect will be that government that we read, "And there
shall be *no more curse.*" Again we must refer to the
first book of the Bible, which tells us when the first
curse was pronounced upon the first human sin. Since
then, the trouble, pain, suffering, distress and death
in the world have been caused by the curse. The last
book of the Bible tells of the removal of the curse because
its cause, sin, has been removed.

The Illumination

A city must have pure water, an adequate food supply, an efficient government, proper lighting and security.
These five requirements are mentioned in the Scripture
passage which we have been considering. We are told
repeatedly that there shall be no night there, and no need
of sun or any other light, for the Lord Jesus, He who

said, "I am the light of the world," shall Himself be
the light thereof.

The passage speaks, finally, of the city's security.
"They shall reign for ever and ever." Men scoff and
make light of this truth, but God says in Revelation 22:6:

> These sayings are faithful and true: and the Lord God
> of the holy prophets sent his angel to shew unto his serv-
> ants the things which must shortly be done.

The Conclusion

Revelation 22:6 to the end of the chapter constitutes
the conclusion of the book, the final summary. Three
times the expression "I come quickly" occurs in this
section. In verse 7 we read:

> Behold, I come quickly: blessed is he that keepeth the
> sayings of the prophecy of this book.

In verse 12 we read:

> And, behold, I come quickly; and my reward is with me,
> to give every man according as his work shall be.

The promise is repeated in verse 20:

> He which testifieth these things saith, Surely I come
> quickly.

It is strange indeed that men with an open Bible before them can deny the return of the Lord Jesus Christ
when God has placed such emphasis upon this truth.
Three times our Lord stresses this final message of the
Bible: "surely I come quickly." He says, as it were,
"Men will deny this truth and scoff at it, and those who
believe it will be sneered at and dispised, but do not
worry, I *am coming again.*"

Today we are beginning to realize the necessity for His coming again. Man has wrought hovoc in the world, and it appears to be doomed unless God intervenes. Even those who do not believe the Bible tell us that we are in desperate straits and that the world seems to be speeding to its end. We Christians have the explanation. Jesus said, "When these things begin to come to pass, then look up . . . for your redemption draweth nigh."

THREE "COME'S"

As there are three reminders of the certainty of His coming again, so there are three "come's" in this chapter:

> And the Spirit and the bride say, Come. And let him that heareth say, Come. And let him that is athirst come (Rev. 22:17).

I like to think that the book ends with a gracious invitation to come before it is too late. To the very end the invitation is "Come! Come! Come!" While the Spirit and the Church cry for the coming of the Lord and say, "Come," those who hear the message cry to a lost world, "Come," and once more the message goes out, "Let him that is athirst *come.*" Moved by what we have seen in this book and the events which are occurring today, we cry to men and women everywhere, "Oh, Come! Come! Come!" before it is too late and the day of mercy ends forever.

THE LAST PROMISE

The Bible ends with the last promise and it is the promise of the return of the Lord. It ends also with the last prayer in the Bible—a prayer for the return of the Lord Jesus.

> He which testifieth these things saith, Surely I come quickly. Amen. Even so, **come, Lord Jesus.**

The final benediction is the benediction of grace:

> The grace of our Lord Jesus Christ be with you all. Amen.

Revelation began with Him, and ends with Him, and is about Him. We have written this book that you who are unsaved might come to Him and that those of you who have come might love Him more and look with new eagerness for His return. In this book we have given merely an outline of Revelation and have made no attempt to give a complete or an exhaustive exposition. Rather, it has been our aim and prayer to create a new interest in the study of the book, the reading of which the Lord has promised to reward with a special blessing, and, second, to give a working outline of the main and general teaching which would help you to study the book in greater detail.

The night is dark, and the world seems to be in the throes of death. Humanity is engulfed by turmoil and confusion. The dark clouds of coming judgment and distress are upon the horizon, and the rumblings of coming judgment may be heard. Men everywhere are wondering about the future, and some are despairing. One of these days or nights, however, while the world is occupied with its frivolities and empty pleasures and scoffing at the Word of God, a form will rise above the lashing waves, as on Galilee, to vindicate forever the devotion and the patient watching of that remnant in all ages who have not abandoned the hope of His com-

ing again, and take them home to the realms of bliss
where sorrow and sighing, loneliness and heartache
will never be known and where, with loved ones gone
before, we shall rest forever in the perfect service of
our perfect Lord. "Even so, Come, Lord Jesus."